To Dick,
Robin with ...

Collected Prose

of a Poet

Cleatus Rattan (signature)

Cleatus Rattan

ISBN: 146629020X
ISBN 13: 9781466290204
Harleman Publishing Company
Harleman.co@bryrus.net
6937 Winchester Avenue
Dallas, Texas 75209

TABLE OF CONTENTS

SHORT STORIES

MEMOIRS

ESSAYS

WHY I WRITE

◾

*O*ne's writings, especially poems, are gestures to scare the dark away, to make room for the light of sanity. A poem is a victory over anxiety, depression, and the fear that comes with the seeming chaos called life. Poems are brief moments of order in an otherwise seemingly absurd world. Or maybe the world is better described as dysteleogically surd.

A poet, like God (according to Genesis we are made in His Image and Likeness) can create a world, then, maybe like God on occasion, transmit the meaning of that world to the inhabitants of this world. Other than that I don't know why I write, but I know I have to. I wrote for years and no one noticed, and I really never expected to have an audience, and though it fun to have people read what I write, it is not necessary.

> "None but a blockhead writes but for money."
> Dr. Samuel Johnson, great 18th century scholar, lexicographer, and wit. (He is wrong, clever, but wrong.)

> "Publication is not the business of poets."
> Emily Dickinson (Nineteenth century American poet)

Emily Dickenson wrote all her life without an audience, without anyone noticing. I expect she had no choice. I doubt that God had a choice about creating this world.

"Being a poet is all; being known as a poet is nothing."
Cleatus Rattan (Internationally Ignored Poet)

"There is no helping the incurious, but then, there is little reason to try."
Sebastian Junger. (I don't know where I got this aphorism I like so much.)
I have some odd sort of dislike for pedagogy. If students are not interested or curious, then leave them alone. What are they worth? Rhetoricians, in whatever manner they are pedagogues are right about one thing: when one gets into the habit of writing, which is to say in the habit of thinking, there is no turning back—one cannot be discouraged.

IN MY CRAFT OR SULLEN ART

---◾---

Dylan Thomas

In my craft or sullen art
Exercised in the still night
When only the moon rages
And the lovers lie abed
With all their grief's in their arms,
I labour by singing light
Not for ambition or singing bread
Or the strut and trade of charms
On the ivory stages
But for the common wages
Of their most secret heart.
Not for the proud man apart
From the raging moon I write
On these spendrift pages
Nor for the towering dead
With their nightingales and psalms
But for the lovers, their arms
Round the griefs of the ages,
Who pay no praise or wages
Nor heed my craft or art.

"When a true genius appears in the world, (sic) you may know him by this sign that the dunces are all in confederacy against him." Jonathan Swift—*Thoughts on Various Subjects, Moral and Diverting.*

"The multitude of men and women choose the less adventurous way of the comparatively unconscious civic and tribal routines. But these seekers, too, are saved—by the virtue of the inherited symbolic aids of society, the rites of passage, the grace-yielding sacraments, given to mankind of old by the redeemers and handed down through millenniums (sic). It is only those who know neither an inner call nor an outer doctrine whose plight is truly desperate."
Joseph Campbell *The Hero with a Thousand Faces*

"The creation of man, whom God in his foreknowledge knew doomed to sin, was the awful index of God's omnipotence. For it would have been a thing of trifling and contemptible case for perfection to create more perfection. To do so would, to speak truth, be not creation but extension. Separateness is identity and the only way for God to create, truly create, man was to make him separate from God Himself, and to be separate from God is to be sinful. The creation of evil therefore is the index of God's glory and His power. That had to be so that the creation of good might be the index of man's glory and power. But by God's help (sic). By His help and in His wisdom." (Sic)
Robert Penn Warren *All The King's Men*

"As a rule a man is sociable just in the degree in which he is intellectually poor and generally vulgar."
Arthur Schopenhauer, German Philosopher 1788-1860

"Seek not the favor of the multitude: it is seldom got by honest and lawful means. But seek the testimony of the few; and number not voices, but weigh them."
Immanuel Kant, German Philosopher 1724-1804

"The vulgar herd can never understand." Commonly ascribed to Baudelaire in "Flowers of Evil," but is actually considered to be the world's oldest aphorism, reputably deciphered from hieroglyphics inscribed within the pyramids. It is a perfect metaphor for dividing humanity into those who rule and those who abide, those who acquiesce, those who promulgate war and those who suffer its consequences.

The Greek historian Polybius (circa 204-122 BC) wrote: "Since the masses of the people are inconsistent, full of unruly desires, passionate, and reckless of consequence, they must be filled with fears to keep them in order. The ancients did well, therefore, to invent gods, and the belief in punishment after death."

The ancient Romans were in agreement. The poet Horace: "I hate the vulgar herd and hold it far away." The Roman orator Cicero: "In the common people there is no wisdom, no penetration, and no power of judgment." And the stoic philosopher Seneca said, "It is proof of a bad cause when it is applauded by the mob." These sentiments were not confined to Western philosophers. Confucius said, "The people may be made to follow a path of action, but they may not be made to understand it," and "Insubordination of the common people is the root of all disorder."

Poetry is the aversion to power; it is the resistance to dominance. It is the act of self-construction in an alien world. Veracity lies in building the word-world, rather than in describing or reflecting. Mimesis may not be enough.

"As democracy is perfected, the office of the president represents, more and more clearly, the inner soul of the people. On some great and glorious day, the plain folk of the land will reach their heart's desire at last, and the White House will be adorned by a downright moron. H.L. Mencken (1880-1956)

"Shall I tell you what I consider to be wrong? What I consider to be wrong is that most of the people in the Western Hemisphere are stark, staring mad, and the few people who recognize this are regarded as lunatics by all those stark, staring mad people."

Ashley Montegue from remarks at the
University of Wisconsin Symposium on
"Alternative Futures for America" 1971.

Sometimes deciphering the world for readers won't do. We must make or create the world for readers. How? I am almost never sure. Sometimes I have moments of clarity, but a writer may create a world that we come to live in and know in our everyday creation of our lives. Minuscule creation is probably enough.

INTRODUCTION TO
THE PROSE OF A POET

———————————————— ■ ————————————————

Jim Linebarger

Cleatus Rattan holds the Mayborn Chair of Arts and Sciences as Professor of English at the University of Mary Hardin-Baylor. He is a former Poet Laureate of Texas and a Distinguished Alumnus of Texas A&M University—Commerce. More than 400 of Rattan's poetry have found their way to print in journals, textbooks, and anthologies. In addition, he is the author of five collections of poetry, and he has authored several short stories, essays, memoirs, and feature pieces. However, he has refused to submit several of his prose works for publication for whatever reasons. Largely, he says he has been too lazy to look for potential magazines to send his prose. "I am a poet," he says "and to teach full time and to look for publishers in addition to scribbling poetry is more trouble than I have interest in or have time for."

Perhaps he is afraid to experience rejection. He once told me that he did not talk to people well and said that he would rather not try. Hence, he says he writes, but the short stories, memoirs, and essays in this collection tell the reader he or she has been cheated out of fascinating values, good humor, and the good sense that most of us want and need.

His short stories are filled with humor and positive observations of charming characters with penetrating insights that amuse and entertain the reader: The math teacher who is precisely wrong in his worldly calculations shows us how we may come to understand his world when a person fails to understand himself. Another character is manipulated by his mother, his high school girl friend, college girls with good legs and firm round breasts, his wife, and the older woman who is the wife of his boss. This character is a Groucho Marx—Woody Allen combination. He is controlled by every woman he ever meets and fails to understand. How sad. How sad he is in a series of marvelous, mishaps. Rattan's characters are more often than not more acted on than actors. The snares of life are hidden or we would never step into them. These fictitious characters are in some ways a microscope and in some ways a telescope focused on us and the traps that await us eagerly.

The memoirs show the reader how the writer has learned to understand the forces he has not always avoided. Moreover, he shows us how some snake pits throw venom on us no matter what precautions we take. Forgiveness, he says, is the point of religion and thus to forgive one's self is an act God not only condones, but requires.

The poet's essays are objective and especially valid insights into the church, the governments, state and federal, and the schools, public and private—high schools and higher education, our heroes, and our philosophers. Perhaps most importantly the essays focus on contradictions and affirmations that abound in both the Hebrew bible and in the New Testament. Then he takes us to the movies with added comments on story telling via Joseph Campbell. In Rattan's hands, storytelling about story telling illuminates the methods and ambitions of story tellers in film and print.

Read these offerings. You will not forget them.
Jim Linebarger, Emeritus Professor of English and Poet in Residence at the University of North Texas, is the author of *Five Faces* and *The Poetry of John Berryman*.

LESSON IN CLASS

—■—

"... no enumeration of the physical qualities of a
beautiful object could ever include its beauty, or give
the faintest hint of what we mean by beauty."
--C.S. Lewis *The Problem of Pain.*

"Can you tell me why I made a D on this test, Dr. Lorr?"
For Blackerby, the tone was curt, even insolent.

"Because I like you, Mr. Blackerby," I said with a twinge
behind my eyes. "But let's look at it. There is always a possibility of error. Let's see," I said taking his blue book. "You
say Beowulf is a braggart and a coward. How do you arrive at that opinion?"

"No one could do what he said he did. You don't believe he swam for a week, do you sir?"

"Leaving aside the question of my beliefs for the moment, Mr. Blackerby, how do you account for his willingness to fight Grendel without a weapon?"

"He was bluffing. His bragging made him have to do it.
He was hoping Grendel wouldn't show up. He was afraid
he would be shown up for the braggart he was. And when
he fought, he did it like a cornered rat. His fear gave him
strength."

"An almost interesting opinion, Mr. Blackerby, but one
I'm afraid that won't hold up. What about his willingness to
fight Grendel's mother? And the dragon? Surely you don't
attribute all these exploits to the fury of a cornered rat?"

"That's my opinion." The absence of the sir was
pointed. "I'm entitled to my opinion."

"Mr. Blackerby, my opinion is that your opinion is absurd. You don't even understand that a literal reading of this poem is not the best way to approach understanding this work, and at this point in our study for you to fail to comprehend the way to read the poem is an indictment of your effort in this class. Mr. Blackerby, my job is to evaluate your opinion. And I have done so. Your grade was generous."

"I'm not used to making grades like this, Dr. Lorr," he said with a touch of menace in his voice.

"You should get used to it, and if your effort does not improve in the future you can expect worse grades to come along."

"Well, perhaps some of my other duties in student government and in the fraternity got in my way. The semester is young; I'll do better on the next test." The transition was too quick to be believable.

"I hope so," I said only somewhat mollified. After he was gone, I found myself breathing hard, and my heart beating fast in anger. I told myself it was a hangover. Surely no one like Blackerby should be able to upset me.

Soon after this unpleasantness, on a golden and red day in late October as I was sitting in my office debating about walking back to my apartment for lunch, there was a timid knock on the door. I said, "Come in," but no one did, at least not for a moment. Slowly, through a small crack in the door, one of my students peeped in through a small crack in the door.

"May I come in," she said.

I have already said so." I recognized her immediately. Her name was Alison Leach. She was the beauty in Blackerby's sophomore class. She always sat near the middle of the room and occasionally looked up at me and the ceiling and me to show that she was thinking. She invariably looked as if she were on her way to pose for pictures in the Neiman's catalogue. She was tall with long black hair that silhouetted her finely chiseled milk-white face. Her eyes seemed to be black, except when they twinkled. She had once or twice laughed at some of my poor jokes, and I tended to be more kind to her than most of my sophomores.

"I'm sorry to disturb you Dr. Lorr."

"I'm not busy, come in." I could have been digging the Suez Canal, and I would have invited her in.

"Well then . . . if you are going to walk to your apartment, I would like to go with you."

She said this without guile, without further explanation, and without a show of shyness. I wanted very much to appear to be a man of the world, but I stammered and

I heard myself say,

"Why?" She looked to be a bit ruffled, but said,

"So I can get to know you better."

"Okay," I said with not too much quaver in my voice.

Even though what she had said would seem to be fairly obvious, I was still apprehensive. I was made more than a bit nervous when it dawned on me I wanted her company very much. But I thought I had better play it safe, so after we had gone down the stairs of Dallas Hall and were out on the campus, I said,

"Is there some assignment I can help you with?"

"No," she said with a twinkle in her eye. I laughed too loud and said,

"Where are you from?"

"Anson."

"Where is that? Is it in Texas?"

"It's north of Abilene about twenty miles."

"Go twenty miles north of Abilene and you will fall off." I said. It was a poor joke, but she laughed a sort of soft laugh that neither went up or down, neither rose nor fell off. It just stopped. I wanted more. We walked to my apartment and stood around for a minute while I tried to decide if it was a quick romp in bed she wanted. I decided against it because she just didn't seem to be that sort of a girl, and she made no further moves in that direction. I was ready to be maneuvered to the bed, but I was not going to try to do the maneuvering.

She had been making As, so it wasn't a grade she was after. I decided, egotistically that she was just what she seemed to be, and that it was me she was interested in. I walked over to the refrigerator, opened the door, looked in without seeing anything, shut the door and said,

"Let's go." She looked relieved.

"No wonder you're so thin," she said.

"I guess I don't eat much," I agreed.

"Can I cook for you sometime" she said, looking slightly shy for the first time.

"Can you cook?"

"Oh yes, I'm a great cook."

"You don't look it—you're slightly thin yourself you know."

"Dorm food."

"I know. My cooking and dorm food are a lot alike."

"How old are you," I said after a short pause.

"Nineteen."

"You must have been the belle of Anson High."

"Well, maybe, but I had plenty of time to learn to cook."

We were close to a barbeque place in Snyder Plaza, a small shopping center near the campus, and suddenly I felt hungry.

"Would you like a sandwich at The Pit?"

"Sure" she said.

Entranced with her as I was, I think I wanted to see some student reaction to our being together. Although we saw several students I knew, we drew no more than quick looks and blank faces. I was trying to find out what sort of reputation she had. Being a sorority girl, she had *some* reputation, but there was no hint for me at The Pit. I made a mental note to ask around, probably the fraternity house would be the best place. Although I had not been in the house for years, enough freshmen let me know they were KA pledges for me to realize my name was mentioned during rush week. I had not hidden my thoughts too well, and then too my next question was not spontaneous enough.

"Do you often invite yourself along with men you don't know well?"

"Just this once," she said slowly. For the first time since we had been talking, she stopped smiling. I smiled in what I hoped was my best mood lightening way and told her the truth—that I was not used to the company of girls, much less the company of such a beautiful girl, and I was trying to find out if there was some "other" reason for her company lest I make a fool of myself.

She laughed and agreed she had been "unforgivably brazen," but that she had tried every other avenue she knew to get to know me. I had seemingly ignored her in class, and she had no friends who knew any of my friends. Caught by her beauty, I sat there too long and almost missed a class. I explained this to her and left some wadded up bills, and asked her to pay as I hurried out. But as I got to the door, I stopped, came back and asked her to go out somewhere, anywhere with me the next night. I was pleased to note that she was pleased to say yes.

I did check up on her, however. No doubt a crummy thing to do, but I called the KA house and asked to talk to a student of mine—one I liked and had a certain rapport with. He wasn't in, but later that evening Blackerby returned the call. I didn't want to talk to him, and I was surprised that he was a KA, but I made the mistake of talking to him and asked him in what I hoped was still fraternity parlance for the "scoop" on Alison Leach, girl Pi Phi. I didn't tell him why I wanted to know anything about her, and he didn't ask.

He said that there was no need to ask around because everybody knew about her. There was nothing to tell, he said. Her first semester as a Pi Phi pledge, she dated some fraternity pledges the social chairperson set her up with, but since her initiation she just stopped dating. As far as he knew she didn't date anyone in particular. I thanked him in a burst of fraternity brother pride.

"Thank you, Dr. Lorr," he said. I wondered why he thanked me. Just nervous, I supposed.

I thought perhaps I had been too brusque with Blackerby in my office. This information was just what I wanted to hear, though. She was an obviously superior person. Couldn't tolerate the callow youths—needed the companionship of a mature scholar—a man in his mid-twenties, at least.

The next few months were among the best in my life. She was a joy to be with. She enjoyed everything. On my salary, our activities were inexpensive, but fun. One Sunday we went to Fair Park to the aquarium and laughed at the fish for an hour or so, naming them for professors and in pseudo-semi-Latin: "Perchous Precipitus," "Flounder About Us," and "Just for the Halibut." Not very funny really, but hilarious to us at the time.

We never tried to hide our relationship from anyone although we thought about it. It didn't seem to us we were doing anything wrong, and we knew of no university rule which prohibited our dating. No one ever said anything to me, neither the Dean nor the Department Head. If anyone complained we were ready to go underground, but we were never going to stop seeing each other, we promised. In class, Alison and I were circumspect, even though there were times when that was difficult. One day as we were discussing an essay that dealt with the author's youth on a farm, a student commented about something from his adolescent farm days, and one comment led to another when I asked Miss Leach about her youth. She in some context or another mentioned her horse, and I foolishly interrupted her proper narrative to ask her horse's name. With a straight, unsmiling face she said, "Herbert Hoofer, father is a Republican."

From that point on the classroom was something of a contest ground, each of us trying to break the other's mask. At the bottom of one of her themes I returned I suggested that a good name for a horse was "Claude Rains," an actor we had recently seen in an old movie on TV. On her next theme she added "J.P. Morgan" and later "Jack Le Mane."

Out of class we were ridiculous gigglers also, but we reserved some jokes to spring on each other. The other students were completely aware of our relationship, and they understood our classroom "games." How well they understood was made clear to me a week or so later when a young lady suggested that horse names were okay, but we could perform a real service by thinking of names for chickens because usually one found many more chickens on farms and ranches than horses. She had said all this with a seriously blank expression, so I thanked her with a mock seriousness that Alison described as my Dr. House manner and vowed to work diligently on this problem that had long plagued American farmers until help could be offered. "As a start," I said, "may I suggest Gregory Peck?" That started it "Gary Cooper" someone said. "Eggward G. Robinson" was another's contribution. Peckahontas, John Steinpeck, Joseph Pullitzer, Henny Youngman, and perhaps my favorite, Fryar Cluck were some of the offerings of the day.

There was nothing accomplished in at least one section of sophomore English that day. Later that night after Alison and I had gone through our critique of the day we were on my bed with our thoughts seemingly far away from what the day had offered us, and I was lost in the mystery of her when she moved away from my snuggling, looked me in the eye with tenderness and love on her face and said, "Of course if you had a French chicken you could call her "Too loose to peck."

It was not long after our chicken episode that I asked Alison to marry me. I doubt that there are many men who propose marriage who have much doubt as to the answer. I know I didn't have any doubts. I think I was in love with Alison the first week I knew her. And I never had many, if any, doubts about her loving me. We had begun to talk about our future in the plural. It was always what we wanted to do. We wanted a small house that would leave her free to do her studying, until she finished her BA. We wanted two small cars instead of one big one and one small one. I knew I couldn't afford anything more, and she knew what my salary was. She did not care that I was in a profession that would never leave her free to spend lavishly, but she looked expensive to me. It had been *we* for a long time before I formally proposed. She said no.

"But I love you," I said. "Don't you love me?" I sounded like a disappointed child. I was a disappointed adult.

"Of course I love you, you know I do."

"Nothing is of course about love, and if you love me, why can't we be married?"

"Well, my father wouldn't like it. He's never met you."

"We can take care of that in a hurry."

"I don't know Clayton, I do love you, but can't we go on like this for a while?"

"Sure we can. I didn't mean we should get married right away. No I'm lying. I hate getting you back to the Pi Phi house at 10:30 on week nights, but, but. . ." I couldn't understand her reluctance. I wasn't prepared for it. She's just a sophomore, I thought. Maybe her parents have planned her debut or maybe a trip to Europe that she hasn't mentioned. But I was hurt and surprised. She kissed me and said,

"Darling let's go visit my parents this weekend." She had more reluctance in her eyes than I thought should be there, however.

The next week was filled with thoughts of Alison saying no, while she protested yes. Then one night close to ten as I was getting ready to walk Alison back to the Pi Phi house two old friends, Louis and Howard, inebriate of somewhat more than air, and debauchees of do, dropped in. At first I was glad to see them because I wanted to show off Alison, but I soon became embarrassed. Louis continually bragged about his things: cars, boats, airplanes, gonorrhea. Howard matched Louis' charm by bragging about his position in the law firm. I made matters worse by making some bad jokes about "firm positions" being "hard" to find. No one laughed, and I cast a pall on the proceedings. I was mad and a poor host and in the process insulted Alison by being the adolescent pouting boy. Even though I had been an ass, I had to ask Howard to take us to the Pi Phi house so I could get Alison to the sorority house before curfew. His car was behind mine. Howard drove too fast, but we were late anyway, and Alison was mad at me anyway for being such a childish ass.

To make matters much worse as I tried to explain on the steps of the Pi Phi house about my jealousy of their money, rather than telling the truth, which was that I was hurt, and I was not making decent decisions because I was hurt, sick, and mad because she had said no. She had not just tried to put me on hold. She had no in her eyes, and I knew it, so I made matters worse between her and me. Then another bad thing happened.

The house mother came out of the house bellowing like a wounded bull elephant about my having ought to have known better. As she continued to gnaw at me, she became more convinced of the moral correctness of her position. She knew who I was and she objected to one of her girls dating a faculty member, especially one who was contemptuous of the rules enough to break one. Years of frustration began to pour out of this old woman. She wouldn't let me apologize or explain, and as she continued to yell at me, I gave her the finger and left with her yelling that the Dean would know about this. I was certain she was right.

Because the porch lights, flood lights, remain on until all of the girls are in the house are in, many girls at other sorority houses were at their windows waiting at first to see who was late. It grew worse. Many boys were waiting in their cars. As I walked back to my hysterically drunk friends, both SMU graduates, horns were blowing wildly with appreciation. I climbed back into the car and directed Howard and Louis to the Killarney Bar and Lounge on Greenville, a place we had way too often visited when we were undergraduates. I joined them in their drunkenness just like the old days.

Explaining the whole fiasco to Alison, my chagrin, my hurt wasn't difficult except I had to do it by phone because she had been campused. Anyway, she was understanding beyond her years. Explaining to the Dean was more difficult.

Dean Cairns called me into his office and asked for my side of the story. I varnished nothing and told him exactly what happened. He couldn't hide his disappointment.

"Dr. Lorr, Clayton, this is bad business I've known for some time that you were keeping company with one of your students, but I had hoped that the problem would take care of itself. It hasn't." He was a gentle man, and I began to feel sorry for him.

"Dean Cairns, I want. . ."

"Let me finish, Clayton. This is important. You could have a good future here, and jobs aren't easy to find. I'm not going to tell you how to live your personal life, but you must be . . . well, discreet. Enough said?"

"Yes sir," was all I could say.

"One other thing, Clayton. I've received a complaint about your grading. There's nothing to it, I'm sure, but don't let the black marks stack up."

Later that evening when I began to put the day in some order, the Dean's last remark began to seem more important. It was not like the Dean to report one remark about unfair grading. It is a common complaint among the disgruntled, and usually it is ignored until many such complaints have been lodged. Blackerby, I thought. It must have been him. He must have gone to the Dean, complained and hinted about alumni power. Blackerby's family, especially the Slaughters, are powerful people at SMU. I went to my desk for a copy of the catalogue. Yes, Theodore F. Slaughter on the governing board.

I met Alison's parents the next week after Alison was no longer captured on campus. I was thrilled in a way and terrified. Alison's father, I found out on the way to Anson had been educated to be an attorney. He never practiced law because his father had died soon after Jerry had graduated from the University of Texas Law School, and Jerry had taken over the ranch. Jerry and Claudette had met as undergraduates at SMU. Alison was a legacy to the Pi Phis and Jerry had been an enthusiastic, active Phi Delt. It would be better, she quietly informed me, not to start on my usual harangue about fraternal organizations. It seemed almost accidental that she had told me all this. Oh my God, I thought, and shuddered at the thought of a weekend with Jerry and Claudette Leach.

As we drove through what must be laughingly referred to as downtown Anson, I could not help but wonder how such a rose as Alison could have been nurtured in such a weed bed as Anson. One had only to look at Alison and talk to her a few moments to know that she fairly reeked with old money, old at least for Texas, but I was not prepared for the sight of her home. As we drove across the flat land north of Anson, her house seemed to grow out of the horizon until I thought it was a joke, a mirage. It was three stories high, and had it been in a city, it would have covered a city block.

"Gaudy," I said without thinking.

"Yes, isn't it? Grandfather built it at about the time I was born. I don't remember him well, but father told me the old man tended to overdo everything." As I pulled into the circular driveway and up to the front door, I fully expected an army of "Negras" to come sweeping out saying Oh Miss Alison wee's so glad you home. Scarlett's Negras never showed, however. In fact, no one came to meet us. I started to ring, but Alison just went in, saying no one ever locked the doors. We walked in through a dark, large living room to a large dark paneled game room.

Here was the Negress I anticipated. A large (fat) old black woman grabbed Alison and squeezed her until she almost went out of sight. Alison's black hair was enveloped like a small fly in a plant the size of a dirigible. The woman was huge. Her arms were covered with enough material to make into a sail for a schooner. I stood there with my jaw dropping lower and lower until they finally acknowledged my presence. I missed the first utterances of Alison's because her voice was muffled in the folds of enough cloth to outfit a platoon of Marines.

"Is this the one?" the old Dilsey-like earth mother said. The one what, I thought, but the old lady's grin, wide enough for a Volkswagen to enter, captured me, and I soon felt at ease (with a servant). Etta, the zeppelin, explained that Mrs. Leach was in town, grandmother was upstairs, and Mr. Jerry was out doing on the ranch doing whatever he was always out doing.

Alison led me to my room on the third floor. She checked to see that the room was in order before she tried to leave me. It was perfect. It was exactly what a guest room should be--private bath, clean linen, bible, Kleenex, and even a tooth brush in case I had forgotten mine. I tried to get Alison on the bed for a moment or two of snuggling, but she said, "What would Etta say?"

I told her that obviously Etta couldn't get up the third flight of stairs without a hoist, and I was sure Etta was just an apparition because the Hindenburg, to my certain knowledge, had blown up in 1937.

Alison left and I looked around the room and out the windows and saw flatness. I showered and lay on the bed until almost dark. I had just decided to dress and go downstairs, thinking I might have been forgotten in the reveries of family reunion when I heard Alison's voice.

"Clayton, Clayton, can you hear me? The intercom is above the light switch by the door." I finally found the switch, muttered some "Rogers" and "Overs," World War II Air Corps dialogue and agreed to parachute down for supper at 7:00. I was in the same position as a novice sea traveler. I didn't know whether to dress for din din. First night out is casual, I decided. Grey slacks, sport shirt, non-nautical, non-rancho attire. However, as I was about to descend the stair with no bald spot yet in my hair, a wave of panic swept over me. How could I rely on my judgment in a situation like this? Clearly my blue serge was called for. After all, these people had their own Negroes.

Although the seat of my old suit gleamed dully like the sides of a hearse, I felt almost confident as I strode in to the dining room to greet Mr. and Mrs. and Grandmother and Alison Leach, all of whom, except for Grandmother Leach, were clad in their best Sunday Levis. "Merde," I muttered, trying to be brave.

Supping was a success. Everyone was gracious, friendly, and warm. Later, Alison said I was almost subdued, only a few puns. Mr. Leach had told me to call him Jerry. Neither of the Mmes. Leach did anything to alleviate

my difficulty in that area, however. Being forced to address the ladies as Mrs. Leach forced me to be sure I had
the eye of the one I was speaking to—a difficulty for me
that neither of them noticed. They all took turns asking
the polite, but ever so important questions. I was twenty-
six, Kappa Alpha, Democrat, and Libra. I just threw the
Libra in, no one asked. Almost blew the warmth. I tried to
find the right blend of being impressed but not awed as
I searched for the right questions with which to appear
bright. To Mrs. Leach, the elder, I addressed the question
of how long she had been in this part of the state. I had
struck the right note with her. She became positively garrulous until Mrs. Leach, the younger put her in her geri-
atric place with a few withering looks. With Mrs. Leach,
the younger, I hit the wrong note by asking her about her
flowers. The house was filled with flowers, and the road, a
long one, the driveway, was lined on both sides with flowers. She told me a great deal about flowers, more than I
wanted to know until she discovered that I knew nothing
about them. Disappointment after having found then lost
a soul mate, I suppose.

So far with the Leaches I was one for two. I noticed that
Jerry seemed impatient with the talk about flowers, so I
supposed him to be a practical man who thought that
everything planted should be a money crop. After supper, as he and I were drinking bourbon and water, and I
was trying to play the part of a practical man, "down-to-
earth," whatever that means. Jerry took this opportunity
to ask me about my "prospects." This seemed to be THE
moment for which I had been invited to Taj Mahal west.

And though I lied by a gross amount about my salary
when I became a full professor, Jerry was obviously not
impressed. Alison, however, seemed pleased and held

onto my arm, so as to say to her father, don't be so rude. Jerry felt better later when he had beaten me a few times at pool and Ping Pong. (I could have beaten him in Ping Pong, but even though I kept the games close, he was the big winner, and damned if he didn't seem pleased with me then.) I thought something less of him, however.

Then we "adjourned" to the living room so Alison could play the piano. I was not surprised to note she was good. At this time, it finally dawned on me, Mrs. Leach, the younger was playing a *Gone with the Wind* game of life while Jerry was playing Rock Hudson's part in *Giant*. I was not sure about Mrs. Leach, the elder, nor was I sure about Alison. Maybe she knew her part, and maybe she didn't. I never mentioned anything about the evening to Alison after we returned from fantasy land.

I felt better later after we had all retired. I heard Alison on the intercom.

"Clayton, can you hear me?"

"Yes darling," I said hopefully.

"Shelley."

"What about him?"

"Not him, silly. Hens are female."

I was even topped by Jerry in the pun department. I was bragging about when my older brother was in his last year of medical school, he began to date his pharmacology professor. I was reliving my greatest pun I thought when I told the Leaches that I had asked my big brother about her family. He had explained that her family were farmers in Illinois. So I bragged: I said that I had said that she was a former farmer pharmacologist. Jerry immediately said, "But she was still outstanding in her field." My opinion of Jerry rose again, but I hated being out punned by him.

The rest of my stay I was given the grand tour of the "place." I was treated cordially by everyone except Aunt Jemima—Etta who was effusive. I took that as a good sign. I was, of course, looking for good signs. On our way back to Dallas, Alison was quiet--no mention of marriage.

The only interesting aspect of the journey home occurred when I saw a car with a decal on its back bumper extolling the virtues of the Winters' "Blizzards." Alison had to explain that Winters was a small town not far from Anson and instead of having a mascot something common like Buzzards or Pole Cats, they were the Blizzards. Bangs, Texas is also in this area and I could not resist the urge to suggest that Bangs should be the Bang's Gangers, gang tacklers, I had to explain. Alison thought this had merit and about twenty miles or so farther down the road, she said, "Pants."

"What's that?"

"Anson's football team," she said looking positively bored. She had won again I was pleased to note.

As the semester came to a close, I saw less and less of Alison. I had told her what the Dean had said, and we were, I thought, being discreet. Then too, I knew she was studying for finals. Whenever I did see her, usually on weekends, if I talked of marriage she grew evasive and changed the subject, but we still had good times in my inexpensive fashion.

One day after class, we no longer left together, as I followed her into the hall Blackerby came up behind her and put his arm around her. I stifled an urge to run after him and throw him down the stairs, but I thought she would push him away. She didn't, but she did look back at me apprehensively. That night I called the Pi Phi house, something we agreed we wouldn't do because many of the girls knew my voice, but she was not there, so I was told. The voice told me she was at the library, but I heard or thought I heard a giggle in the background. Soon after that I put a note in one of her themes asking her to call me. After a few days with no call, I resolved to catch her after class—to hell with the Dean.

"Miss Leach, may I see you for a minute after class?" She was obviously startled and not pleased, but she waited patiently until a young lady ran out of questions to stall with and finally left.

"Well?" she said.

"You're getting pretty friendly with Blackerby, aren't you?"

"Oh that, my father and Franklyn's father are good friends. I've known Franklyn since I was a little girl."

"Oh," I said somewhat shocked. "How well do you know him?"

"What do you mean by that?" she asked with obvious irritation in her voice.

"It's a simple question. I haven't seen much of you then I see Blackerby with his arm around you, acting like he knows you very well. What's going on?"

"A gentleman would never ask a question like that."

"To hell with gentlemen."

"Two gentlemen I know agree in their opinion about you too."

"Two gentlemen? Who do you mean, your father and Blackerby?" I could see I had struck home, though she did not answer. "Okay, so maybe I didn't pass the test with your father, but Blackerby doesn't like me because he's a crummy student who is used to making good grades because he's polite, usually, his grandfather's on the governing board, and he says yes sir a lot. And in my class that crap won't work, so he's out to get me with the Dean and you. He uses politeness as weapon, Alison." I had begun to plead so I shut up, embarrassed.

"You don't understand Franklyn," she said very coolly. "He's not out to get you with anybody—he's not that sort of a person."

"Bullshit."

"You know for a person who is supposed to have read a lot, your vocabulary is often limited."

"Alison, call me tonight. You know I can't call you."

"If I can."

"What could stop you, Blackerby? Alison, don't let that shithead come between us."

She did call, although I was sure she wouldn't. We didn't have much more to say, however, and in fact, we said nothing of importance, but we were civil. And I hoped that meant something.

Blackerby had begun to act smug in class lately, though his grades remained borderline. I first assumed his smugness came from the low Cs he had been making lately, or his talk with the Dean. Perhaps his grandfather had been talking to the Dean too. More likely grandpa was talking to someone on the board who was talking to the president.

When the phone rang that night, I grabbed it quickly, hoping it was Alison.

"Dr. Lorr, this is Franklyn Blackerby."

"What can I do for you, Mr. Blackerby?"

"You may come to the house this Friday evening. Several professors will be there. It is the annual end of year appreciation dinner for some faculty members, surely you remember."

I started to decline. I wanted to decline, but I remembered there are several KAs in my classes, not just Blackerby, and I thought the Dean might be impressed that I was invited.

Friday came slowly. Alison didn't call all week and kept her distance after class. And Blackerby smiled all too complacently.

As I walked toward the fraternity house in the darkness, my heart began to beat rapidly, and I thought about going back to my apartment, but I didn't. It was rather like looking over the edge of a cliff. You're afraid, but you continue looking.

A pledge met me at the front door and had a name tag ready for me. I strolled about the house and noticed that not much had changed except some furniture and the carpet in the years since I was last in the house—almost five years ago. I greeted faculty members and students in a jocular mood—them, not me. I saw Dean Cairns as I entered the game room in the back the house. As I stood talking to him, Alison, on the arm of Blackerby, came in the back door behind the Dean and in front of me. Blackerby must have been waiting outside the game room windows. He timed his entrance carefully.

"Dean Cairns," said Blackerby, not looking at me, "I'd like you to meet Alison Leach. We were pinned last night."

Later, Louis who as an old KA, had invited himself and Howard to the party told me that I said in a clear and especially loud voice, "Blackerby, you mother fucking son-of-bitch."

That night Alison called me to tell me that she was sorry about what happened but she was sure Franklyn hadn't planned it.

"Horseshit," I said and hung up. The Dean called next and told me not to expect to return to SMU the next fall. Howard and Louis were with me, and Howard suggested I go to law school. Louis offered me a job in one of his Savings and Loans and promised me I would be making more next year than the Dean.

I suggested we all walk the ten blocks to the Killarney and get drunk. As we walked along, the moon came out and bathed us in an eerie glowing silver-grey light. I felt surprisingly calm and clear headed. After all I had three months' pay coming; surely I could find some university with low standards that would want me. And oh yes, Blackerby, the mother fucking son-a-bitch, failed English that semester.

Stunning

Her hair was dark, almost black and was smooth, soft.
The perfect hair was not long unless you think to the shoulders
is long. The hair tried to cover her gently rounded shoulders,
and stayed together, each strand loving the other, protecting it.
The shoulders when she talked, tried to meet in front
of her words as if they were forming a gentle cool wave.
A soft downy breath uttered pure distinct syllables
that hesitated to leave pink, sometimes red, round lips.

Words can do nothing for features that are symmetrical,
neither side of her face ascendant. Her eyes needed no help,
but if she had worn glasses they would have been straight as virtue
across her face. She never gave in to earrings, fingernail polish,
or perfume. She never had that vapid look of models in magazines
that sold sex. Thoughts flashed through her eyes.

Her waist indented flatly, her hips sufficient to support all eyes
descending to do her homage. The legs under all pulchritude
were symmetrical as her face, smooth as her hair, held her
about 5'7" above a fortunate floor. When anyone,
professors included, didn't stare, he was pretending
to be cool. Eyes yearned to leave a recalcitrant head
that wouldn't bend or twist. Alison Leach was,
perhaps still is, the name for a rare fortuitous blend
of genes that did not return to SMU for a third year.
The buildings mourned with doors hanging open,
windows weeping dust.

CLAYTON

■

Prologue

Clayton Lorr was admitted to a selective college, but he was on a waiting list and lucky, he knew, to get in, even at the last minute, and he was lucky that his mother insisted that he attend this expensive private school. Clayton's father did not want to send his son to a private university. Clayton Sr. was unable to say no to Mrs. Lorr.

Clayton had trouble packing, and his mother told him what to take to college and what to leave, except Clayton couldn't leave without having Sandra at his house all morning as he was packing. Clayton knew that his mother wanted the time to be alone with him for last minute advice and an affectionate hug, but he couldn't control the situation, so his mother pulled him into the laundry room and said her tearful, huggy goodbye, slipped him more money, and tried unsuccessfully to remember what Greer Garson had said to her son on the eve of the Battle of Britain.

As Clayton pulled out of the drive with "things" bulging from his classic 1960 Ford Thunderbird, Sandra was in the front seat with him. They went to Sandra's house where Sandra's mother had left more food for him.

Later that afternoon, when Clayton was finally able to leave for the twenty minute drive to Dallas, Sandra cried and asked him not to go. He was relieved to leave her standing in the driveway, her hair asunder, pledging her love forever. Clayton sniffled and pledged his undying love and repeated his vow to be home for the weekend when the high school was having its first football game. He headed east to the big city.

That evening as Clayton was unpacking his "bird" and meeting his roommate the roommate's older brother came into the overstuffed dorm room and said that he had promised two dates for his girl's sorority's pledge dance. His little brother and Clayton would have to do, he said.

Clayton was unable to come home for the football game, which his old high school won easily, his mother and Sandra told him on the phone.

Ten years later

In Texas, September and most of October are as hot as July and August in most other parts of the country. As Clayton Lorr was walking to his first class of the new school year, he pulled on his collar and resolved to remove his tie after the ten o' clock convocation. He could feel his blown-dry black hair falling limp on his collar. When he turned the corner at the library, he saw Ginny coming at him. He felt like turning back, but it was too late. She saw him.

"Oh Dr. Lorr," she called.

"Hi, Ginny," he said smiling.

"I'm enrolled in your romantic poets class."

"Oh good, that's nice. I'll see you there . . ."

"I tried to call you once when I was in Dallas this summer, but your mother said you were at the library."

"I spent almost the whole damn summer at either the SMU or the UNT library. I'm sorry I missed you." As he looked at Ginny, he felt his firm resolve melting. At 5'2" Ginny should have been in the cute category, but she was far from being merely cute. She had long brown hair, a light complexion, and a face that often appeared mildly Eurasian. A lucky blend of genes, he thought. She had a perfect figure, good legs, her best feature, and full, round breasts. He was always surprised that she was short. He always remembered her as tall until he was next to her. From his height of 6'2", he looked down on her as far as her cleavage.

"Did you get anything published this summer?"

"Too soon to say. I have hopes."

"I just know that everything is going to work out fine for you."

"I certainly hope so. I'll see you in class in a few minutes. I've got to go to my office," he said as they climbed the stairs of Dallas Hall.

"Okay. I saw Pete and Billy at registration," she yelled after him. "They say they are going to be in your class too."

"Great." He smiled back at her as he rounded the corner to go up the stairs to his office.

Ginny was one of two work-study students who had worked part time for the English department as communal secretaries last term. He had hoped she had not been placed at the English department again, but she would have said so if she had not been assigned to the department. It is going to be hard to ignore her, he thought.

To get to his office, he had to pass by Dolores' open door. He couldn't risk trying to sneak by. He stuck his head in the door: "Good morning, Dr. Plyburn."

"Good morning, Clayton," she purred. "Have you got a minute?"

"Well, I've got just a minute or two before class, yes."

"This won't take a second." She came from behind her desk to the doorway, slyly looked both ways down the hall and pulled him, ever so gently, into her office. She straightened his tie, stood on her toes, and gently kissed him on the cheek. "I loved last night." A woman of few words, he thought. "And you made a big hit with Mrs. Cullmer, I know. She went on and on about how handsome you are."

"She certainly likes to dance the slow ones. I was afraid you or Dr. Cullmer might think it strange, our dancing so much."

"Nonsense, Clayton. I wanted her to see you."

"I know I've got you to thank for the invitation."

"I can be a big help to you, Clayton."

"I don't know. Can you help me get something published?" He said with what he hoped was a boyish and guileless grin.

"Maybe I can."

"I hope so," he said, "but right now I better not be late to class. Cullmer wouldn't like it. I'll meet you after class, and we can walk over to convocation together, if you like."

"Yes, let's do," she said returning to a business-like tone.

The first class of the year was easy enough. He acknowledged a few friendly faces, gave them his office number, the office hours he didn't intend to keep, assigned the text, and tried not to stare at Ginny's legs.

"It's all in the syllabus." he said to every question. When he tried to end the class with the purely rhetorical "Are there any questions?" Pete Laughlin raised his hand

and said," Dr. Lorr, did you know that the radio station in Armageddon is KEND?"

"I can see how you spent your summer, Pete. We better go."

"How about KKKK in Selma, Alabama?" Lorr heard as he was walking out the door, smiling in spite of his intention. "KDUM In College Station?" Lorr hurried his step, but found that Ginny was beside him. Pete was close behind her, but she gave him a stern look, and he trailed away.

"Did you get your old apartment back?"

"Yes, didn't give it up. How about you? You're not in the dorm are you?"

" No, I have an apartment close to yours. I knew you didn't give it up."

"Roommate?"

"One, but she is not going to be here weekends, she says. Her home is in Dallas, and she'll spend her weekends at her house or traveling. She's got a boyfriend at Austin."

"Good, I missed you this summer."

"I missed you too. Here's my number." She put a folded piece of paper in his coat pocket and strolled away as Lorr reached his office. When he looked back at her as she reached the end of the hall, she looked around at him with a sultry look that he knew she had rehearsed. She had been gone about thirty seconds when Dolores stuck her head in his office door.

"Finished early, did you? Thought you might. Ready for convocation? Dr. Cullmer's speaking."

As he sat beside Dolores, not listening to Dr. Cullmer's attempts at drollery, he wondered how he could get things so muddled the first day, the first hour even. He looked at Dolores intently listening to Cullmerisms and decided she was about thirty-five. He had started dating Dolores during the summer when he was bored. He enjoyed her company for a while, a few dates. She was often witty, intelligent, and she liked him. That was about all he really required.

She had already been a big help. Cullmer would never have given him, an untenured young assistant professor, a junior / senior level romantic poets class if Dolores had not spoken for him. But what will happen to me, he thought, if Dolores finds out about Ginny?

One evening during the summer Dolores had taken his arm and by her actions broadcast to the college community that she had a man, a younger man at that. Okay, he thought. I'll stay away from Ginny. Cullmer and his insane wife both love Dolores, and she is not too bad looking. Good figure, nice boobs, thin. If only her face weren't so long. She looks a little like six o'clock. She's shy and inhibited compared to Ginny, but who isn't? Madam Pompadour?

Predictably, it had been the third date before he got Dolores into bed, but he had not predicted how she would take over his life, possess him and hint about their impending marriage. If he started up with Ginny again, Dolores was sure to find out. She'd be devastated again like last year with that musician, and she would tell Cullmer. Cullmer was sure to be fussy about professors sleeping with students, and he'd be through. At age twenty-nine, he'd be selling encyclopedias or maybe he'd have to teach in a junior college—God forbid.

Okay, break off with Ginny, carefully, get some things published, but avoid marriage. He looked over at Dolores again, returned her smile, and then saw Ginny across the aisle staring at him.

II

"Come in Dr. Lorr."

"Thank you, Dr. Cullmer"

"Now let's see, what can I do for you?"

"You sent for me, Dr. Cullmer."

"Oh, did I? Of course, of course. Now let's see, I have your file right here. Uh, Miss Pirtle?"

"Yes," came a voice from around the corner.

"Why do I have Dr. Lorr's file?'

"I'm not sure sir, but Mrs. Cullmer called to remind you that you have the weekend party on the seventeenth." Miss Pirtle appeared at the door, straightening her dress, and fluffing her hair.

"Oh yes, thank you Miss Pirtle." She remained in the doorway. "Mrs. Cullmer is having some friends out to our lake cabin next month. Mrs. Cullmer hopes that you and Dr. Plyburn can attend. I have forgotten the exact date, but I'm sure we can let you know the particulars later."

"Thank you, Dr. Cullmer. I'm sure that I, that we, Dr. Plyburn and I can be there. Won't you be there, Dr. Cullmer?" Miss Pirtle laughed and started back to her desk.

"Of course I'll be there. It's my house, isn't it? The better question is have you heard from *Victorian Poetry*? Of course you haven't. Be sure to let me know when you have a favorable reply. Dolores says that your article is on . . ."

"Houseman, sir. *Elements of Classical Rhetoric in the Poetry of A.E. Houseman.*"

"No, that's not it." Laughter came from around the corner. "Dr. Plyburn tells me that you have quite a good chance with your article."

"I hope so sir."

"Well, you mustn't let me keep you Humphries." More soft laughter from around the corner.

"Uh, no sir. I must get to class."

As Lorr was leaving, Miss Pirtle smiled broadly at him then laughed out loud. Lorr reflected that Dolores must be wrong. The man must be senile.

If, however, he did have a good chance with the Houseman paper, the reason was that Dolores had written almost the entire paper. She had tactfully suggested that she might help him re-write certain parts of the article, but as each night grew longer she took over more of the task until it was far more hers than his.

Lorr was, he decided, paying for the service.

It was a rare evening when he was not at Dolores' house. He had begun to cook the evening meals and, of course, wash the dishes. Then while she was typing and editing, he swept and often mopped the kitchen and dining room floors. He needed to do something, and she didn't seem to need or want his help with the article.

Some evening they went out for the evening meal, other time he cooked in the outdoor grill and always, always they went to bed. At midnight or one or two in the morning, he would wearily get up, dress and go home. Dolores insisted that he go home before sun up. Her reputation.

Dolores was compulsive about almost everything, but she had little experience with men, and she was not sure about the frequency of sexual activity. The only man she ever talked about was the one she could not deny. The year before Clayton joined the faculty, Dolores had been engaged to an instructor in the music department who left her for another man. In addition to being jilted, she had to deal with the certain knowledge that everyone on the faculty knew of the situation.

When Clayton first met Dolores, she had just emerged from the Timberlawn psychiatric hospital. Cullmer and his wife, Inez were protective of her. They, Mrs. and Dr. Cullmer had hired Lorr and presented him to Dolores. Everyone knew this but Clayton. The first year he was on the faculty Lorr ignored Dolores completely, and his stock had gone down with the Cullmers considerably. Clayton couldn't understand why he had become such a pariah. He might never have known if a Madam Mosher from the French department had not told him. Told him all. Still, Clayton did very little. An occasional phone call, and afternoon concert, and a movie now and then were about all Clayton had in mind until one night in the summer when she had asked him if they were going to continue to see each other.

Lorr responded in a casual manner that he had always enjoyed her company.

The next day Cullmer called Clayton to the English office and invited him to a party Mrs. Cullmer insisted on giving. As Clayton was leaving, Cullmer told him that Mrs. Cullmer was looking forward to seeing him and Dolores. Clayton and Dolores were a package deal. Almost anyone could have seen it coming.

Realizing that he had to make the best of an extremely bad situation, Clayton increased his attention to Dolores. He found that he had a willing, warm, but inexperienced sex partner. Dolores had apparently decided that every day was a new test of her sexual attraction.

She initiated most of their sexual activity after their first few nights together, never doubting that he was ready and eager. One night after a long spell of typing, she told him not to be impatient that she was coming to bed soon. He pretended he was asleep, but that did not deter her. She caressed him awake and did what she obviously considered her duty. Lorr longed for a different kind of relief that would not hurt Dolores' feelings and his job chances.

Lorr, whose sex life had previously been sporadic, had always thought of himself as insatiable. He found that he was saturated and satiable—with Dolores.

When the Houseman paper was finished, he had hoped for some respite, but Dolores had "given" him another idea for a paper on Heller's Yossarian as an extension of Hemingway's Fredrick Henry who was in turn an extension of Crane's Henry Fleming. On they worked night after night each doing his or her best at his or her specialty. Lorr wanted to run from battle too. He suggested to Dolores that he was taking too much of her time and that she had her own career to think of. Here he had made a tactical error. She responded that their careers might become, as they—one. Then too since she was a tenured full professor, his argument lacked urgency.

Lorr did not want to hurt Dolores, but he did want tenure. The trouble was that Ginny looked better to him every day. From that first day at convocation, he had meant to call her, but it was almost impossible. His mornings and early afternoons had to be spent on campus, and Dolores occupied his evenings and nights.

About two weeks after school had started, Ginny had come by his office. She shut the door and asked him why he hadn't called. Lorr looked at the closed door nervously and told her the almost truth. He told her that he was in a panic about his job and that he and Dr. Plyburn were collaborating on a job that if successful would earn him tenure. And since he was in the third year of a three-year tenure-track job, his success had to be now. Although the matter of tenure was arcane to her, she sympathized with him for having to spend so much time with "ole horseface" and said she understood.

Outside of class, he had not seen her except when she was working in the English department office. She began to come into his class and go out on the arm of Pete Laughlin. Lorr remembered last year, winced, sighed, fantasized, and began to seriously resent "ole Horseface."

III

"Hello, Ginny?"

"Yes."

"This is Clayton."

"Oh, I thought you had lost my number, Dr. Lorr."

"Come on Ginny. You know the spot I'm in."

"I've heard your story."

"Look Ginny, my parents live in Irving, and they're going to be out of town this weekend, and I thought we might have the weekend together. . . "

"You sure you don't need to be working with Dr. Plyburn this weekend? I see your car at her house every night."

"As a matter of fact, I do need to be working, but I miss you. You know it's hell for me to see you every day and not be with you.

"I can just imagine."

"It's true, Gin. You know if I don't get tenure, I won't be here for your senior year. We'll have the house to ourselves, Gin. We could go out to dinner, maybe take in a movie, and then come home together."

"Well . . . I do have a date with Pete for Saturday. His fraternity is having a party at the lake."

"Okay Ginny. I was just hoping."

"But I guess I could break it."

"Great. I was hoping you would understand. If I gave you my parent's address, could you find their house? It's easy to find, and we don't dare go together."

"All right. What is the address?"

"1708 Glen Valley. It's two blocks off highway 183 in Irving, right off of MacArthur Boulevard. Just past where Texas stadium was. I'll put a map in an envelope in your box at work Can you be there about noon Saturday? I've got to work Friday night."

"Okay, if I don't get lost, I'll see you Saturday."

"I can't wait, Gin. Look, if you do get lost, call me. My parents are In the book—1708 Glen Valley. Sure you've got it? Call me if you get lost, but you won't."

Now, he thought, the only problem is what to tell Dolores, but Dolores proved to be less problem than he anticipated. He explained that he had to spend the weekend with his parents to help his father with some work and that his mother wanted him to spend the night and go to church with them on Sunday. He'd call her when he got back on Sunday.

Dolores suggested that this might be a good time for her to meet his parents, but he explained that his mother was determined to make some repairs to the house before she met his girl. With that, Dolores brightened considerably and told him to go and be a dutiful son. She needed to do some shopping Saturday for some new clothes and beach wear for Cullmer's party the next weekend. Maybe she could get Inez to go shopping with her. With that consoling thought, she bid him on his way.

Saturday came slowly, but by nine o'clock Saturday morning he was on the road to his parents' house. He decided that he and Ginny could stay in the guest bed-room. He'd be sure to wash the sheets after Ginny left. As long as he left the house reasonably clean, he couldn't foresee any problems. From experience, he knew that Ginny's perfume was apt to be the only difficulty. His mother had a good nose, but if he washed the sheets, the central air conditioner was likely to filter the problem. Then too, he'd leave his parents a note telling them that he had come home that weekend so that anything unusual could be explained. He simply wouldn't mention that he had brought a guest. With all this resolved, there was noth-ing to do but wait.

After two hours of pacing and looking out the front win-dow, the doorbell caught him by surprise. With a forced calm, he opened the door, smiled and said, "Hi Ginny. Did you have any trouble finding the house?" Her calm was genuine and after a few perfunctory remarks about plans for the evening, he showed her the house and took her to bed. A hang up call bothered him slightly, before the big moment, but he answered after deciding that one of his mother's friends might be calling. Better to answer than to be asked by his mother why he did not. Probably a neigh-bor has seen my car, he thought, but there was no answer to his hesitant "Hello."

Afterwards, while he lay on his back and watched his heart slowly give up trying to come through his chest, Lorr relaxed and began to be his old punny self—a side of him that Dolores tried to discourage.

"You know, Ginny, with the advent of women's lib there ought to be a special decathlon for women."

"What do you mean?"

"There should be special events for women."

"Like what?"

"For instance, the breast stroke," he said as he reached for her bare breast.

"Oh you, but I see what you mean. Of course you'd have to have the broad jump." She was always quick.

"The one hundred meter douche is a must. And of course, we'd have the twat put." Ginny decided that she had had enough and left him laughing at his own jokes as she grabbed her bra and panties and headed for the bathroom. Lorr lay there for a moment feeling very pleased then decided to go to the bathroom in the hall. He had just picked up his underwear when the doorbell rang. Startled, Lorr thought that one of the neighbors had seen his car and come over to say hello. He thought about not answering it as he rushed to get dressed, but then decided he had better, he didn't want one of the neighbors telling his mother that he had refused to come to the door. "Besides, it's just a salesman, probably," he told himself. "Or maybe two nice-looking, well-dressed young men bicycling themselves toward heaven with a message from Joseph Smith. No Jehovah' Witnesses, please God," he muttered. When he opened the door, Pete Laughlin pushed himself in.

"I know she's here, Dr. Lorr. I followed her, and found your name in the phone book. Just as I thought, you answered."

"Look here Laughlin, I don't know what you think you have to accomplish by busting in here, but this isn't what you think. Miss Walker just happened to drop in as she was in Irving shopping."

"Horseshit, Lorr. I knew about you and Ginny last year. 'Miss Walker,' what a bullshitter you are. And she's my girl now."

"Laughlin, if she is your girl, she isn't here. Ginny isn't here. She and my mother have gone shopping. Now get out of here before I call the police."

Later, Lorr reflected that at this point he seemed to be ahead on points, but then Ginny strolled in from her shower, hair wet, wearing only bra and panties, saw Pete and screamed.

The remainder of the encounter was a bit blurry in Lorr's memory, but it seemed to him that the three of them were outraged from completely different points of view. Each yelled his argument paying no attention to what the other two were saying. Lorr gave up and sat in his father's recliner and moaned.

Ginny was indignant that she had been followed and yelled that Pete had no right to interfere in her life. Pete was outraged that she had broken a date with him to spend the weekend with Lorr. Lorr pleaded for reason, though he couldn't seem to think of any reasonable arguments. There was a minute when Ginny and Pete both looked to Lorr as if they expected him to say something significant. When he couldn't think of anything to say, they ignored him from then on.

After the first shock of seeing Ginny in a state of semi-nudeness, it did not seem strange to any of them that she returned to the bedroom with both of them following. They all continued their monologues as she finished dressing in their presence.

Pete left in a rage, threatening to go to the administration about Lorr, and while this argument had little effect on Ginny, it terrorized Lorr. Ginny steamed about the house, trying to get her hair dry while Lorr, who felt weak and exhausted, returned to his father's recliner.

The following Monday Lorr approached his romantic poets class with great trepidation, but both Pete and Ginny sat in their usual places as if nothing had happened. That day every time his phone rang Lorr felt his heart become staccato, but the ax didn't fall. That night, at his apartment, he had told Dolores he wasn't feeling well, which he reflected was true, Ginny called and told him not to worry because she had talked to Pete after class, and although he said he didn't want to see her again, which she said was all right with her, he didn't seem to be planning any vendetta against Lorr. Clayton wasn't positive that Ginny was right about Pete's intentions, but he felt somewhat better. The remainder of the week, he resumed his old role of being sometimes the man of the house, and at other times the housekeeper for Dolores.

Saturday morning as he was packing for the weekend festivities at Cullmer's lake cabin, he decided he couldn't risk angering Ginny. In order to pay some attention to her he called and asked if there were any new developments that she knew of. In addition, he told her to feel sorry for him because he had to spend two boring days with faculty members. Ginny seemed pleased that he had called and told him that she had not seen Pete. Ginny asked when they could be together again. Lorr was evasive. The truth was that he didn't have any desire to see her again. He hoped she would fall in some gaping hole, get married, or find someone she liked better. However, he lied as usual and told her that he'd see her as soon as reasonably possible. He was eager to see her again, he said. Lorr shouldn't, couldn't make her mad, he knew.

"It may be sooner than you think," Ginny said. Lorr didn't push the matter, but wondered what she meant. It was just one more thing he had to worry about. On his way out Lorr stopped to check his mail. A letter from *Victorian Poetry* was the only letter in the box. It has to be an acceptance, he thought. The big envelope he had enclosed his article in was not there. He fumbled and trembled slightly as he struggled to open the letter. He read the brief, business-like non-personal note three times before he picked up his bag. He felt tension drain from his big toes into the carpet at the notice of the acceptance. His mother would be so proud of him, he thought.

The carpet put the tension back into him like static electricity when he remembered Ginny, Pete, the scene at his mother's house. Cullmer's face loomed large in his picture. The face would remember what he wanted to say this time; Cullmer would love to tell him he had violated the moral clause of his three-year contract. He could see Miss Pirtle laughing as she made out an advertisement for an opening in the English faculty.

He pushed the scene out of his mind and hurried to pick up Dolores and tell her the value of her work. Dolores could tell Cullmer of his success as he stood in the back-ground seemingly unimpressed with himself.

He always knew whatever he wrote would be accepted. He might just become one of the editors of *The Norton Anthology* someday. Normally one article wouldn't mean much, but in a three-year tenure-track job it just had to mean something to get into *Victorian Poetry* with a long article. What the hell has Cullmer ever published? He got tenure before it was tough. Cullmer only saw his name in print in the phone book. "I will get tenure," he thought.

Dolores was more excited than Lorr appeared to be. "Oh darling, how wonderful!"

"I have you to thank, Dolores, and I want you to know how much I appreciate it—you, how much I appreciate you."

"Nonsense, Clayton. It was your idea. I just helped with a few little ideas here and there." He knew better, but he shut up and allowed her to play the role of helpmate, filling the cup of male ego.

"What perfect timing. I mean right before we go to see Cullmer and Inez."

"Yes, I thought of that."

"You did?"

"Yes. I think this will be the perfect time to make our announcement."

"What announcement?"

"Why to tell everyone of our marriage, silly."

"Oh. Well, hadn't we better hold off on that? After all, we don't know for sure that I'll get tenure, and I'm only an Assistant Professor and . . ."

"Don't be silly, Clayton. You're bound to get tenure and be promoted, and I think *American Literature* will take our article on Hemingway, Crane, and Heller too. This is just the beginning, Clayton. Why soon you'll be one of the most published members of our faculty. Cullmer will see that, I know. And it won't hurt that you are going to marry me," she said, counting her toes in her sandals.

Lorr tried to smile as he raced to think of a way out. A car wreck before she fastens her seat belt. He heard the click and thought: no, too messy. I'll have a heart attack. He dismissed that idea too and, suddenly religious, looked to heaven for help. Dolores held on to his arm, even though she had to lean against her seatbelt to do so, and she put her thirty-five year old head on his shoulder. All the way to the lake, Dolores hummed what was for Lorr the death march from Lohengrin.

IV

Lorr had heard the stories about Dr. Cullmer having married wealth, and he had noticed that Cullmer's house in town was obviously expensive, but he was not prepared for the sight of Cullmer's "cabin." It was a large brick hugeness that was probably twice the size of Cullmer's town house. Dolores was not awed by the mansion and said that she had been here many times. They had entered the "place" by going through wrought-iron gates that Lorr had assumed were the gates to an addition, but which were the gates to Cullmer's estate. As they continued on the only driveway Lorr had ever seen with posted speed limits, Dolores explained that although Cullmer and Inez had been married for fifteen years, Inez's first husband had been a wealthy oil-man who had died from a heart attack while in bed with another woman. She had since sought stability by marrying an academic man whose behavior was more predictable.

An interesting story mused Lorr, but his mind was filled with his own disaster. He had decided that there was no way out of announcing his engagement to Dolores, but that didn't mean that he would marry her. A long engagement could be broken in a few months or in a year after tenure, at worst.

Inez answered the door and before Lorr could get the bags in from the car, Dolores had told all: publication, engagement, everything. Inez, still an attractive woman even at age fifty or so, was properly delighted and patiently listen to Dolores tell it all again. Only this time the details for the wedding were included. Lorr accepted Inez's congratulations with a weak smile and agreed with Inez about how lucky he was. Even though it was still early, Lorr had a beer after he and Dolores had been shown to their separate rooms. While Dolores was freshening up and hanging clothes, Lorr went downstairs to find another drink, bourbon and water this time.

They presumed they were the first guests to arrive and Cullmer had gone to town to pick up some supplies that Inez knew they needed but had forgotten. Lorr found his drink and headed to the back of the house until he came to a large room with sliding glass doors overlooking the lake and Cullmer's boat house. He went out the doors and was standing on the patio, looking morosely down at the dock when he saw the form of a young woman sunbathing in the still warm November sun. Lorr put on his glasses and stared. He heard the glass door slide open behind him and looked around to see Mrs. Cullmer with a strand of gray-black hair blowing over into her face, coming toward him.

"I'm glad to find you alone, Dr. Lorr. There is something I want to discuss with you." Lorr had trouble taking his eyes off of the reclining young woman, but he turned to Mrs. Cullmer, forced a smile and said, "Yes, Mrs. Cullmer, what is it?"

"You probably don't know it, but Miss Pirtle, my husband's secretary, was once my first husband's secretary. After he died, I became somewhat responsible for her. In fact, it was I who secured her the position she now holds at the university. Consequently, she feels a certain obligation to me."

Lorr couldn't imagine where this was going, but he had always thought Mrs. Cullmer was eccentric as her husband, so he listened patiently, though occasionally stealing a glance at the form on the dock.

"One day this week," Mrs. Cullmer continued, "Miss Pirtle received an anonymous note to my husband stating that you have been having an affair—last weekend to be specific—with one of your students, Ginny Walker."

"Mrs. Cullmer, I assure you . . ."

"Let me finish Dr. Lorr. I also know that last weekend you went to your parents' home in Irving, and I know that Ginny was out of town for the weekend."

"How do you know that?" Lorr said, seeing his life flash before his eyes.

"It was easy to check on. Dolores told me where you were, and as for Miss Walker, I simply called and told her that I had tried to call her last Saturday and Sunday to ask her and the other young lady who works for the department to come here to help with this weekend. She told me that she had been out of town for the weekend. She seemed awfully glad to come here for this weekend, however. Perhaps the extra money was an inducement, but somehow I don't believe money was the only attraction. Maybe the promise of an early afternoon swim was enticing," said Mrs. Cullmer seeming to enjoy having this fish on the hook.

"Mrs. Cullmer, let me assure you . . ."

"However, Clayton, may I call you that? Since Miss Walker arrived I've talked with her about the reported affair between you and her, and she denies it. She says that she knows the young man who wrote the note. He is a disappointed suitor she says who has made up the whole thing. I'm inclined to take her at her word, and because of my feelings for Dolores, I've decided not to show the note to my husband. By the way, that is Ginny you have been staring at on the boat dock. Let's walk down to see her," Mrs. Cullmer said as she took Lorr by the hand and lead him down the path.

"Ginny, Ginny darling," crooned Mrs. Cullmer, "I've brought your professor down to see you." Ginny looked up casually and said, "Oh, hi Dr. Lorr."

Lorr sensed the possibility of survival and said calmly, "Hello Ginny, nice to see you. I hear you've come to help this weekend."

Mrs. Cullmer was struggling with her hair and said, "Let's step into the boat house. The wind is destroying my hair. That's better," she said as she shut the metal door behind her. "Ginny darling," said Mrs. Cullmer, putting one obdurate strand of hair almost back in place, "Dr. Lorr and Dr. Plyburn are going to be married. They have just now announced it."

For once, Ginny's aplomb failed her. Her eyes widened then filled with tears of undeniable hurt and anger. "How nice," she muttered as she grabbed her towel, opened the door and ran up the stairs to the house.

"I see," said Mrs. Cullmer as she shut the door again. "Then it is true."

"Mrs. Cullmer, there's nothing between Ginny and me. We had a little, hands off flirtation last year, but nothing came of it. Why, I've never even held her hand." Lorr lied valiantly, hoping yet to be able to salvage the day. He had come so close, he thought.

"You needn't deny it now. The truth is obvious."

How bad can junior colleges be, thought Lorr. Then Mrs. Cullmer came close to him, put her hand on his lapel, looked at him and said, "I still may not tell my husband, Clayton, if you'll be a very good boy." She kissed him lightly, looked at him and kissed him again, and then he kissed Mrs. Cullmer, Inez, passionately.

Epilogue

Clayton continued. He had an affair with Mrs. Cullmer whom he continued to address as Mrs. Cullmer even in private. He married Dolores, wrote a book, or was given credit for having written a book on the poetry of John Berryman, received tenure, was eventually promoted to Associate Professor. At about this time a son was born unto the Lorrs. His name is Dallas.

Lorr continued to have affairs with students because . . . because they wanted him. But times changed. The girls he knew told their friends of their affairs with him. The friends told other professors who told the chairman of the department.

Dolores heard of his affairs, usually from the wives of the other professors. Dolores was brave. Everyone said so. She sighed, decided that her tragedy was that she had neither loved well, nor wisely. She then turned her full attention to Dallas.

At about age forty-five, years after Cullmer's death, Lorr discontinued having affairs because . . . because no one wanted him. He began to write poetry, some of which was published, and then he died a failed associate professor. Sandra, without any of her family—not her husband, not her sons, was one of the few people in Clayton's home town who attended his funeral. Dolores did not notice her.

Dallas became a MD with a general practice. Dolores was proud then she died. Dallas retired from the medical profession, opened a little art shop in Snider Plaza, very close to SMU. Sandra was one of his best customers. He grew to like her very much. She never told him that she had once known his father. Dallas never married.

MYRA

———————————————————◾———————————————————

*C*layton Lorr stood up, looked in the large mirror over his desk that had BILLIARD PARLOUR, LADIES WELCOME written on it in large gold letters. He pulled in his belly. He straightened his shirt by inserting his thumbs in his pants and sliding them around each side. After he made sure that his shirt edge and fly were in line, he put on his black camel hair coat and regarded his image. *I like gray in my temples. I remember once thinking I might put that gray there, but that would have been silly.*

He stepped out in the hall and looked for Grady Stevens or Jim Linebarger. They used to go for coffee with him every MWF at 10:30, but lately Stevens had stopped joining them for coffee, and Linebarger was nowhere in sight. Lorr felt for his pipe in his empty coat pocket. He had quit smoking two years before, but he regretted losing the look the pipe gave him. No one smoked now.

As he was standing at the corner waiting for the traffic light to change, he saw her. She was across the street in front of the student union, looking straight at him. The crowd began to move forward into the street. *I could turn back. No. Better to walk on, ignore her.* He could see her out of the corner of his eye. He passed her without looking directly at her, but he could feel her following him. *I can hear her footsteps, even in this surging crowd. I know she is there.* He didn't dare look around, but he listened for her voice. *Silly. She has nothing to say to me. She's better now.*

Only when he stepped into line for coffee did he turn around. *No. Of course she is not here.* He sighed and looked for an empty booth or table. When he sat down in the booth, he saw her at a table to his left, not more than three tables away. She had not taken off her hat and coat, and she had no coffee in front of her. She was staring at him. For a moment he couldn't think of her name. *She wasn't even last year's. . . what? Woman? Paramour? Piece? Girlfriend maybe, but she was no girl. She looks worn, battered, much older, and heavier. Her hair isn't combed. It is trying to escape in all directions from under that tired old hat. The part of the dress you can see from under her coat is not pressed and looks as though it hasn't been pressed for a long time. Neither the coat nor the hat has any shape, no form, and they're cheap looking. She has a blank look.*

"Dr. Lorr, can we join you?" Lorr, startled, spilled coffee in his saucer.

"Sure," said Lorr, reaching for napkins. It was a teaching assistant, working on his doctorate and Bailey, this year's girl, also a Teaching Assistant. He couldn't think of the young man's name, so he looked at Bailey. *She is not beautiful, but she is trim, neat, good figure, good legs. Bailey dresses well, lives alone, and worships me. That's all I require, a little worship.* Lorr smiled at his joke, talked and laughed with the TAs and forgot about Myra. *Myra, that's her name.* He looked at her table, but there were five or six undergraduates at that table, talking animatedly. Lorr looked everywhere for her on his way back to his office, and asked Mrs. Blinn, a communal secretary, if he had anyone waiting for him.

"No one," she said without looking up.

His Romantic Poets class went well that afternoon, and he was pleased with his performance as he walked back to his office, talking with Bailey.

"Why don't you come over tonight? We'll cook out on the patio, if you like, have some vin ordianaire rouge, listen to Vivaldi. The prospect of such an evening would usually bring an adoring smile to Bailey's face, but not this afternoon.

"Oh, Clayton that sounds great, but I've got to finish my paper on Yeats for Dr. Linebarger."

"I can get Jimbo to give you a few more days on that paper. He's not so tough as he seems in class. Really, he won't mind at all. I'll call him now, if you like."

"I can't Clayton. I've got it all in my head right now, and if I wait for a few days it might be gone. I don't think I dare." Their affair had just begun and usually in the first few months with a new girl he could prevail, but not this night. He sighed, decided to watch Monday night football and wondered if he had any beer in the refrigerator.

Lorr's apartment was on the edge of town, and it would have been a perfect place to live but for the traffic. The highway was so loud that on the patio, he had to talk between trucks. *Hurts the atmosphere of cooking out and drinking wine.* "Too hot anyway." He decided he might catch a quick nap before the game and lay on the divan with his head propped upon two, too quickly worn red pillows with white large white flowers on them, pillows that came with the divan. He lay there and looked at the stacks of books that were piled on the floor beside the dining room table, and he quickly glanced at the un-graded themes on the table then averted his eyes to the TV. *Just as well she didn't come. I would have had to clean the place.*

He couldn't sleep. There was nothing on the tube before the game, and he didn't know who was playing. "Maybe Dallas." The phone rang. Lorr answered eagerly.

"Hello."

"Dr. Lorr? Clayton?"

"Oh, Myra, is that you?" He could hear someone breathing softly, slowly. "What is it? Myra, are you there?" *I don't have time to waste like this.* "Myra, do you want something?" He hung up and stared at the phone for the first quarter of the Giants, 49ers game. At the end of the first quarter he went to the Town and Country for a six pack of Coors Lite. The game was on and the attendant was watching closely. "What's the score?" Lorr didn't hear the answer, but smiled knowingly and left to drive by Bailey's apartment. The next day, Tuesday, he had only one class, a freshman composition class. He usually dreaded this class, but he was looking forward to it today. *If I could just get something more published, articles, a book maybe, I could get my teaching load reduced, get away from these freshmen. A pay raise would be nice. Get away from the highway.*

Myra was standing in the hall, just next to the door to his classroom. Both his hands started to tingle. *Catch hold. Again a plain dress and that unkempt look. Without books in her hand she stands out. Everybody must wonder who she is. She's staring at me.*

He started toward her, but she looked horrified and darted down the stairway. He stopped. *Don't want to catch her. Mustn't run after her because she runs. That's like an animal. Time for class. Mustn't look odd to the fresh-men. Breathe deep, slowly.*

After class he looked hard for her as he walked quickly to his office building. He looked for her close, behind trees, behind cars, in passing cars. He developed the 1000 yard stare, scouring the trees at the edge of the campus. He looked at windows of all the buildings close enough to see in. Checked every window. *Damn fool. This isn't Hue. Get your head out of your ass.*

Sitting at his desk that afternoon, he frequently looked out to the hall. He walked to the door and told Mrs. Blinn that he had some phone calls to make and shut his door. In front of that door, she was staring at him oddly, he knew. He usually just shut his door when he wanted to. *There is no need to tell a secretary what you are doing or why. I'm not sure why I shut that door. Why doesn't she call? What does she want from me? Why call and not say anything? Why did she run?*

She was always strange. She cried easily, even when things weren't bad. If she made a B on a paper or on a test, there was no way to convince her the world hadn't just come to an end. She had never seen herself in any true light. Everyone knew that. Everyone on her com-mittee anyway. I never gave her a B in a course. It was Stevens and some others. I couldn't give her a B. She owned me from the first. She let me know that she was willing. The way they all do when they are willing. She was good-looking then. When was that? It wasn't last year. I was with the Bawcome girl then, and the year before. My god, it's been three years. No wonder I didn't know her. She was tall, thin, and had perfect hair, every hair in place.

That night, as he knew he would, he jumped a foot when the phone rang.

"Hello."

"Dr. Lorr. Clayton." her voice was slight, lacking in breath, but urgent as if she were afraid somebody on her end was listening.

"What do you want Myra? Myra, you must tell me what it is that you want." She hung up, but the click was soft. *She was always strange. That was why I got rid of her. No, no. I didn't get rid of her. She couldn't pass the comps. I wasn't the only one who could see that on the comps. I wasn't the only one who rejected her work.*

He sat there for a moment, then walked in to the kitchen, opened the refrigerator and looked in without seeing anything. He shut the door and decided to call Bailey. *I should have called her earlier. She doesn't have to work every night, all night.* The phone rang as he put his hand on it, and he screamed the scream he heard from himself when was a kid and came across a snake in the pasture. He was then surprised at how calm he was when he said, "Hello Myra, is that you?"

"Yes."

"Myra, there was nothing I could do for you. There were five people on your doctoral committee. I was just one vote. I voted for you, you know. There was nothing I could do. You know that." She did not respond. The silence was accusatory. "Where are you working, Myra?" He tried to sound calm, but his voice had too much urgency in it, he knew. A sob or some strange sound from her or the phone engulfed him. It didn't sound human. He was inundated by it, overcome. "Myra, this is a harass-ing call. There are laws. For God's sake, Myra." She hung up.

He looked at the phone. *It wasn't my fault. I usually want women younger than she was then. Why, she was almost thirty-five. She was good-looking though. Tall, firm, dignified, unless she was on one of those crying jags. I wanted to know if she could be reached under all that dignity, resolve, confidence. She had recently been divorced and all that self-possession was an act. I could see it in her essays. Her whole life was just an act. She was always on the verge of coming loose. As comps came near, she became erratic. She stayed in my office all one day. I had to go home, for God's sake. Had to hide.*

I remember I called back three times to see if she were still there. I couldn't have that, could I? She had to flunk the comprehensives. Her thinking wasn't right. We couldn't turn a woman like that loose on unsuspecting college students, could we? It was easy to show that to the others. They understood. A woman crying in my office all day? Looked bad. The others knew about her and me, or they thought they did. She created scenes. She was always unstable. I couldn't go to bat for a woman like that. I knew her best. I had to be objective and make the others see she was neurotic. Can't turn a neurotic loose to teach. Just because I went to bed with her a few times and tried to help her with her studies doesn't mean I have to be responsible for her all her life, does it?

He was afraid of her, he knew. *Violent? What do I mean? Knife? Gun. A knife is not a woman's weapon, is it? A gun. She could carry a small gun in her purse. She's crazy enough. I didn't know she was crazy. How could I know?*

She was a good-looking, mature woman. I'm not married any more. Wasn't then. Hell, I'm not a priest. It's not my job to be a priest. I could call the police. She may have been in a psychiatric hospital for the past three years. No, no I can't call the police. What would I tell them? She hasn't threatened me. The campus is public. She can come in the student union and the class buildings, I think. No law against it. Besides in a town this size, the Dean would know everything in a week or less. Many of the police are part-time students. Affairs happen all the time. Everyone does it. She wasn't married; neither was I. Still, there are ethics. I'm sleeping with my students. She expects to pass. Can you flunk sex? Feels good to smile. That's it. Right after a jarring divorce, her professor uses her, gets rid of her. Uses her, but doesn't help. Hurts in fact. Maybe I better carry a gun. Where is my twenty-five caliber "boot pistol"? I could scare her, if I have to. In the hall? in the student union? Maybe she'd come to my office. I could leave the gun under a piece of paper on my desk and in my open brief-case on my desk in class. She could wait for me by my car though. Could be behind any of the cars. She knows where I park. I could start parking here on the street here beside my apartment. There are side streets I could use, here and at the university. And I could take a different route every time I come and go. Be a pain in the ass for a while, but worth the peace of mind. She could still do it, but I could carry the pistol under my arm, cocked. No, not cocked, what am I crazy? But it would only take a second to crank a round in the chamber. How far can a bullet go in a second? Sixteen hundred feet per second for a forty-five, and that's a slow one. It wouldn't be a quick draw contest though. She would want to see me squirm first.

He could see the look on her face as the bullet entered her body. *She'd be shocked. She'd know I was too much for her then. She'd know then that she was no match for* me. He began to feel better. *I've handled all this pretty well, thought it through.*

He slept with the gun by his bed, and he practiced finding it in the dark. He visualized, and his muscles knew where to go for the gun. In the mornings or at any time, every time, he looked out the window very carefully before he went out the door. He dug out his field glasses, scanned the front of the apartment for anything suspicious, anything different in the day. He saw accomplices hiding in cars that were parked or driving by slowly, and he was ready for them. Ready to jump into action. He had been a Marine; he was ready.

In the parking lot, he had the key to the car in his hand when he arrived at his car. There would be no unnecessary fumbling, looking for keys. Everything would be quick and smooth. The key to his car he kept in his left hand while he had his right hand on the pistol in his coat pocket. *No unnecessary chance taking. She might get me, but I'm ready.*

He began to vary where he parked and the time of day he did everything, changed supermarkets, barbers, everything except go to classes. And even then he took different routes. *I'll trade cars, get one she doesn't know. Had this one too long now.* He felt good about his precautions. He'd be too quick for her; his planning was too good. *There would be a scandal, of course, but I can't help that. Better a scandal than a funeral, my funeral anyway. The student paper might even make a hero out of me.* "Ex- Marine Professor Protects Himself."

Feeling better about everything, he forgot about Myra until the next day at 10:30 when it was time to go to coffee. *Is it wise to be so predictable, but she shouldn't be able to dictate my life.* He put his pistol in his coat pocket and looked at his BILLIARD PARLOUR mirror to see about the bulge. *That looks all right. I can say the bulge is my old pipe if anybody asks. Nobody will, of course. Decision made. Strategy planned. Commit. That's the Marine Corps way.* He slowly stepped into the hall and sighed with relief. It was empty.

Halfway down the hall, past the point of no return, the empty hall seemed unreal. He began to sweat. He looked nervously behind him and quickened his pace. At the glass door he paused, looked all round carefully then strode out with an air of unconcerned purpose, heading for the street. It had rained all night and he could not avoid the puddles that formed in the sunken parts of the old sidewalks. *The grass is too high on either side of the walk. Makes lakes to walk through.* He smiled thinking about walking on water. Watching his feet, trying to dodge the gathering water, he forgot to look around as he walked. At the streetlight where the crowd gathered waiting for the light to change, he remembered to look up. There were no recognizable faces across the street.

The light changed and as the crowd surged forward, he heard a soft voice almost in his ear. "Dr. Lorr, Clayton" He stepped forward and looked backward at the same moment. His heel slipped on the curb, his knee buckled, and he pitched forward, sliding on his stomach and chest in the water. The crowd parted around him. He lay there for an instant and reached for the gun, which might have slid from his coat pocket. Lying on his side in the wet street, he looked up to see Myra standing above him. His hand was in his pocket, gripping the gun. He kept his hand on it as he sat up in the street. She laughed. She stood there, and she laughed.

Everyone stood there for the moment, parted around him, and laughed. Then the crowd came together, passed him, and he was enveloped. Myra continued to laugh as she walked down the sidewalk and into the parking lot by the student union. He stood up, dripping, looking briefly into the faces of the gawkers who passed him, smiling at his discomfort. He saw Bailey standing on the curb, looking in amused disbelief. He was still dripping, standing on his tiptoes, and he watched Myra's car come out of the parking lot. He watched it slowly disappear. He could hear her laughing long after he could no longer see her. He turned to search for Bailey.

DIZZY

———————————————■———————————————

*T*he first time I saw Daniel Zurcher Myers was the day he and his wife moved in to the house directly across the street from me. I was coming home from work and trying to get into my driveway, but I was blocked by his moving van. I sat in my car for a few minutes before I realized that the men I saw coming from the house across the street were coming for another load, not to move for me. I had honked, but they ignored me. I live on a cul-de-sac, and I suppose the driver and his minions were content to block just one driveway, and they really didn't have much choice. They had to block somebody and I was he.

The new owner came out to apologize to me as I was walking up the lawn to my house, and I looked at his furniture as he introduced himself and tried to engage me in friendly banter. I was neither friendly nor unfriendly and not upset. He told me his name and said he would try to hurry the men. I told him not to bother. I think he wanted to talk some more, but I wanted to get into my house to see my wife and our son, who would want to play catch.

I had gazed at his furniture, however and it was odd. Much of it looked as if it had written "Souvenir of World's Fair," on it, but some pieces were obviously expensive. I saw a chair and a sofa that were Chippendale. In the house, I remember I bet my wife that somewhere in that collection we could find a print of Gainsborough's "Blue Boy."

As the weeks passed, I tried unsuccessfully to ignore D.Z., but no one could. He put up a mail box that seemed to be supported by a loose chain. Not only was the apparition of a floating mail box startling, but he had his name painted four inches high and he had the D and Z put too close together. It seemed to say "Dizzy." Hard to say DZ rapidly without sounding like dizzy. I thought it possible he might put his name in neon so passers-by at night could see his name, but we had no passers-by who did not live close to us.

There is something about the house in front of you. You tend to focus on it, even when you don't want to. It is always in front you when you open your door. There is no getting away from it. When it changes you can't help but notice. It is a kind of haunting. The picture is always changing, and you can't help but wonder about it.

One matter I was forced to wonder about was his brick walkway, concrete was called for. Dizzy had put in a brick walkway from his floating mail box to his front door. The Association's rules are quite clear: all walkways must be concrete. No grass where it should not be, between bricks. Since I was secretary of the association, I was asked to write a letter to him telling him he must remove the bricks, and if he wanted a walkway, concrete was called for.

A month later, almost at the time for another association meeting, there was a knock on my door late one afternoon. There was Dizzy standing at my front door in an expensive dark brown suit with a red vest. Wing tip shoes and a cigar completed the picture. After the suit, the first thing I noticed about Dizzy was his age. He must have been in his late twenties, I guessed. I had long held the position as the youngest man in the addition, but Dizzy was at least ten years younger than I.

"You're Lorr, aren't you?"

"Yes," I drawled refusing to mention my name on my mail box as well as on the letter I had sent him.

"I'm Myers. I wanna talk to you about that letter."

"Come in," I said. Then I noticed the cigar. "But leave the cigar outside." He looked at me, trying to decide how to handle the matter and decided to throw the smoldering thing on my Bermuda. I showed him in through the entry to the living room. I remember looking him over carefully. That was the first time I realized that he was short. He couldn't have been more that 5'7" or so. I doubt that he weighed more than 140 pounds. From a distance, I thought him to be taller. His hair was black and combed straight back without a part. He had put something on it to give it a wet look. I asked him to sit, and he looked around the room and chose a comfortable chair that swallowed him.

"I got a room like this, you know, one that nobody uses. Cept I got some heads on the wall." He wanted some reaction to that statement, but I didn't know what to say.

"What did you want to see me about Mr. Myers?"

"You can call me D. Z. Yeah, this letter," he said pulling my letter out of his coat pocket. "This isn't too friendly. I've lived here almost two months and nobody says boo to me cept for this letter telling me what I got to do."

"Your realtor provided you with the regulations, Mr. Myers."

"I know all that. I pay my dues on time. Five hundred a month–that's some dues, you know."

"It's necessary for security."

"Yeah, I think it is a good idea, but I rate more than a letter. You could have just walked across the street, you know. Anyway, I wanted to meet you and tell you that I'm having the bricks taken up next week. I'm having a special thing put down like they put around swimming pools so I can walk down to the mail box and not burn my bare feet. It looks like concrete, you know."

"I'm glad, Mr. Myers."

"You're not going to call me D.Z.?"

About an hour after he had left, it dawned on me that when he came in, he was angry. Something, the cigar maybe, had taken his mind off what he had come for. Why was he mad a month after he had received the letter? Dizzy was clearly a strange little man whose nose was too big for his face. Maybe he's mad about his nose, I thought.

It took two months and two more letters for him to get his new walk completed. And it looked like plain concrete to me.

My wife, normally a sensible and intelligent woman, was on his side from the first. She thought the brick walk was perfectly acceptable and that we had been heavy-handed with him.

"Invite him and his wife over for dinner," she said. The point was that she thought we should make amends.

"We don't know him," I countered. "He could be anything or anybody. He's a Yankee and obviously ill-educated. There is no telling what he does for a living. Nobody can be making an honest living, living in a house like that at his age." I immediately shut up after I said that. I knew what she was thinking. If I had not stayed in the Marine Corps, and if I had taken the job with her Dad's ad agency five years sooner, we could have been living as we do now at about that same age. "Well, not many people can marry as well as I can," I said. She laughed, and I agreed to invite Dizzy and mate to dinner.

I started out the front door to Dizzy's house thinking what a lucky man I was to have such a beautiful, sweet, intelligent, and rich wife. There were, however, many aspects of the life about the Marine Corps I missed. Now I had to pay to belong to a club where I could jog. With all the running and walking and jogging in the Marine Corp, it seems ironic. It was the camaraderie and the feeling what I was doing was important I really missed. Spending one's day, every day, in pursuit of money seems trivial compared to what one does every day in the Corps' life and death endeavors.

From the Kappa house to a Second Lieutenant's billet was a difficult adjustment for Brenda, except for a few teary months, she handled the transition well. I was proud of her. When I was in zone for captain was the time we had our first serious argument. I was a company commander as a First Lieutenant and was thought to be a "Fast Burner" by some. I wanted those captain's bars badly. After I made captain a few years went by and I was still a few years away from the Oak Leaves of a Major. Brenda wanted to go home to Dallas. After a few years her Daddy's money became too much to say no to. Our son, Ryan, was no doubt better off in Dallas at St. Marks than he would have been changing schools every three years while I traveled around the world, but I often missed the good times, the feeling of having proved myself a man every day. I missed the Corps, but I was doing the right thing, I knew.

Dizzy couldn't hide his surprise at my being at his front door.

"Clay Boy. Come on in."

"Call me Clayton," I said.

"Okay, Clayton it is. What are you doing in my neck of the woods?"

"I live close by."

"Yeah, well it is good to see you. You see I got that walk down,"

"It's very nice."

"I guess you guys are happy now, huh?"

"Well, pleased, I guess."

"Can I get you something to drink?" I started to say no. Every instinct told me to run, but thinking of Brenda's admonition I said, "A drink would be nice."

"How about Scotch?" he said jumping from his chair.

"I'd prefer a glass of wine."

"Sure, what do you want, red or white?"

"Red will do."

"Gotcha." He reminded me of a ferret as he hurried back to me with a glass of cold, bubbly something I could barely get down. He looked eagerly at me as he sat down holding a glass of the same concoction.

"I came to ask you and your wife to dinner."

"Hey, that's nice of you Clay Boy. What night you want us?"

I hadn't thought of that.

"You know, I forgot to discuss that with my wife. Will it be okay if I call you in a few minutes? I'll call you as soon as I talk with Brenda."

"Sure, say let me get my wife in here and introduce you." With that he jumped up and ran out of the room much as he had before. I wondered if he ran around the house often.

I used the opportunity to look carefully around the room. I had never seen such an amalgamation.

Obviously expensive furniture sitting next to junk. I saw a Chippendale sofa and chair. It didn't make sense. Dizzy came hurrying into the room dragging a mousy, stooped shouldered, fuzzy-headed woman he introduced as Brenda. He though it funny that our wives had the same name.

"I'm glad to meet you, Mrs. Myers." She smiled weakly. Dizzy was standing beside her, supporting her. I don't mean emotionally, but It seemed as if he were her physical support.

"Call her Bren, I do. I told you we'd meet some nice people here in Texas, honey. Clay boy has asked us to dinner some night soon."

"Oh?" she smiled again.

"Yeah, isn't that great." Dizzy said. "Can we bring something, some wine, maybe?"

"No," I said glancing furtively at the glass I had left half empty. We were all standing and Dizzy said,

"Sit down, Clay Boy. Is Texas as hot in the summer as everybody says"?

"It's much too hot from April to October," I said.

"That will be good for us, won't it Bren? We're used to long winters with lots of snow and ice."

"Oh, where are you from," I said trying to direct a question to Brenda.

"I'm from Sacramento but Bren here is from Massachusetts. We've been in Rhode Island the last four years though. I was in school there."

"Oh, where?"

"Dartmouth." I almost fainted. "Dartmouth, how nice, and what brings you to Texas?"

"Southern Methodist, I teach at SMU." This was turning out to be one of the most shocking days of my life.

"I graduated from SMU. I taught there for one year after the Marine Corps," I said a little dazed.

"Yeah, good school," he said patronizingly.

"What do you teach?" I knew it would be engineering or business.

"History, he said. "I teach history. That's what My PhD is in. I specialized in medieval monasticism."

His wife again smiled weakly as he squeezed her shoulders from his perch on the arm of her dollar and a half chair, which I thought might break from their combined weight of about two hundred and fifty pounds.

We talked on until I recovered enough to make the walk home, a full forty yards or so. What I learned and told to my Brenda was that Dizzy was a poor boy from California who had earned academic scholarships from Princeton and Dartmouth. Dartmouth was where he had met a rich man's daughter, his Brenda, and he married her. He wanted to teach, but she was unhappy in Texas and eager to return to her Daddy and Massachusetts. It was all reasonable, but odd and shocking. Dizzy sounded like a B movie character, not like an Ivy Leaguer. Upon closer investigation, he was really quite knowledgeable and a sharp person. I could just imagine the impression he made on his parvenu SMU students, however.

My Brenda tried to extend herself and make the dinner party exceptionally nice to entertain them, but I'd say we met with only modest success. Dizzy monopolized the conversation and he lectured more than he conversed. The two Brenda's looked slightly sad and defeated. I tried to change the conversation to include the ladies, but I got caught up in Dizzy's lecture and listened intently.

After dinner, (I was actually calling him Dizzy now and he persisted in calling me Clay Boy). Dizzy and I shot a few games of pool. He was a good pool player, and we began to be friends. I could sympathize with his problems with his wife wanting to go back to Massachusetts. After a few glasses of a good merlot, I told my new friend to stick to his guns—to do what he had prepared himself for. Sure, it was hard on his wife having to stay around the house while he was out meeting people and teaching, but she would adjust and after all she was living pretty damn well, I told him.

"Just what I needed to hear Clay Boy. I spent a lot of years getting this job, and I like it. I never did fit in her family anyway. They want me to go to work for them. They think a PhD is a silly waste of time. What do I know about furniture anyway?"

"That's what they do, manufacture furniture?" I laughed.

"Yeah," Dizzy laughed too.

That evening I was going to tell Brenda what I had learned about them, but she wouldn't talk about them, she wouldn't talk about anything. I shrugged, had another glass of wine and ran the table before I went to bed. All the next week Brenda was slightly distant and seemed sad. I came home from work early, picked up Ryan at school all week and tried to find out what was bothering Brenda.

One evening as Ryan and I were playing croquet, Brenda came out, stood awhile and watched, then took my hand as we watched our son make the winning shot. "She is going to leave him, you know."

"Who?" I said.

"Brenda. Brenda is going to leave Dizzy."

"How do you know? Did she tell you?"

"No, but I know."

"Is this more of your intuition?"

"I suppose so, but it makes sense."

"Makes sense because he is doing what he was preparing to do when she married him? I don't believe that she is that unhappy or that spoiled."

"Maybe not," she said as she went back toward the house.

"Wait a minute," I said following her. "I know he's a little coarse, but surely she knew that when she married him."

"It's not that as much as it's . . . well, she is alone here."

"No more than he is." I said on very weak ground. "They have each other. He's interested in her. He always talks about her. Tries to make things better for her. He loves her, I know."

"He might just be worried about losing her."

"Losing her money, you mean."

"That could be it."

"Maybe," I said slowly. "Was I ever afraid of losing your money?"

"Never, you didn't seem to care at all, not at all."

"See, she has to try. Have they joined a church, a country club? They know us."

"That poor little thing is not going to join a country club. Country clubs are not like officer's clubs, you know. And they go to Temple Immanuel, but it is reform, so they don't go often. He grades papers when he's home."

"That's his job, his career."

"They can't make friends anywhere, she says, but that doesn't bother her. In fact, it once brought them together. To hear her tell it, he was the only social life she ever knew."

"You weren't gregarious either, but you didn't think of leaving me."

"How can she think of leaving him?"

"Now he has his work and doesn't need her. A woman needs to be needed. I remember when you loved the Marine Corps."

"I still love the Corps. It was good to me. I was successful there, and I haven't really been successful anywhere else. I could stay at home from work and your dad would continue to pay me, or give to me. Except for you and Ryan, I haven't really accomplished much, you know."

"Are you that dissatisfied?"

"No, I did the right thing, but sometimes that has a cost associated with it. We just can't be two people. I sometimes wish we could. Dizzy is doing the right thing. She has the cost this time. He will change if they have a baby. He'll have new responsibilities, and then he may do what she wants, but she has to love him enough to wait. And she should be happy, and I'm not sure she would be happy anywhere."

"You don't know that."

"Of course I don't, but she has to try. That I know." She put her arms around me and put her face on my chest. "What are we arguing for?" I kissed her until I felt Ryan pulling on my hip pocket. "Let's play again, Daddy."

The next Sunday, despondently thinking about Dizzy, I climbed into our low roofed attic to clean it out of old worthless items so we could put new worthless items in it. I had been promising Brenda I would throw away our old junk for the last six months. Ryan followed me and played with dusty old toys he had outgrown. He seemed to want to keep some of them, so I let him. With Brenda's old stuff, and mine, I was ruthless.

Ryan uncovered an old trunk of Brenda's that she had when we were in college. It was locked, but the hasp had broken, and he opened it, looking for new old treasures.

We looked in the trunk together. Under some clothes was an old purse. I opened it and found some letters to Brenda from a Lieutenant I knew in another battalion. Letters filled with someone else's love.

They were dated at the time we were at Camp Pendleton in California. The letters talked of places I knew, movies I remember, and of love that I thought was exclusive. When I was on long training missions, she was with him.

Ryan was pulling on my arm. I looked at him, at a boy who was my son, perhaps not sired by me. Ryan continued to pull on my arm, bringing me back to a reality that would never again be quite so nice. Love is, I decided, what I say it is. Love built on strands of time since that time at Camp Pendleton will hold if I say it will. I put the letters back in the purse, shut the trunk, and tried but failed to stand up straight, banging my head on a rafter. I fell on my knees and was slightly woozy. After a minute or two I slowly stood up again, but not quite so tall.

"Where are you going, Daddy?"

"I've got to see Dizzy across the street and tell him that now I am not so sure what he should do."

ARCADIA

---

*W*hen Biford Bickford Bosse graduated from Southern Methodist University, our entire fraternity mourned. I think I mourned more than most because Biford and I had a falling out of sorts in a situation where I was entirely in the wrong, and I wanted to apologize in person.

It had finally dawned on me that I was wrong a few months after I graduated, but I left the country soon, the next day after my graduation. I arrived back in Dallas on the day of Bosses' graduation and attended the ceremony intending to catch him after the ceremony, but I missed him. He graduated in absentia; I should have known. Sitting in the McFarland auditorium, I was desolate, but I had high expectations of a joyous time watching whatever Bosse had in mind to disrupt the evening. Nothing of note happened. I was disappointed twice that evening.

I had expected hundreds of toy soldiers parachuting down on the audience, or maybe "Little Darling" by the Diamonds played in ear shattering volume. "Highly amplified music inundating the unsuspecting," he had once said about the best way to enjoy graduation. I thought it would happen even if he were not there. I was almost heartbroken at the boredom; I stayed through the nonsense to see the "happening." Sad, sad, sad.

I knew that night that it was all over; the legend had ended. As an undergraduate, Biford had become a legend, a tradition, a duty, even an obligation in my fraternity, dating from the first day he arrived in Dallas. Some say the story of his arrival is apocryphal, but it is true.

On his way from Bosse, Indiana to Houston and Rice University, Biford grew tired of driving, stopped in Dallas and enrolled in SMU. The assistant Registrar was a grad student who was a member of our fraternity. He told our fraternity and ultimately the whole school the story about the new student who told the normally formidable Dr. Nystrum, the Registrar, that his religious preference was none of SMU's business. Dr. Nystrum might have reasonably argued the point since SMU is private and a so-called Methodist university. (Actually, SMU is about as secular as schools can be.) The campus had only two rules: Don't drink on campus, and don't throw beer cans out of your car or dorm windows.

Nystrum, however, was too shocked to do anything but smile. Biford had a disarming way of appearing as innocent as Billy Budd, so that many people doubted what they had heard. Something about his actions and his appearance seemed incongruous, so that many unsuspecting persons were always concentrating on the relationship of Biford's words to his other words, and his actions failed to register until later when response was, as is almost always the case, too late.

SMU requires a 1200 SAT, but Rice requires something more. Biford had a copy of his SAT scores. That was enough for Dr. Nystrum. SMU always recognizes real ability, and Biford had the ability to write a check for his tuition, so the interview was a hurried and forgone conclusion.

The first semester a student is on campus he or she is required to live in a dormitory. The only exceptions to the Dorm rules are married students and graduate students. Transfer students are all classified no better than third year students. All students earning an SMU degree must do the last two years work at SMU. About these rules, SMU is adamant, no exceptions. Biford moved into the dormitory in his fashion. As soon as he had unpacked some things in the dorm, he drove off to find an apartment. Biford always kept an apartment even after the first semester when he moved into the fraternity house. "Just need the storage space," he would say when asked about his apartment that everyone knew about.

The one thing about Biford that very few realized, and it is a grievous oversight for some, that money was never a consideration for him in any decision he ever made. He had an unlimited supply. He did not look poor, but nothing about him spoke of money. Biford was . . . unprepossessing.

He was about 5' 10", maybe he weighed 160 pounds, had fair skin, and light blond, already thinning hair. He usually wore long-sleeved shirts in summer and winter, and never a tie except at black or white tie affairs. I thought he bought his clothes at JC Penney's.

I once ran into Biford at a clothing store not far from the university, near the Village Theater, and he looked to me to be embarrassed. After he left, a clerk told me Biford was well known at that store for buying six shirts at a time. To buy six shirts at a time may not be strange, but Biford bought six at a time of exactly the same shirt.

Usually he requested some strange combination of colors which had to be ordered. After that, I noticed that he would wear the same oddly colored shirt day after day. I hadn't thought about it, but I began to notice and think about it, but he would have to be washing and pressing the same shirt night after night if he had not owned several of the same color or, more likely, colors

I thought at one time that his weight varied a great deal, but I decided he could not always obtain six shirts of the same size, so he bought three of his size and maybe two or three of the next larger or smaller size. Most often he wore khaki slacks, neatly pressed, white socks and jogging shoes. Neat, clean, and plebian.

His car was homemade. A neighbor, Biford said, built it, and he bought it for three thousand, and it got forty miles to the gallon in the city. It looked as if it were built by Spanky and Alfalfa. It was only a two-seater, but it had a very large trunk. The trunk was the most pleasing aspect of the car, Biford said. I think he might have been able to carry a Shetland pony in it. The cab was box shaped with corners that came together at sharp angles. It was yellow, hideous and apparently ran well. In the three years I knew him, I rode with him only once. My car failed to start one afternoon at an impromptu TGIF party at the White Rock Terrace. Everyone else had gone, so Biford gave me a ride back to the campus. The car had strange gauges and knobs, but if the car had any special abilities neither I nor anyone else knew what they were.

I don't believe Biford ever drove faster than 55 miles an hour. We all thought Biford was a timid driver. When he got out of his car, he seemed timid too, but I saw him challenge a bigger and known tough guy to a fight. The guy turned down the opportunity. We all sighed. The guy might have had to fight several of us had he hit Biford. We never knew what would have happened, but Biford had no bluff in him, that I learned.

Biford stuck his chin out when he walked, so that he looked as if he was looking down his nose at everybody, or maybe he looked as if he was looking out the bottom of bifocals, but he did not wear glasses. His two front teeth were a bit over long which gave him the appearance of a desiccated Bugs Bunny. He was not an impressive looking man, but he impressed almost everyone.

B. B. Gloriosus

I'm not sure what attracted the fraternity and Biford to one another, but it proved to be a strong love affair. I was a sophomore when Biford came through rush, but he was older than I. He was twenty when I met him. What he had done from prep school until SMU, no one ever knew, but the rumor was that it had something to do with computers or electronic devices and other arcane things.

One story was that he had been a radio operator in the merchant marine. Could be. His father owned a shipping line. There were other stories too. We all guessed, but he would never deny or confirm all these rumors. I think he liked the attention and the mystery, the awe we felt for him.

The rush party where I first met Biford was at George Hutchings mansion on DeLoach street. Everyone, members, rushees, and pledges were looking very spiffy in their best dress, except for Biford. Biford was in one of his many colored shirts, standing in the shade by the pool talking to James Flynn. Flynn was a senior engineering major who was a tall, thin, dark-haired, quiet sort who somehow commanded respect. Whatever he had done to command respect had been accomplished before I came to fraternity life. As I walked around the Hutchings house, I saw them talking all afternoon. If it had not been for Flynn, no one would have thought of pledging Biford. When Flynn said that Bosse was a rare find, no one disputed him.

How I became Biford's big brother was Flynn's doing too. I think he thought I wouldn't be too demanding on the pledge. He was right; it wasn't long before I became, as most people, obedient to Biford. I once saw Dr. Lawrence Perrine apologize to Biford for having to give him an A- on a theme. Biford was, as usual, gracious.

Why Biford chose to be a "Fraternity Man," was something of a mystery to me at the time. He didn't seem to be the fraternity type, and I am not sure the Phi Delts for instance would have had him. He had no recommendations; he wasn't a legacy; and it took some time, usually, to get to know him.

It was my junior year on the Hilltop when some strange things began to happen. One especially strange thing to me was that the most beautiful girl on the campus, Jackie D'Ellis broke up with Erwin Innan. Innan was a predictable Phi Delt. He came from a "good family." He was tall, lean, and muscular. He had curly blond hair and a complexion that could not be called fair, but he was not dark skinned either. Erwin had been an excellent prep school quarterback who refused a football scholarship to SMU. Biford once said of Erwin that Hitler would have loved him.

Of course, Erwin dated "The Choice Jackie D," usually just known as The Choice. Jackie was from Spokane and had conquered SMU for her own from the first week she arrived. She was a Kappa legacy who was just like all of them, but more so. She was tall and flat bellied with longish dark hair. She worse semi-loose sweaters and worked at seeming maidenly. She was better than most of the seemingly maiden Kappas at seeming maidenly.

The Choice Jackie D was tall, about 5'8" or so and artfully proportioned. Her skin was so rich and creamy looking that you would want to bury yourself in it. Her dark hair flowed down to her shoulders where it didn't spread across her back but stayed together without being tied or bunched in any way. Each strand acted as if it loved the other. On a campus literally filled to the brim and above with beautiful women, she was the consensus choice as The Choice. If anyone didn't turn to look at her when she passed by, he was pretending to be cool, professors included. Eyes yearned to leave a recalcitrant head that would not turn to stare. When she left a classroom, the doors hung open, the windows wept dust.

When The Choice Jackie D broke up with GGE, (Greek God Erwin), she began to keep company with Biford. I had rarely seen Biford with dates before, but now he and The Choice Jackie D were going everywhere together. "She went from GGE's BMW and Izod sweaters to a homemade car and sears specials," moaned the Kappa sisters' chorus.

As far as I know, Biford and GGE only spoke to each other on two occasions that I witnessed. The first time was in Professor J. Lon Tinkle's French class when J. Lon asked GGE to read the sentence that Biford has translated to French on the board. The sentence in the text read in English: "The girls are pretty, aren't they?" GGE read: The prostitutes are pretty aren't they? J. Lon smiled broadly, two Kappas blushed, well-rehearsed blushing, and GGE was obviously pleased. At J. Lon's gentle prodding, GGE explained that in Paris idiom, girls must always be spoken of as young or everyone understood them to be prostitutes or at least women of low social rank. Biford returned GGE's smile and said, "How do you know how to talk to prostitutes, Erwin?" J. Lon changed the subject, but both my crowd and the Phi Delts believed their man had emerged on the field that day as triumphant, but it was a minor joust.

Not long after their classroom encounter, they bumped into each other, literally, at Gordo's Bar and Grille. Biford was standing by the bar taking to some blue-collar friends when GGE came to the bar to pick up four mugs of beer for some other Phi Delts seated at a table. Biford turned his back on GGE partly to make room for him, and he turned sideways so GGE would have room at the bar, I think.

GGE was convinced he had been snubbed, and as he turned quickly with the four full mugs in his hand, he sloshed some beer on Biford's back. Biford turned around slowly like in a dream, GGE apologized in a perfunctory way, and then he asked Biford to join him and his friends at their table. It may have been a pretty big attempt at rapprochement on Erwin's part, but Biford said slowly and in a loud clear voice. "No thanks, I'm waiting for friends." The "friends" was strongly emphasized. GGE's mistake was to say "O, la fille est tres jolie, n'est-ce pas." He had just called The Choice a whore. Biford suggested that they step into the parking lot in back and discuss the matter further.

GGE was closer to the door, but he suggested Biford precede him. I rushed to the door beating GGE's three friends out the door by a step. I thought it was going to be four against two, but Biford actually ran about three steps out the back door before he turned to greet GGE. GGE stopped, and the matter might have ended there but for Biford's insistence on an apology. GGE declined and Biford put up his fist in a manner much too like a 1910 fighter's pose. GGE laughed and then I saw GGE's head pop back with a red smear on it, and then Erwin fell forward. As he staggered up, Biford kicked him in the stomach and that ended it. I looked at GGE's brothers, but they had no inclination to fight, and I was relieved. Biford went back into Gordo's and washed the blood off his hands. GGE was a bleeder. I wanted to leave before the cavalry arrived, but Biford refused. He never appeared worried. I was worried enough for the both of us, so I called the fraternity house and asked for reinforcements, thereby strengthening Biford's place in the Parthenon of Kappa Alpha history. GGE was 30 pounds heavier than Biford and had a reputation based on prep days that he was a hell of a good athlete. If someone had made book on a fight between those two, I have no doubt the smart money would have been on GGE, and the ones who bet on Biford would have had to have had odds, good ones.

A few days later, I finally had the opportunity to ask Biford what had happened in the parking lot, and he casually explained that GGE began to draw back his right hand to hit, so Biford hit him with a left jab I missed seeing, followed by a right cross. Biford explained that if GGE had fallen on his back as Biford expected, he would have dropped on GGE's belly. As it was he had to wait for GGE to try to get up before he could end the fight with a kick to the breathing apparatus. I asked Biford where he had learned to fight, and he said from reading Batman comics. On some subjects, one could never expect a straight answer from Biford. That night, the "friend," The Choice I assumed, never showed. Biford later said she was not supposed to meet him there. I asked Biford what The Choice thought of the fight, but he said he had never mentioned it to her. The only thing Biford ever said about GGE again was that he was a smug asshole.

It had always been noticeable to me and to everyone that the fraternity, except for the president, was run by the junior class. Freshmen were too stupid, sophomores did the work and vied with one another for power, but the decisions were made by the juniors, and the seniors shifted the focus of their lives somewhere outside the fraternity. As usual, Biford did something different. He became more occupied and enamored with the fraternity as time passed. He only made quick trips home during vacations and was always the first to return from any vacation, Christmas included.

Biford spent his mornings in class, his afternoons studying, and his evenings at the house or at Gordo's Bar and Lounge. Biford usually had lunch at the house where he presided. He would appoint the pledge to say the prayer and then go to Momma D's apartment—her name was Mrs. Delone–to escort her to meals. Momma D was the house mother who was a garrulous old woman nobody but Biford liked much. He was always on his best when she was around. The pledges learned quickly that would-be witty prayers brought quick retribution if Biford were at the meal. Otherwise, short witty prayers were appreciated.

Biford like most family men tried to keep his two loves together. He began to bring the Choice Jackie D with him to the fraternity house at night. He would lounge around the family room, den, or game room with The Choice Jackie D on his arm or sitting at his feet on one of the many foot stools or on the edge of his chair while he held forth on any subject that came up. We all always enjoyed seeing The Choice assume her poses. Kept many of us out of Gordo's.

The esthetics were too much to miss. It would have been like walking through the Louvre with your eyes shut. We tried hard not to drool or moan too often but with limited success. And she knew and loved the act she put on, but she was good at it. Her eyes never darted around to notice who was watching. She knew.

The evenings were just a casual hour or two of shooting the bull, but Biford was as entertaining as Jackie was beautiful. And there was no entrance fee, and no cost to park. It was a hell of a deal.

I was almost never sure Biford's ideas were sensible, but he was an iconoclast of the first order. I remember one night when a picture of one of our brothers was in the "Hoofprint" shown drinking champagne out of a girl's shoe at a party. We were slightly embarrassed and saying dumb things like "That was sure a dumb picture." Biford interjected: "I hope he comes down with athlete's mouth." The remark may or not have been witty, but it was a better shot than anything the rest of had mumbled, and it was on target.

Some dumb butts thought that hanging around the house was a cheap date for Biford, but they just didn't know him. Some of us worried slightly that The Choice was going to become bored, however. I knew she loved being the Queen of the KA's, but being a Queen is tough, and one may become surfeited with too much homage and become distrustful, and our supply of homage was unlimited. In addition, most of us were secretly proud that The Choice was dating a KA, and that she had dropped a Phi Delt to do so.

Biford had become the royalty of the fraternity, however much he was unlike the royalty of other fraternities. We had our GGE types too, but we much preferred Biford. He had a few jealous detractors in the fraternity, but the great majority of us loved him and thought the detractors were jealous, which they were. Perhaps Biford might not have become our royalty if The Choice had not seen something in him. Myself excluded, many members might not have seen him with new eyes if The Choice had not shown us another lens to see him through, though his trouncing of GGE had put him up on many shoulders, figuratively.

Biford was like an adult playing with children. He would start the game then sit back and enjoy himself enormously. He was, in a sense, our gadfly. When we began to take ourselves too seriously, we could count on him to put the world back into a perspective we could understand. He would whisper, sometimes yell: "Fame is fleeting" over and over again to us, though he was no slave.

One night at a chapter meeting during a very important discussion about fraternity pride George Hutchings, a pre-law student with political ambitions, began to lecture to us on the importance of fraternity pride, especially in the building of a home-coming float. When George began to love the sound of his own voice and drone on and on, Biford stood up, put out both hands as if to demand quiet. He then stood on a small table that did not appear to be able to support him, turned to face the startled Hutchings, and unzipped his fly in a series of several jerky movements. When the fly was completely unzipped, he zipped again with a flourish and stepped down.

Maybe because the gesture had no meaning, and maybe because it was absurd, Hutchings floundered.

He couldn't think of any way to counter such absurdity and consequently he was destroyed. Some of the brothers closest to Hutchings began to laugh and then everyone roared. For the remainder of Hutchings time at SMU, including law school years, when two or more KAs met Hutchings anywhere, on the campus, at the house, or in Dallas anywhere, they unzipped, zipped in salute.

I have thought of going to Hutchings law office recently for a salute in remembrance of Biford. I know he would have laughed. A tribute is a tribute.

We broke with tradition that semester by electing The Choice as KA Rose. Normally the election is held in the fall, but traditions are meant to be broken. Biford taught me that traditions become outdated and they die, except in College Station where anything that happens twice becomes a tradition. The Aggies notwithstanding, The Choice prevailed.

The afternoon after the last final was over we had another C function at the White Rock Terrace. It was here that we told The Choice that she was our choice once again. We surrounded her, and she behaved beautifully. She laughed, she cried a little, and reigned supremely. It was here we learned that Biford was to pick up The Choice early the next morning to take her to DFW for her flight to Spokane for the summer.

When Biford rolled to a stop in front of the Kappa house the next morning, twenty or so of us were standing in front of the house sipping champagne. He was slightly disconcerted, but brave, I thought. We cheered when he came out the door the first time with her luggage. Each trip brought new toasts and cheers but no help with the luggage. The Choice came over to us at the curb and told us that she loved all of us and hugged and kissed some of us. I was first in line. Biford's large trunk was stuffed, but we decided to follow them to the airport where we behaved obnoxiously and sophomorically. We cheered again as Biford kissed her goodbye and as soon as the plane was in the air, we grabbed Biford and took him to Gordo's.

In the summer, little goes on at the house. Most of the members and pledges are gone for the summer. But the house remains open largely because Momma D lives there and a few students remain for summer school. No meals are served and the house is far too quiet.

During this summer, order began to reassert itself. Erwin began to call Jackie, and he flew to Spokane several times. GGE laid siege to The Choice in a manner that was uncommon for him. Those of us who lived in Dallas were given little nuggets of information by a friend of the Phi Delts whom several of us knew well from our days at St. Marks.

We worried; we calmed ourselves, and we worried again. We finally decided to tell Biford what was going on. One night at Gordo's I said, "Biford, I've got some bad news for you." I paused for dramatic effect and a few of the brothers snuggled closer. Biford looked interested, but with a group of KAs listening, his eyes darted around the group surrounding us and a bored look came over him.

"Well?" he said.

"I have found out that GGE has spent a great deal of time in Spokane this summer." Nothing registered. "Well, aren't you concerned?"

"Nope," he said as he walked over to the bar.

"He's hurt," I said to the group around me. I had no idea what he was feeling, but everyone was looking at me as if I had an elephant gun and they wanted me to shoot it. In a minute, Biford came back over to where I was standing by the large round booth in the corner and said to no one in particular.

"Did you know that GGE was nominated for president of Phi Delt? If he wins, he gets the corner room, you know, and it has a private staircase."

This puzzled us all because we all knew GGE was probably going to be the Phi Delts new president, and we all knew their president lived in the president's private room with the private bath and the private staircase leading to the Phi Delt parking lot. Maybe Biford was in shock many thought. I thought differently.

The worst happened. GGE and The Choice were reunited. I was not sure how Biford felt about this, but several of us were devastated. The KA Rose was pinned to a Phi Delt. It was too too humiliating. If only we had waited to hold the election in the fall.

Biford showed up one night at Gordo's with a mousey little blond independent he had met in computer class. We were all shocked and hurt as we read the "Dear John" Biford received just before fall classes were to begin. Biford left the letter on the bar. He had corrected her grammar, but as far as I could tell it was the standard letter of its type. She had not meant for this to happen, but she and GGE could not help themselves, and she was sure he would understand. I think he did understand.

Biford seemed impervious and that irked several of us. He didn't realize what this had meant to the fraternity. And he was with an independent.

B.B. Immolatus

For two years Biford had been our child, our parent, our teacher, and often our jester who was the only one who could tell us the truth, but now love died between

Biford and the KAs like a child and the parent who had left him out of his will. If he had been inconsolable, we would have consoled him. If he had been mad or indignant, we would have reasoned with him to protect him. He was none of these things, so we were. He made us look silly, we thought, and he did not seem to care.

One night after a chapter meeting a few of us were standing around on the front lawn planning to go to the Killarney Lounge when Biford passed through us. It would have been easy to walk around, but he never took the easy path. He stopped and turned to me and said, "Why don't you make out a bill and send it to me? Yeah, calculate what I owe you and let me know." Then he walked off as I was trying to decide what to say.

At midterm Biford moved out of the KA house and into his apartment full time. He maintained his membership, paid his dues, and occasionally attended a few parties and maybe even enjoyed the parties. I couldn't decide. Momma D cried when he moved out and certainly no one was ever quite so nice to her again. After graduation, though I didn't see him, he packed the same peculiar little car he arrived in and left town. I have never seen him or heard from him again. I always regret I failed to apologize.

Epilogue

That fall semester of Biford's junior year, the senior year for GGE and me, a strange thing happened that the Phi Delts still talk about. One Saturday afternoon in September when SMU was playing a home game at Texas Stadium, many workmen in two eighteen wheelers showed up at the Phi Delt house from what was advertised to be a well-known construction firm in Dallas and remodeled the back stairway to the president's room. The workmen completely enclosed the stairway, installed a luxurious carpet, beautiful light fixtures, and two magnificent heavy oak doors. One door was placed at the top of the stairs from GGE's room to the stairway, and the other at the bottom of the stairway, leading to the parking lot. It was said that twenty or so workmen were working furiously as the seven dwarfs rushing to protect Snow White.

The Phi Delts were first pleased. The few students in the house at the time of the installation had asked the workmen what they were doing and were told that the firm had a rush order for this remodeling and showed a work order to a largely disinterested few. The students shrugged and went to the library to study in peace. No one had noticed the signature on the work order. The Phi Delts first thought the wealthy Innan family had given the stairway to them for their son's use and ease because a plaque on the bottom door plainly and proudly proclaimed the gift to the Phi Delts from the Innan family. Now GGE could walk down his private stairway and not get his carefully coiffed hair mussed by the nasty ole rain. No matter that the Innan family denied the gift. Because their family was large and because they lived in Vancouver, each member of the family suspected a wealthy aunt or a distant cousin had made the gift. Could be, thought GGE. Certainly no bill ever came for the door, so the few Phi Delts who thought the doors a mystery decided all was well.

In November a strange thing happened that the KAs continue to talk about occurred on the eve of the Manada Carnival. As GGE was leaving his room to go to Manada, he and The Choice Jackie D had been named King and Queen of Carnival, GGE became trapped in his own personal stairway. Both great doors had become locked somehow, and GGE had missed all of Manada and a large part of Sunday. The Choice Jackie D was said to have been severely pissed off.

It was late Sunday afternoon when some pledges in the parking lot finally heard GGE's weakened pounding and yelling through the almost sound-proof stairway. They had to break down the bottom door to extricate him. They, the pledges, had been reluctant to break down the door so a few more hours went by before some persons made the decision to break it down, which proved to require some professional help—the doors were solid and especially sturdy.

Many months later the story got out despite GGE's threats. The dead bolt locks were powered by a computer. Someone outside the house locked the doors. The Phi Delts and the Innan family hired detectives to find out who had falsely imprisoned GGE. GGE believed his life had been threatened because the rug on the stairs had been treated with some chemical that when mixed with urine turned the stain, normally a shade of yellow one believes, to a bright red and stunk unbelievably. GGE had been gassed, he thought. The stench was noticeable all over the Phi Delt house for weeks. GGE was now often known in some circles as PPE.

I was positive that the Phi Delts and the Innan family were wasting their money and that no trace of the culprit, or the workmen, or the trucks would ever be found.

OVER THE EDGE

■

When Charles de Gaulle was told that he was a modern-day Robespierre, he sighed and said, "Ah, how little one knows oneself. I have always seen myself as Jeanne d'Arc."

Francis T. Caston, PhD was a precise man who was long leery of trying to measure time, so he compulsively always knew time and distance. He knew he was a precise man of fifty-two years, four months, and thirteen days on the day he packed his lawn mower and gasoline-powered edger into his 1988 Ford Ranger pick-up and headed for his church. Making his last trip out the door with his almost forgotten cap in his hand, he looked at Mrs. Caston asleep on the divan with *Shakespeare* open on her bosom. *She reads too late into the night—misses the good sleep.*

The morning air was cool. He felt the cool metal on his underarm as he rolled down the driver's side window and leaned on the door to his old, cream-colored, dented, often-scratched pick-up and drove just below the thirty-five mile hour speed limit.

He felt the wind blowing through his thinning gray hair, and he put on his blue baseball cap with the red T on the front, proclaiming some slight allegiance to the Texas Rangers baseball team. Francis saw Sam Beggs in his pajamas hurrying across his front lawn trying to get his morning paper before anyone saw him. Francis smiled and waved then scowled, thinking the paperboy should throw the paper closer to Sam's door. *Poor Sam nothing to do but wave.*

Francis made the calculatedly twenty-minute drive in eighteen minutes, twenty-two seconds without speeding. Francis looked at his watch and noted with satisfaction that it was 7:04 as he invaded the driveway of the Parish House. He was ahead of most of the early-morning traffic this Friday morning, the sixth of June. Francis sat in his pick-up and smiled. He had, in fact, seen only four cars on his journey, and they were headed to the truck stop on the interstate.

Too early to mow, but he could go into the church kitchen and make a pot of coffee. He had planned to be early. Francis liked to pray in the church, and he liked to be alone. He did not want to disturb anyone's sleep, so he was happy to make coffee, pray and admire the Gothic beauty of the Holy Trinity Episcopal Church.

The church was set deep on a street covered by trees that seemed to be always bowing to one another across the pavement. Except for the church, the street was residential until it stretched up the hill into the business or downtown area, as it was commonly known, some twelve blocks from the church. The church street, Seamen, then became the main street of Hadley-Prairie. Just barely on the north side of town as the city limits ended and gopher holes, unrepaired by the county, Seaman street, now road, slowed the traffic leaving town.

It did not seem strange to any of the twelve thousand indigenous folk or the almost three thousand college students to see Gothic architecture in a little west Texas town some eight hundred miles from the Gulf coast, the nearest sea.

Francis felt peaceful in the nave, and he loved the high ceiling with its dark-stained wood beams running the width of the church. One lone, large beam ran the length of the church and was the focal, attachment point, for all of the other beams. The middle beam was directly above the middle aisle where it held everything together. One had only to use a little imagination and limit his scope to see a cross of enormous proportions above those who hoped to be the forgiven, the would-be faithful. Without an optimistic imagination, someone might see a long spider with its eight legs extending from a wide firm body.

After two cups of coffee and a long prayer in which he thanked God for everything he could think of: wife, sons, parents, health, job, friends, and for protection for all of these loved ones, by first and last name, the quick and the dead, Francis determined that at 8:10 he could crank up his mower without disturbing the sleep of anyone except those who should have gone to bed sooner on a weeknight, besides after mowing, he had to hurry home, shower and get to his first class at 11:00. He went out the back door from the church kitchen to cross the wide lawn to the Parish House garage where he had parked his old friend of a pick-up. Francis lifted the three-horse-power mower with ease and placed it gently down at his feet.

Francis lifted weights regularly at the university Fitness Center and was pleased to see the looks of admiration that he could sometimes detect on the faces of students in the weight room. Francis jogged regularly, noting time, distance, pulse rate, and recovery time. Francis' father, an immoderate man who smoked, drank beer, and cursed, had died at age fifty-six of a heart attack. Francis did not know if his father had accepted Christ, and Francis prayed for his father's soul daily and resolved never to be like him in any way.

Like all of his machines, the mower was in good condition and Francis was proud of it as it started on the third pull. Francis began as he always did on the little strip of land between the Parish House and the only neighbor the church had on that side of the block. The neighbor's house was a large, painted white-brick structure that housed the Baptist banker, who had recently moved to Hadley-Prairie from Boston. Clarkson, the banker, belonged to every civic club in town and was a cheerful, condescending man who hated west Texas and everyone in it. Everyone in town loved him immediately, cheerfully spoke of him, and invited him to every social function. Everyone was pleased at how generous the man was with his time and money for town charities. And everyone vowed that Clarkson, that Yankee son-of-a-bitch, would never make a dime more than they could keep from him. "Thwart the Yankee bastard" was the un-shouted battle cry. Francis refrained from letting such thoughts run loosely in the dark corners of his mind, clicked clucked his tongue, mentally tsked, tsked, and removed the empty cans of Coors Lite, which often littered the hedge between the Yankee-son-of-a-bitch-snowbird's Baptist's house and the church.

Clarkson was a tall, thin man with a slight pot belly. He had dark hair that was obviously thinning because of the part that was almost down to his ear. He looked frail as though he never did anything more strenuous than open mail and cans of Coors Lite. Francis once knocked on Clarkson's door to ask him about the beer cans. Clarkson denied that he ever drank anything alcoholic. Francis pretended to believe him, but hoped that his polite asking might end the cascade of several empty beer cans that were always slightly closer to Clarkson's side of the hedge on that side of the church.

As Francis began to mow the familiar ground, he smiled and thought of what people driving by this end of town who saw him once again mowing his beloved church's lawn must say of him. *Eccentric is the word they must use.* He thought the townspeople must have thought of him as a *slim, muscular, decent, though eccentric man working for his church on a hot day, with only slightly thinning gray hair. That is how they must see me. And those who know me may admire me.* Francis, slightly embarrassed, decided to change his thoughts.

Francis remembered one hot-beyond-belief day, the summer before when he was literally soaked and dripping from the hours of mowing and edging in the middle-of-the-June-day sun. On that day, on the way home, Francis stopped to fill a prescription at the Hadley-Prairie drug store when Mrs. Squires, wife of the pharmacist-owner, looked at his wet, bright-red face, his dripping wet t-shirt and asked him what he had been doing. Francis replied that he had been at church. Mrs. Squires was obviously puzzled. Francis told her that he had been at choir practice, and they had worked on a particularly rousing version of *Stand-Up for Jesus* until everyone was exhausted. As Francis was walking out of the store, he could hear Mrs. Squires say, sotto voce, "I never know what Dr. Caston is talking about." Francis was content.

I was twenty-six when I moved here. Wife and only two young sons at that time when I came to this little backwoodsy town, thinking I would finish my dissertation and be out of here in a year or two, thought I would be off to a selective private school or a large state research university.

But Francis came to like the little town where everyone knew his name, where he was respected and people liked to think of him as their eccentric. Larger cities had eccentrics, and Hadley-Prairie needed one. Francis was just fine. He could forget his billfold, and the lack of money, ID, and credit cards would make no difference in his day. There were no lines in the post office or in the courthouse. The lines in either of the two supermarkets, however, rivaled those in the big cites. Francis thought of the supermarkets and sighed that some lines were as ubiquitous as the iniquitous.

Ah, but the roads, that was where they beat the big cities. No one ever thought to repair the city streets or even the county roads in Hadley-Prairie. A truck came by after some, not all, of the infrequent west Texas rains and threw some black stuff in the potholes that hardened almost immediately then melted the next day. After the next rain, the black stuff went somewhere, a present to the gods who were thought to inhabit the slight hills just north of town where the Comanche village had been.

The natives of Hadley-Prairie took rare sojourns to Ft. Worth or Dallas to reassure them that they were God's chosen people. *Life is too short to be lived in Dallas.* And so the little town with its little traffic never troubled with roadwork and yellow flashing-light signs narrowing traffic to a single lane. When the citizens of Hadley-Prairie were in Dallas or Ft. Worth, not realizing or anticipating the constant road work, they thought that they had arrived on one of the worst days, and that the traffic jams on this day were one of the prices the gods of Dallas or Ft. Worth inflicted on travelers for failing to worship daily at the crowded big-city shrine.

Hadley-Prairie county roads helped make country life bucolic, if bumpy. Francis silently vowed to offer a prayer of thanks for the roads and the ten-minute rush hours after he finished mowing.

Francis' sons, all three of them, had grown to manhood here, and by their athletic prowess, kindness, and good grades in school had made Francis well known for fathering. Francis served on the grand jury about every three years. He had been Senior Warden at his church six of his twenty-six years of membership. And Francis had spoken three times at the high school graduation.

Francis liked to mow the church lawn. The mowing was good exercise because the church-complex was on three lots. The church sat on two lots, and the Parish House was on one. It took Francis three hours, and twelve to sixteen minutes to mow and edge. This included a twelve to thirteen minute water and rest break, sitting in the shade of the Parish House garage in a light aluminum folding chair with eight wide straps as a person container. Francis brought the chair and a thermos, filled with cold water.

Francis liked to mow because in addition to the good exercise, the church would have to pay at least $100.00 a week to have the large lawn maintained. The church saved money and Francis deducted half that amount from his tithe. He had three sons in college, two in medical school. His investments through the years had been good, and he owed the Lord a great deal of money every week.

By the time his reverie ended, Francis had mowed the Parish-House lawn and made a good start on the north church lawn. It was time for his break. As he sat in the saggy-bottom chair, sipping from his thermos, Francis looked at the Holman house across the street. It too took up three lots. It was the largest house in town. Mrs. Holman, a widow, was well known as the richest person in town. About twenty years older than himself, he guessed, Mrs. Holman was highly regarded as a gracious lady of gentle manners and good taste. She was reclusive, however, and Francis had never formally met her, though he had seen her countless times around the small town.

Francis had met her son, Bill Jr. a few times. Bill Jr. was an attorney who kept an office though he did not need the income from his law practice. Once Francis had sought some free legal advice from his second son's father-in-law, the district judge, but what he got was "Go see Bill Jr."

In a matter that Bill Jr. could have reasonably asked a fee of several hundred dollars, Bill Jr. charged Francis thirty-five dollars—a real deal for an eccentric with three sons in college.

Francis stood up, screwed the cap back on his thermos, folded his chair, put it back in his pickup, and turned around to walk back to his mower when he saw Mrs. Holman almost upon him.

A tall, slim woman whose gray hair was pulled back in a loose ponytail, Mrs. Holman must have been a beautiful woman in her youth, Francis thought. She was wearing a long, loose, dark skirt that seemed to have some Spanish influence. It had many pleats, and it had spangley things on it—decorations with no meaning Francis could discern. Her blouse was white and loose.

"You there," she said. "I'm Mrs. Holman from across the street." She nodded toward her house. "I've seen you working here many times," she said with a pleasant smile. "My gardener has to be gone a few days, and I'm giving a lawn party next week. Would you be interested in helping me? If you have the time?"

"When?" It never occurred to Francis to tell the truth.

"My party is next Saturday morning," she said patiently. "Any time before then." Francis quickly calculated that his last class on Thursday ended at 1:00. He could be at her house by 2:00 easily. Francis could see the making of a joke here.

"I can come on Thursday afternoon at about 2:00 or so. Would that be all right?"

"Perfect," she said. "Would you like to come over to my house now and let me show you what needs to be done? Then you can tell me how much you charge."

"There will be no problem about money, Mrs. Holman. Could you show me on Thursday afternoon? I'm behind schedule here now," said Francis, looking at his Gucci.

"Fine, I'll see you Thursday afternoon then."

"Yes Ma'am. I'll be there." Francis hummed and sang the parts of *Men of Harlech* that he knew over and over as he finished the remainder of his chosen work for that day.

That night as he told his wife about what he was going to do, he was surprised to see that she could not realize the humor in the situation. She was sure the idea was not funny, and she said that the idea was not particularly nice. Francis thought that his wife of twenty-eight years was an otherwise perfect woman who had no sense of humor.

Can't she see that when Mrs. Holman tries to pay me, and I tell her who I am, the lady will be amused? And when I tell her that I can't take her money because her son has been so very nice to me, she will realize that Episcopalians are especially fine people who know how to repay their debts. She needs a gardener; I owe her son a favor, and the whole thing is funny. I'm lucky to have this opportunity. Francis snorted slightly in his wife's direction and went to sleep, smiling.

Thursday afternoon Francis stood and gaped at the Holman back lawn. He had known how large the front lawn was, but he had not computed the sidewalks around the pools in the back, one heated, one not, the decks around the greenhouse, and the labyrinthine garden with its angular walkway. The work to subdue nature here was not on a scale and scope that Francis had foreseen, nor could he have imagined. In addition, the sidewalks were not straight as anyone would have a right to expect them to be, but they curved sometimes gently, but at other places they rivaled Lombard Street with their tortuous turns. The machine Francis owned with its metal blades would not do much of what was required for edging. Francis would have to use Mrs. Holman's weed eater, a contraption from hell that required as much wire as the front lines across France in World War I. The wire had to be continually re-wrapped around a spool that was hard to manipulate, open, and close. *God Himself might lose patience with this machine and forgive far less than seventy-times seven.* Francis struggled with himself for thinking, not saying, angry words in the heat of the day and the many moments of battle with the wire.

Francis could not finish his edging on Thursday afternoon. With his Texas Rangers baseball cap in hand, playing his part just as the sun was going down, he rang the doorbell.

"Mrs. Holman, I ran out of daylight, ma'am, but I'll be glad to come back tomorrow afternoon and finish." Mrs. Holman was not pleased, but she continued a weakening smile, and Francis went home scowling at the dark.

Francis' MWF classes didn't end until 3:00, and it would be 4:00 before he could get to the Holman house unless he turned his last class loose early, or cut it entirely. He decided on a short Friday class, snarled at himself in the bathroom mirror, showered, and bounced the formerly sleeping Mrs. Caston as he sat down hard on the bed. She merely turned her face to the wall, and a book fell to the floor.

This is too much work to be as much fun as I thought it would be. I expected to finish the lawn in about three hours, and as she was making out his check, I would tell her I could not take her money. She would recognize my name, and I would tell her that I was the Lone Mathematics Professor and ride off in my cream-colored, dented, old Ford faithful pick-up with a hardy "High-Yo Ranger" resounding through the neighborhood. She will be smiling on her front walk long after I drive off. Not enough.

The next day, letting his class out shortly after roll call and a library assignment, Francis sped to Mrs. Holman's house quickly and began edging with the machine from hell. Just before dark, Francis breathed deeply, rang the doorbell to announce that he had finished. This was to be the time for the payoff. Waiting for someone to answer the door, Francis remembered that one of five spaces in the garage was empty. There was no one home. Francis slowly packed his mower, unused chair, empty thermos, and started inching home, keeping his eye on the drive-way in his rearview mirror as long as he could before he turned the corner.

Great. No pay off. How can I come back to her door to play good neighbor if I am not going to accept money? What would be the point of presenting myself at her door? I have the knowledge of a good deed done, a debt paid. Not enough. A cheerful heart is one thing; a weed-eater from hell scourging me is another.

Six weeks, one day, and twenty hours later, Francis T. attended an annual charity function that he would normally have missed. This time though he listened to Mrs. Caston and put on his evening wear, and dutifully stood in the den of the town's only osteopathic doctor, talking to the Yankee son-of-a-bitch-snowbird-Baptist banker. Francis was slowly drinking a glass of ice water in an amber-colored glass with a sprig of something green in it, barely listening to Clarkson sing of the virtues of small town life. Francis wished he were at home in his den reading when he saw the normally reclusive Mrs. Holman across the room. For the first time in his tenure in this town with the bumpy, sometimes impaired, un-repaired roads, Francis had run into Mrs. Holman socially. *God is telling me something.* Francis made his apology to the Yankee son-of-a- bitch-snowbird-Baptist banker and began to make his way toward Mrs. Holman. *This is where the fun begins.*

She might not recognize me because I am not sweaty, pauperish, and I won't be as servile as I was during previous conversations. I am not even smelly this evening. Ah, the occasion has its charm.

"Mrs. Holman," Francis said, "I'm Francis T. Caston." The name did not mean anything to her. "I mowed your lawn a few weeks ago and edged it."

"Yes," she said seemingly unconcerned.

"You weren't home when I finished." Mrs. Holman smiled but appeared to be untouched by the news. "I teach math at the university." He urged her by his pleading voice to acknowledge some sort of oddity or obligation. Francis hated himself for not having enough cool to keep his joke to himself, but he was a man now on a mission, and the urge was growing stronger. "I mow for my church as a service, not for money." This half lie convinced

Francis, but Mrs. Holman remained impassive and quiet. "Weren't you concerned that the man who worked so hard on your lawn never presented himself for his money?"

"No" Mrs. Holman said. "I just thought that you did such a poor job with the edging you were too proud to take money. . . but you don't want money, do you?"

Francis turned red and while trying to think of something to say he felt a hand on his shoulder. He turned to see his worried wife, who slid between Mrs. Holman and Francis. Francis glared at, through, and around Mrs. Caston. He could see the red of his face, he thought, in his wife's frilly white dress. Then he circumvented her to reach for Mrs. Holman, who was making her way to the door. Francis expelled enough air to fill a football, tugged Mrs. Caston with him, and caught Mrs. Holman in front of her hostess, telling the town's only osteopathic doctor's wife how she had enjoyed the evening but had to leave early.

"Mrs. Holman, may I present my wife, Mrs. Caston."

"I've known Mrs. Caston for many years. It is you I've never met, though, of course, I've seen you many times." Mrs. Holman continued toward the door. Francis caught her again.

"May I offer you something to drink? You've seen me many times?" Francis looked back hopefully at the buffet table in the dining room, but it was empty. There was nothing yet offered to eat, and Mrs. Holman lost her wispy smile. "Did you know who I was when I agreed to mow your lawn?"

"No, but I recognized you later when you were mowing my lawn."

She walked off, her ponytail bobbing. Francis vigorously shook off his wife's pull and stood alone and shouted loud enough to stop the party: DAMN!

Francis T. stood at the spot where Mrs. Holman had left him for the safety of the door, and Francis peered into space for a long time—a minute or two. *I didn't tell her about my debt to Bill J.* The party stopped as everyone watched Francis do nothing but turn redder and puff his cheeks like an adder.

Francis T. stepped out the front door onto the town's only osteopathic doctor's well mowed and adequately edged lawn and cursed the heavens to the top of his considerable voice. Francis took the Lord's name in vain several times and used his complete repertoire of curse words, which everyone who had spilled out of the front door marveled and then agreed that his knowledge of the world and its seamier lexicon was complete.

The door was held open by the Coors Lite drinking, Yankee-son-of-a-bitch-snowbird-Baptist banker with thinning hair that fell down on one side of his head, exposing a small scalp spot. The Yankee-son-of-a-bitch-snowbird balding Baptist banker agreed with everyone on the lawn that Dr. Caston had exhausted the possibilities of English language cursing.

Those present, who could talk, especially liked the part about smelly fluids flowing upstream. "That part seemed spontaneous," the gleeful, Yankee son-of-a-bitch- snowbird balding Baptist banker said.

"I saw him speeding on a Friday afternoon not long ago," said Raisley Calvert, Sheriff of the county. Heads turned toward Raisley.

As Francis turned back toward the town's only osteopathic doctor's front door, many of the crowd parted into red impatiens-filled flower beds, while others almost stampeded toward the safety of the punch bowl and the recently served little crackers with something smeared on them that was smelly to the serving girl. On the steps, Francis looked back at the starlit sky, expecting a sign— perhaps a star falling in the east. The heavens were as inactive and quiet as the town's only osteopathic doctor's wife's living room. She sat down too hard in a hard chair and noticed her broach that looked a little like Raisley's badge, fell into the dusty looking white carpet where it was half covered.

Most of the conversation after the Castons went home was about how and why the party improved without them. They agreed that Francis might actually be of some danger to the community. Hadley-Prairie was better off without him.

On the chilly drive home, Mrs. Caston was quiet and did not ask Francis to raise his window. Francis T. looked at his watch and adjusted his speed. Later, on the divan, Mrs. Caston picked up her book, settled in for a long night of reading, read: "He hath ever but scarcely known himself," and her eyes began to droop.

HART

――――――――――――――― ■ ―――――――――――――――

My little brother just died. The accident was an odd one of some kind. His horse returned to the barn without him, and my nephews and their mother, my sister-in-law, set out to find him in the pasture. Rianza in the pick-up and Jason and Randall on horseback. Hart had hit his head on a rock after, one supposes, his horse had thrown him. He was the best horseman I knew, and it would have been difficult for any horse to have thrown him, but his favorite horse, the bay he named "Best" was usually calm and tractable. We thought of asking for an autopsy to see if he had fallen for some other reason, but we decided that no matter the reason, he was gone, and only horse-men's egos would have been salved, so the death did not warrant an autopsy. He was gone, and he was a hell of a good horseman.

Many years ago, my brother when he was eleven entered his first rodeo as a roper in the ages eleven to twelve category in the then little town of Euless, Texas. I remember the night well.

I was just starting my second year at Southern Methodist University in Dallas, but Euless was no more than twenty miles from Dallas, and I had entered that same rodeo at the same slight age of eleven. I wanted to see how little brother was coming along on the road to being a roper, a passion we all enjoyed.

My father was an executive with a large corporation in Dallas, but he was first generation off the family ranch in East Texas. After a few years of climbing the corporate ladder, Poppa decided that his sons should have the opportunity to become cowboys, so we moved "out" and became cowboy sons on the gentleman rancher's "place." We, my brother and I, learned every aspect of ranch life and thought, like all cowboys, that ranch life was the only good way to live. At age eighteen, however, my father sent me to SMU and told me to take a break from ranch life and see what else was available to a young man. I was at first scared, then sad, then excited with the parvenu crowd of the fraternity, sorority, and academic life, but I missed the ranch life.

When my brother, nine years younger than I, entered his first junior rodeo, I was there. My Poppa had provided "Hart," Hartley with a superb horse, and he had given to Hart, as he had given to me, many lessons in the home-made perfect arena, with lights. Roping lessons, and much practice in roping both in the arena and in the pasture was a large part of our lives. We roped almost every day. After a day in the pasture, we came back to the arena near the house at night and roped under the lights. Mother always watched approvingly.

When I came home from college, as I frequently did, I would always have trouble finding Hart. He was always "in the pasture" mother would tell me. I would saddle whatever horse was close and begin to search. When I found him, he always had a rope in his hand and a huge smile on his face.

But that night when Hart was eleven, he roped the calf perfectly, was down the rope like a pro and found the calf was too big for him to throw and tie. Someone had made a mistake and put a calf that must have weighed three hundred pounds, maybe more, in with the calves for the younger boys, and Hart was there straining even to reach over the calf to find the flank to lift. After giving up on trying to throw the thing, he tried to get some slack on the rope so he could get his rope free, but as the calf pulled, the well-trained horse backed up, and Hart was there with no solution and the crowd was laughing. With a red face and tears beginning to form, Hart kicked the calf then he kicked the thing again and again. The announcer said, "Son, we don't treat animals like that." My Poppa often kicked hell out of recalcitrant calves, and they always became less obdurate. These calves are to be slaughtered.

The announcer was in the middle of telling the pick-up men to go out and stop that boy when I saw my father, a big, strong, lean man striding across the arena. I had not noticed that he had left my side. When Poppa reached Hart, he kicked the calf so hard that it dropped to its knees. Poppa then threw the calf on its side and motioned for Hart to sit his horse and loose the slack. Hart did, and Poppa took the rope and threw the end of it to Hart to coil.

As Hart was riding out of the arena, Poppa stood in the middle of the arena and raised his large bony middle finger high in the air toward the announcer. The announcer started to apologize, but my father reemphasized the gesture then stood in the lights and made that same beautiful gesture to everyone in the now quiet crowd. Poppa completed his 360 and walked out, slowly, dignified, following Hart. I made my way toward the trailer.

On the way home, Poppa, drinking a beer smilingly told Hart that he was proud of him. Soon Hart and I were laughing at Poppa's antic in the arena and how quiet he made them all, and we knew who was proud, we were.

For years Hart and I told that story to his sons and mine, and they were always polite enough to listen again and again and to laugh at just the right time.

On the day of Hart's funeral, I heard Jason and Randall, Hart's sons now in their twenties tell that story to their friends, who had probably heard it before, and they too were polite enough to listen to the entire story and laugh at exactly the right time.

TEXAS DOG FOOD

―■―

My father was a cowboy who had been forced at the age of sixteen to come to the city of Dallas to seek, not fortune as much as sustenance. He was the fifth son in a ranching family caught in the slowly industrializing Texas of the 1920s. Except for the opportunity to watch Southern Methodist University play football, he never liked living in the city. And when I was nine or ten years old, we moved out of Dallas and began to pursue the gentleman rancher's life just outside of the then very small town of Irving, Texas.

There for the next nine years or so I was at first a fledgling cowboy, then a full-fledged working and rodeo cowboy. By the time I was sixteen though, in spite of my father's best efforts, which were considerable, Irving surrounded us and forced us away from the rustic life. We became more Dallas than my father wanted. Texas seceded from us. We were forced to surrender.

My father sat in his rocker on the front porch and emitted sighs that could have been heard by the cursed Flying Red Horse that was the symbol of Dallas on top of a building that was a full 20 stories high—unbelievable, unacceptable. It was small consolation to him that his ranch land was becoming very valuable. I, on the other hand, don't remember shedding a tear or a sigh or even being slightly distressed that my horses and the cursed cattle were gone. I wanted a car. I didn't question or curse a bountiful fate. Now I had time some days to goof off and go girl hunting—the car was a help. Girls hardly cared about horses, I found. The cowgirls made the transition to city life quickly and easily, I noticed.

After SMU, the University of North Texas, Texas A&M University at Commerce, and five years in the Marine Corps, I began to become my father. I yearned for little or no traffic, no noise, and for the pleasure of working my own land. One hundred and forty miles west of Dallas and its tentacles, I began to teach English to a very polite, rural, and disinterested group of rural high school graduates at an undistinguished Jr. College. Not teaching at a selective or research oriented university was fine by me. I was about to become a rancher again.

I lived in town for a year and thought myself clever to hide my real desire in moving to the hinterlands to seek the best place to start my ranching empire. As always the best places are not for sale. "A man won't sell you his best cattle," my father said. He isn't likely to sell you his best land either, unless he gets too much for it.

After what seemed to me to be a long and careful search, I found what I wanted. The land, water, fences, barns were good. What it didn't have was a house, at least not a house my wife, not a cowgirl at anytime in her life, would live in. Money that I had set aside for cows, pens, tractors and a few good horses went for the building of a very nice house. Mr. Blandings spent too much on building a house again. The house grew from the original plan to what my father would have called a show place. It was the swimming pool I hated the most. I never looked at it without flinching then shuddering. My wife was worth it all except for the God-damned swimming pool. It had no place being on a working ranch and reminded me daily of a fool I knew, me. If I looked at the water, I saw King Lear, Harlequin the Zanni, The grave diggers, and most frequently, Polonius. The house I could have afforded if only it wasn't sitting on 600 hundred far too expensive acres.

I had used my inheritance to support my wife, and now three sons through my ten years of college. The last of the Sears, Skillerns, and Walgreen money, the ones among others, who bought Poppa's pasture land so as to transform it into a good portion of Irving, Texas. The money was in the house, the land, and the swimming pool. I don't even know how it happened. "Oh what a rogue and peasant slave am I." "Confound the ignorant." Still, if I were lucky, very lucky I might be able to pay off the bank in a few years. I needed to get about 90% calf crops from my expensive cows each year. Expenses had to be kept to a minimum.

It occurred to me that my sons were living out my young life except they were living in a very nice house, at least until drought or some such happened. Because I had been imprudent with the house, we barely scraped by each month even though we produced many of our own needs. In college for ten years, and I had never studied finance, agriculture, nor veterinary medicine. Perhaps my mother's family was right; I just wasn't smart enough to get out of school.

One expense I knew I couldn't handle was the veterinary bills. Most small ranchers do their own doctoring because they can't afford to do anything else. The cost of birthing one calf by a vet is about the same as "the profit" the calf would bring after a year of nursing, grazing, and growth. Besides my Poppa had taught me pretty well, so I thought. He had passed a test and had thus "grandfathered" his way to a Vet license in Texas In 1921. He had taken a correspondence course in Vet medicine. How he learned enough to pass a test I don't know, but I think the state wanted the money for the license rather badly in those days. And he had worked for a Vet somewhere outside of Pecos, Texas for a year after the correspondence school. He never had graduated from high school or any other school I knew of, but all his friends called him "Doc" and sang his praises. I think his fees weren't much. When he wanted to make some real money, he gave up Veting and went to work at a restaurant supply company that hired him as a high-priced executive because of his friendship with some especially bad and dangerous people. Then was when he could afford to buy the pasture land that made him rich.

He had lost interest in veting until he was sitting on that rocker cussing (cursing) the Flying Red Horse. He became obsessed then with trying to teach me to take care of animals right after we had very few of them left. He was a horse and cow man. His attitudes about dogs was that they were shit-eating animals and a 22 bullet cured their diseases right well. Unless a dog helped him with the cattle, and we had several that did, he didn't want them around. I remember a collie I loved who wasn't much good with the cattle, except for getting them out of the brush. The dog followed me everywhere I went on horseback, and I loved him. He was sick for a few days once, and I slipped him to a vet's office in Irving then gave him to a friend to keep for me until he was well. Poppa never noticed he was gone.

Anyway, Poppa's real legacy to me, one I couldn't mishandle, was my knowledge of caring for, and treating sick animals, and how to safely get them into this world so we could all have hamburgers. (I have become a vegetarian.) The idea now of eating animals makes me sick. Strange change.

I bought this cow about three years ago when she was a "coming four-year old" in cowboy parlance. She had already had one calf, so I was surprised when about a month after I bought her, she began to have trouble. When she was "springing," i.e. about to give birth, she became prolapsed, which is to say her uterus hung out. At that time I put her in a pen so I could watch her carefully. I set my alarm every two hours all night. I'd check on her and go back to sleep on the couch, fully dressed, of course.

The next day I decided to put her uterus back where it belonged and sew her up. I had to drive to the Veterinary Supply Store in Abilene where I could buy the equipment I needed for such a procedure. When I got back from the two hour drive, I saw a new calf. I was lucky; one can only imagine the disaster of a poor cow trying to deliver with a sewn in uterus. In my defense, I had no way to guess when she was due, and I was watching her closely enough to cut the stitches if she began to labor. Then too she was more than a month away from her due date. I was both lucky and relieved when the problem resolved Itself; however, the next year, the problem, like a poor cousin returned.

Although the she was prolapsed again, this time I had the advantage because I knew when she was due. I had been smart enough to have had her artificially inseminated, and because she was almost two months away from delivering, I decided to sew her up—a standard procedure in a case like this.

I had the necessary equipment and even the experience for this job. The equipment consisted of a bottle of epidural, a pain killer and muscle relaxer I got from a friend whose name I can't mention. The needle used in such an operation is five inches long and about an eighth to a quarter inch wide. The thread is only slightly thinner than shoe laces for tennis shoes. The needle is bent in such a manner to make it appear in the shape of a roof top, or if the two ends were placed on flat surface the needle would resemble la circonflexe dans l' alphabet francaise. Properly equipped, I put the cow in a chute in such a way she could neither advance nor retreat. Next came the odious task of washing the protruding uterus—I used soapy water and a disinfectant. Ole cow was a mite touchy, but the washing was a necessity for two reasons. She protruded so far that she defecated on herself, and I needed a lubricant to help her put her uterus in place. The pushing was a difficult job. She pushed back even after 5 ccs of epidural. In fact, our pushing contest lasted almost half an hour. I had unfortunately forgotten to remove my watch, so I kept up with the time quite well. I stood there my left hand out of sight in her, looking at my watch. The watch was pushed far back on my arm.

Finally I won. She took the sewing well, only twitching occasionally. One interesting aspect of the sewing ordeal was that in order to keep the stitches from ripping out as the cow continued to strain, she was certain to do so, I broke off two short sticks from a nearby mesquite tree before my operation began and sanded off the ends so they would not be pointed. Then I placed the sticks vertically on each side of her vagina and sewed around them in a figure-eight manner, thereby strengthening the stitches. During the stitching process, when she strained to expel the uterus, she sprayed a malodorous fluid on me. Sometimes the stream was strong. Pity. On the operation day and for each of the next three days, I gave her an injection of 20ccs of combiotic. Alas, five day later, she died.

Had she died of some communicable disease, I would have burned the carcass, but I hate to do that. The burning process is long and almost as smelly as letting the poor thing rot. Plus, the rotting process is lengthy too. I called the county agent to ask for advice, and he suggested that I call Texas Dog Food Company in Weatherford, Texas—a semi-large town close to Ft. Worth and about eighty miles from my little home town. At least the town I live closest to. I called them, all unsuspectingly, and the lady with whom I talked told me that they, the company, would like to have her, but that they would have to charge me ten dollars to come to Cisco, or close to Cisco, to pick her up. This price seemed strange to me because I was providing them the very substance of their business.

However, the voice on the other end assured me that ten dollars was reasonable because the distance the truck had to come could only be defrayed, not totally accounted for by ten dollars. Still odd, I thought, but after the haggling ended, I agreed to the price, and she told me the truck would be in Cisco the following morning. We then agreed that the driver would call me when he arrived, and I would come get him and show him the way to my ranch, not an easy place to find or to give directions to because of the complicated nature of the trek from town to my place.

At one o'clock the next day, I had not heard from them, so I called. Truck trouble, I was told. The voice on the other end began to talk to the driver, and I heard him assure her that the truck was almost repaired and that he would be in Cisco no later than 10:00 that night. I was dubious about this because there are no lights, or at least not much in the way of lights to the pen where the cow was. I communicated this reservation to the voice that in turn relayed my thoughts to the driver. There came an echo-like reassurance that there would be no problem, no problem. "Okay," I said "have him call me when he arrives."

When the phone rang that night at 11:00, I had been asleep for an hour. It was the driver and now even though I could talk to him directly, we continued to have problems communicating. He told me that his assistant driver, who was also his fiancé, had become ill earlier in the evening, and he had taken her to the hospital. Now with her somehow restored to health, they were on their way. He would arrive at three in the morning he said. I should have told him to go to hell, but I didn't. I doubted I should ever hear from him again, but I told him should he arrive at 3:00 to give me a call and I would meet him at the truck stop, which, even he couldn't miss. Then I told him I doubted his arrival, but If he should arrive anytime before breakfast to call me. Otherwise, not to bother me again.

He called precisely at 3:00 am. He told me at which service station at which I could find him. I was wrong about his missing the truck stop as big as the Louvre, and I told him I was on my way. It was at this time he asked me if I owned a rifle. Without thinking, as usual, I said yes. He asked me to bring it because he had picked up a cow that was not quite dead, and he needed it for her. My wife said, quite reasonably, that it might not be smart to arm somebody at 3:00 AM whom we did not know, considering we were miles from any neighbor. I put my pistol in my boot and left my rifle at home.

I wasn't positive he would really be at the service station, but he was there along with his assistant / fiance who seemed to be in a fitful kind of sleep. As he and I talked by the truck, she would sometimes roll into the window so that I could see a portion of her face and hair. Because it was a very cold morning, her window was fogged over. Seeing her was difficult, but I remember black roots, very long and greasy blond hair.

He followed me to my ranch by a different method from the one I used to get to town because I needed a better road than the one to my house– one that I had built to get cattle trucks to my pens if the roads were muddy. It took longer, but it was safer for him to find his way back to the highway on this hot-topped road. I planned on a shorter route back to my house to try to get some sleep before the freshmen began to try my patience too.

At the gate, I got out to hold the gate for him to drive through, he stopped, got out and came around the truck to tell me that his flashlight had just stopped working. He wanted to know if I had one. I did not. Since my house is four miles by road to the pens, I had no intention of leaving him and the grease pit alone while I went back for one. It was also at this unpropitious moment that he asked me for the rifle. I told him that I had forgotten it and asked him to drive on through the gate because I was freezing.

In the pick-up I put my boot pistol in my coat pocket and drove on to the pens where the dead cow was. I left my headlights on so he could see which pen was the one where the dead cow lay. He had to back up to use the winch which was to lift the body with. At this moment he got out of his truck again to explain that the last cow he had picked up was not quite dead. I took my pistol out of my pocket and showed it to him and explained that was all I had. His eyes got bigger looking at the pistol, which was the reaction I wanted. He had tried, he said, to hang the cow that only had two broken legs, but he was unable to kill the beast. I now wished I had brought the rifle because I could hear the poor beast moaning. The boot pistol would not be enough to go through her thick skull, and he and I knew it. At this point it occurred to me that I could use the rifle on two poor dumb beasts, but after he finished his hanging tale, he proceeded to back up until he backed into my corner post and knocked it down.

If you have never worked on a ranch and built many cross fences for pastures and such, you cannot know how much trouble corner posts are to plant. After a cavalier apology, I'm afraid I was no longer what one would call a gracious host, but I restrained the urge to hang him by his own winch. Captain Vere would not have blamed me. *

We tried to continue with the task. We found with the help of my headlights the correct pen, and we were able somehow to put the cable around her hind quarters, no easy task. His winch broke. At 4:30 in the morning in freezing weather and a knocked down corner post, it became impossible to lift the cow into his truck.

After a few minutes of staring out into the cold dark corners of the universe and my own mind, I began to congratulate myself on my self-control. After all, put into proper perspective this could be funny. As I was trying to congratulate myself on my self-control, the driver timidly approached me. His timidity was to his credit, considering his size, half mine, and his request. He explained that he had only two dollars on him and that he needed about twenty dollars for gas to get back to Weatherford. He asked me to loan him the money.

I am not sure of my exact words, but I believe it is safe to say I was rude. He hurriedly left; I went home. As I sat on the side of my bed, putting on my pajamas, telling my wife all that had happened and explaining all the early morning farce, I noticed a frown of disapproval from her, not the congratulatory sympathy I expected. In fact, she gave me a much needed lecture on Christian charity. I relented, re-dressed, re-drove to town; and as I expected I found the driver and his still sleeping grease pit at the service station where I had first met them. The driver was trying to call someone and was not particularly surprised to see me. I gave him all the money I had on me, twelve dollars. He thanked me, took down my address, and promised to send me the money back as soon as he reached Weatherford.

I received a call from Texas Dog Food a few days later. The same voice asked me if I still had the cow. I said that I did, but I told her I had pulled the cow off to a part of the pasture far from my house and the pens—a present for the coyotes and the buzzards, I told her. She said they would still like to have her. I resolved to change the diet of my collie. She asked if they could come the next day to pick her up? I told her yes, but I would not pay her the ten dollars, and I wanted my twelve dollars back. She agreed to all this as usual. As usual, I told her to have the driver call me when he arrived in Cisco. That was two years ago, and I have yet to hear from them.

Frankly, I must admit that I had no intention of answering the call when and if the driver arrived. Revenge is never satisfying but when one plans it and fails to achieve it, the pain is worse. And one other thing, I saw the county agent one night at a high school football game, and he asked me if I had called Texas Dog Food. I told him I had. When this was not enough of an answer for him, I explained that their service was more than I expected. He looked pleased and wanted, I think, a thank you.

GOTCHA

───────────────■───────────────

*L*ast week at my high school class reunion, I was got a good "gotcha" by a dead woman who, apparently, held a grudge until the day she died and maybe for a few weeks thereafter.

The tale begins, I think, as all tales begin, in one's earliest memories. I was born to what people in Dallas society call a "good" family, which means that my mother drove a Cadillac, and it also means that I attended a private school.

School for me was a matter of fun and academic competitiveness at ages five through ten. I did what I was told, as did all the well-behaved little rich kids. If rich kids are not all good little boys and girls today, maybe their hell-raising days begin after age ten. At least my surmise about the rich kids being good seems correct for the period of time after the Korean War. Who knows about today?

My father was first generation off the ranch, and as I grew older he began to feel uneasy about my being a pampered kid, so we moved from Dallas to an area about thirty miles southwest of Dallas where I could go to public schools and gather "ranch experiences," to use my father's often-used expression. My mother didn't like the idea, but there we were in the hell of Norman Rockwell gone sour. The population of my new little hometown was about two thousand at that time.

The move to the country was a kind of "gotcha" by fate or by my father, who thought I had some bad times coming to me because we had always had indoor toilets. I don't know why he was mad at me. He was the rich guy.

Anyway it took me a few years of being bullied and unpopular to learn the rules of the rural school game as played by the barefoot crowd. The prime directive of the overalls gang was that teachers were no damn good, and one must resist learning so as to make them look bad. Then too, there is nothing of value to be learned in school because teachers had ostensibly learned and they were no damn good for anything.

I finally and painfully became popular in the burg milieu because I became a troublemaker. I continued to wear shoes because there is just so much one will endure even to become popular. Besides, I lived in a big house on a large ranch, so there was no denying I was the shoe, now boot, type. However, I talked back, got into fights, and I broke all of the rules of which I was aware. The more rules I broke, the more fights I got into, the more popular I became.

My most famous moment in high school came my sophomore year during a baseball game with a Dallas high school team. THE moment of my high school career came when we were ahead by about ten runs in the late innings. I was stuck into the game as a substitute because were ahead, and our pitcher was un-hittable. The first and only time I came to bat (that season) I walked. I was disappointed because I knew I could hit this pitcher, but he walked even me, a sophomore substitute player. I was on first base, cursing just loud enough for the first baseman to hear, pretending to be more upset than I was when this friend of mine, though he is no longer a friend, hit a single. I had read about Ty Cobb who once scored from first base on a single, and I wanted to try that. We were ahead by a large margin. Why not try? I ran hard and didn't look up until I was about halfway between third and home when I saw the catcher standing there, blocking the plate and waiting for me. I lowered my head in the best Ty Cobb, fullback–fashion and ran into him, trying to knock the ball from his hand. He rolled up into a ball like a doodlebug and stopped rolling close to the backstop, but held onto the ball.

The umpire grabbed me under my left arm and lifted me to my feet, hard. He was mad and trying to take my arm off. He was a big strong man. I was over six feet tall even then, but this giant umpire was jerking me around like a hooked carp. My coach came onto the field to protect me, and as he was arguing with the umpire who had finally let me go, the catcher recovered enough to come at me as though he wanted to fight. I hit him in the side of the head with a strong right cross. He went down and stayed down. About a half hour or so later, an ambulance came for him.

I have no idea to this day as to the extent of his injury. I suppose he was all right because no police ever came to take me away, though I was afraid for a few days. Ah, but the umpire—he forfeited the game to the enemy, and I was no longer on the baseball team.

I was allowed to play the next year because the baseball coach was also an assistant football coach, and he liked me. He was the only one who did. I was surprised to note that the other members of my team disapproved of me, but I just thought that was a brief anomaly.

A few weeks after the baseball incident I kicked a girl off of a truck-pulled hay wagon on a gravel road as we were going about twenty miles an hour. It was an accident, though I don't believe many believe me to this day. She was trying to untie my shoe; I didn't know how close to the back edge she was. The hay slipped off the back, and she with a pile of hay that did nothing to protect her, went into the dark of the night, bouncing slightly.

I was pushing her with my foot, but just to get her away from my shoe. It was a reflex; I had no intention of hurting her. I certainly wasn't mad at her. Some parents took her to the emergency room where the doctor took gravel out of her head for what seemed to be a long time. She had long beautiful golden hair; at least she had long golden hair when the evening began. Most of it was left on the floor of the emergency room. A few stitches to her head, a few months to re-grow the hair, and she was fine. So she wore scarves for a few months when she finally came back to school, her family didn't move to Hawaii as everyone said they were going to.

That night at the emergency room some parents hustled me out of the hospital before her father arrived. I remember I wasn't afraid of him, and I think my lack of fear translated into a lack of concern about Goldie's injury. The parents who were on the hay ride thought I should have been more contrite and more concerned. Perhaps I should have been, but I had to be cool, and I explained many times that night that it was an accident and that I was sorry. That's all I could do. It was a dark night; I didn't know how close she was to the back end, and she was untying my shoe. It was a reflex.

The next week there was an editorial in the school paper that was a thick, not thinly veiled, attack on me.

The title was *ENOUGH*. I still have it, crumbling away and yellowing in my dresser. It was written by a girl who was on the hayride, but who was not likely to have been untying my shoe.

Her comments listed problems with America, problems with our town, and problems with our school. I, my type, was the root of all of society's problems. She never mentioned my name, but there was no one who did not know to whom she was referring. I think she confused me with Edward G. Robinson in *Key Largo*, but the editorial was effective.

I began to slide down the popularity scale again, just like grade school days. As my classmates were becoming more mature and as my supporters were becoming fewer in number, some were already out of school and studying felonies and misdemeanors. Some former fence riders began to have the nerve to disapprove of me publicly, though not to my face. I pretended not to care.

The only people who would have anything to do with me then were the obvious criminals, many of whom died early or went to prison or both. The prospects are not mutually exclusive, I've noticed.

The girl who wrote the editorial was not a very pretty girl who was mad at me because she was not a very pretty girl. She was mad at me in grade school, she was mad at me in high school, and she is mad at me today. The girl who bounced off of the hay wagon told everyone she held no grudge. In fact, she and I became close friends before we graduated from high school. Really, "friends" is not an especially descriptive word. You can say that we were close, a year later, after her hair grew back. But she is mad at me today too. Almost everybody in my high school class is mad at me, and I haven't seen most of them in years.

My recent difficulties began years after we were in high school, and after I had learned how to behave so as to please myself. No longer the rebel, I thought I had learned how to stay out of trouble.

Eve Ann Earlach and Warren Odom married right after high school. They were both in my class from the sixth grade through high school. I barely knew either one. I didn't know they dated in high school, and I didn't know they had married until years later. I don't even remember when I learned they had married. That's how little I thought of either of them. By little, I mean infrequently.

Eve Ann was not pretty or close to being pretty. She was tall, thin and had a round face that sat at the top of a long skinny neck. She was gawky, not talented in any noticeable way and was a very nice girl as I remember.

Warren Odom had his few minutes in the sun. He had been a good athlete in jr. high, but he didn't grow and was too little to play sports on the varsity level. I think he was a back on the JV team until our senior year when he was forced to give up. He became sulky and never spoke to anyone his last year of high school. I remember that Eve Ann was taller than Warren.

After high school, SMU, and the Marine Corps, I returned to graduate school and never caused anybody any trouble. I settled down to a quiet life teaching in a Jr. College and ranching. After I had lived close to my little college town for almost ten years, I received a call from Warren Odom early one Saturday morning. Unknown to me this little town was the home of Eve Ann Earlach Odom's mother. I have no idea how they knew I lived close to Little Burg, Texas, but they were visiting momma and wanted to come over and say howdy before they left town. Understand, they called early one Saturday morning and invited themselves to my house. I was asleep when they called.

I was shocked to hear from Warren. I mean I would not have called him if I found myself in his hometown, wherever it is or was. I don't remember ever socializing with either of the Odoms at any time. I tried not to be rude, though I think it was rude of them to call me early on a Saturday morning. And I knew that my wife would be less than thrilled to have guests early on an unkempt morning. She was asleep with no makeup on. This is a woman who puts on makeup to look into the mirror, and if her house doesn't look as if it were ready for a visit by the Queen she is frantic. She is frequently frantic. In short, I turned down the Odom's offer to visit, and I made a pair of enemies.

Before Warren and Eve Ann left town that morning they stopped by the Dairy Queen for some coffee and gossip. They asked the girl serving them if she knew me. Of course, she did. This is a *little* town. The girl had been in one of my classes and was glad to hear the story of my high school life from the folksy Odoms. They told her everything, bad grades, fights, expulsions—everything. There was no corner of my early life left private. I had gone, all unwillingly, public. Soon many, if not all the residents of my little adopted hometown knew of my checkered, and ever spotted, past. Warren and Eve Ann had warned the girl that I was volatile, and they couldn't believe I had changed much. They warned her to be wary.

Many people, apparently, paid little attention to the popular, and probably amplified stories, floating around about me. I laughed them off, lied, and denied. Some folks kidded me about the stories, but I really didn't care much. It all sounded like folklore or high school lies to most people. However, I was slightly irked with the Odoms.

My class reunites every five years, and at the next reunion after the "visit" by the Odoms, I wrote on the questionnaire that comes with the news of the reunion that one of my hobbies was keeping up with the travels with those jetsetters Warren and Eve Ann Odom. It wasn't much of a joke, and I forgot about it, but the comment was published in the bulletin that functions much like a yearbook for the reunion attendees.

I didn't know that my weak attempt at humor was in the bulletin because I did not attend that reunion. At the next reunion though, the one held last week, Warren asked for the microphone and read a moving letter by Eve Ann who had just died of cancer some few months before the reunion. Her last wish, Warren said, was that I was to hear her letter. I had completely forgotten my attempt at retribution humor, the jet-setter remark.

Some of her comments blurred by me, and I only vaguely remember some of what she said, but I remember that she said, in a very moving letter, that she had always been plain, she knew that. And because of her less than imposing physical appearance, she had never been popular. That too, she knew. But she said that she didn't deserve my cavalier treatment. I had refused to have her and Warren in my stately home. However, they had driven to see the estate where I was denying them welcome and found that my mansion was indeed beautiful, at least from the outside. The image here is of hungry little waifs, their distended tummies pooching and their noses pressing against the glass. I thought I was too good for them, she said. And I didn't think that they deserved to be in my mansion.

How could they get that idea? I told them the house was a mess, and that my wife would need some time to prepare for guests. I remember that Warren had said on that Saturday morning that they had not come to see the house, but that they had come to see me. Oh yeah, well it didn't sound like that in the letter.

My house is not a mansion nor is it close to being one, but if it were would I be obligated to have them visit? Is there some noblesse oblige about high school acquaintances that I don't know? If they had given us some warning, or agreed to wait an hour or two, I would have been happy to see them. They said they had to hurry back to Dallas and couldn't wait for an hour or so. They spent some time in the Dairy Queen, though.

This letter from a dead woman was a good one, but didn't she have more important matters to attend to? Like letters to her children for God's sake? I suppose she probably did write letters to her children. Well . . . it was a good "gotcha." After that great letter-reading moment even my wife was looking at me strangely. There's irony for you. If I had not been thinking of her, I would have invited the Odoms over even if the living room were plumb full of hog shit.

No one came within fifty yards of my loosely connected, non-handholding wife and me as we walked through the parking lot after the reunion. I am unpleasantly reminded of Browning's "My Last Duchess." "Who'd stoop to blame/ this sort of trifling?" I damn sure stoop, and I would go and profane Eve Ann's grave, but I bet it is booby-trapped, and I am sort of a booby.

You know what I think? I think the letter was a joke. I don't think Eve Ann was upset that I didn't invite her to my house. I think she was playing one last practical joke on me for the "jetsetter" remark. I think she was slightly torqued about that, and I think she wins.

My wife, however, has a "gotcha" coming to her, and I have planned a visit to my lawyer soon for a change in my will. I will have a large wooden box hidden somewhere on my ranch. My departure instructions will specify how to find the box. The box will be located with a witness, my lawyer. The large box is to be placed solemnly, unopened, on the blazing outdoor grill—a grill large enough for a whole beef. It will be lippin full of fireworks. Two can play at this final joke game–my instructress buddy, Eve Ann, and me.

MARINE CORPS EXPERIENCES

---■---

Why I love the Corps

*U*nderstand that at any time during my first two years in the Corps if anyone had told me I could go home that person would have been in danger of being swept up in the vacuum of my disappearance.

To love the Corps takes some time because the initiation period is lengthy. Boot camp for me in the so-called peace time was fourteen weeks. I knew exactly what it would be like. My father and my uncles explained to me the entire process. It was a time of challenges—an overworked word but applicable here. The challenges are mental and physical. I was ready for both. I was in perfect physical shape, and I knew how I would be harassed all the time. I didn't mind, and I thrived. What dad and uncles must have forgotten to tell me was that after boot camp when I expected to be warmly accepted as a Marine, I, all of us "boots," were held in contempt by the "salty" Marines we met during the extremely difficult six weeks of infantry training that follows boot camp. Okay, I thought, I will handle this too then I will be accepted as one of the Corps. Didn't happen.

The school I was sent to after Infantry training, a school cleverly–note the irony—was named ABCD School, which stands for Atomic, Biological, and Chemical Defense

School. After being prepared for learning by Southern Methodist University, I thought I would now be able to relax. The school day for two months was from 8:00 until 12:00 and from 1:00 to 5:00. Then study until taps at ten. We could leave the base on weekends if our grades never dropped below seventy. The course was crammed full of math, chemistry and what was then called electronics. And the school was dangerous. Among many other dangerous tasks we had to be able to identify what kind of gas was being used to attack us, and we had to detoxify it. The emphasis on learning was practical.

Often in the middle of difficult classes instructors from other schools walked behind our classrooms and threw in teargas grenades. We had fifteen seconds after we heard the spoon pop to put on our gas masks and clear them. More than one "shook" student who was unable to fit his mask in time ended up jumping out of the window to escape the gas. The classroom was on the first floor for just such emergencies, and we were close to the base hospital, which often held some of our former students. I say former because dropping out, a few times was literal, and was common. Seventy-nine of us began the school, but only fifty-one graduated, and I never left the base. I spent my weekends studying. After gas attacks, the lectures continued. Fully masked we took notes furiously. At night when we entered our barracks, tear gas was noticeable as were trying to sleep.

In Marine Corps schools, the graduates cross the stage in order of class standing. I graduated close to the top of my class because of diligence born of fear. I was met by my new company commander, his executive officer and the first sergeant of my new company—Kilo Company, 3rd Battalion 5th Marines, 1st Marine Division. They were mildly congratulatory and told me to pack then turned me over to a Sergeant who was to be my platoon Sergeant. My graduation celebration lasted for the several miles by jeep to my new barracks–Camp Margarita or 33 area.

After eleven months in the Corps, I was promoted to private first class. And most of the year had been tough, really physically tough as well as mentally tough—no one liked "boots," new Marines which continued to require mental toughness to endure. Thirteen months later I was a Corporal. It was about then when I began to be accepted as a Marine. Hell of a hell week extended to slightly more than two years. My former fraternity knew nothing about initiations, I decided.

Episode One: The good stuff began about that time. I will describe as best I can three episodes, chosen from many for me that made me love the Corps. The first pleasant moment that began to change my mind about life in Corps began while I was at home on leave. My father had a serious, nearly fatal heart attack. I could not make myself leave him and my mother. I adored both my mother and father. They were, I believe, perfect parents, and if they had any flaws as human beings, I never saw them.

I did what I had been taught to do during an emergency on leave. I contacted the Red Cross and asked for an extension of leave time. I had the time on the books; I was eligible for the extra days and the Red Cross was able to check my story. I had little doubt I would be granted the extra leave time. My request was denied. I took two more days, however. I was scared of brig time. No one ever wants to be in a Marine Brig. The Marine Brig makes the army stockade in the movie *From Here to Eternity* look like a play house, but I stayed. When I reported two days late, I remember the look on the gate guard's face. He was not surprised. He was shocked. I was in shock too. Very little happened though for about two months. No one chewed me out; no one seemed to care about my disobedience. One day though I was told to appear the next day before the regimental commander who could have punished me, or he could have recommended a summary court martial. I remember when I was standing in front of him I was so scared my lower lip was frozen, and I hardly recognized my own voice. My Company Commander, Captain Reich, was with me. I did not know him well, but he was a good officer, knew his duty and always did it. He was slight of build but always impeccable and tough. I respected him, but I respected all Marine officers. I didn't like one, but I respected them all. He was standing by my side. Most junior officers stayed behind their troops in this situation.

When I was on leave, my battalion was aboard ship ready to attack the coast of California. We attacked regularly. We usually spent about a week on ship then went over the side in all kinds of weather and darkness to get into little boats that never looked sea worthy to me. I tell this because when my telegram requesting leave extension arrived aboard ship, the Officer of the Deck failed to do his duty and send it along to Captain Reich.

Captain Reich explained this to the Regimental Commander by the name of David Schmuck. I am not kidding. His real name was Schmuck, and he was well known in the Marine Corps, a much decorated war hero. Colonel Schmuck listened to Captain Reich patiently explained that if the Navy OoD had done his job, the captain would have extended my leave. The Colonel said, "All right, Captain I will leave the punishment to you, but Corporal Rattan was wrong to take those two days." The Captain saluted, and we turned to leave. I sighed with relief. I knew my punishment would be severe, but it would not be the brig and neither would it be on my permanent record. When we were barely outside the Colonel's door, my Captain told me that my punishment would be that I would be charged with two more days leave.

He risked his career to do what he thought was right for a hard-charging Marine as I had become. He was a gutty son-of-a- gun, and I loved him then and now. I would have followed him to hell. I saluted, said, "Thank you, sir," did an about face and left.

Episode two: A few months later after I had made sergeant, my company went on an afternoon beer bust. Lots of free beer and about two hundred drunk Marines out in the Boondocks (in the country, singing and urinating in the woods). In theory, there is no rank on a beer bust. If a fight occurs the typical Marine attitude prevails, the fight is finished. A person, admittedly stupid, could challenge the Company Commander if he wanted. I saw that happen once. A 6' plus about 190 lbs I would guess and a boot not long out of Infantry training, challenged Captain Reich. My guess is that the captain weighed about 150 lbs and he was maybe 5' 9". The captain never flinched, he never waited for a discussion, he kicked the man in the chest and the fight was over. The Captain was the first man I saw who fought with his feet. Quite a sight. All the NCOs loved the Captain and the boot was lucky. If he had hit the Captain there would have been a race of mean, salty Sergeants to beat the man to some sort of pulpy goo— one at a time, of course. The guy was lucky he stayed down. He was hurt.

Marine Corps fights are not like high school fights where some twosome throws a few punches and then growl at each other after they have been pulled apart. It had never occurred to me before, but those high school fighters are usually expecting to be pulled apart. The Marine Corps method is different. If a fight starts, the combatants are made to finish it. Somebody is seriously hurt. Thus the Corps is most often a polite place to be, unlike the Navy. Tired at the end of the day with one's manhood again affirmed, most Marines want two beers and as much sleep as the Corps allows, which is not much. However, I have digressed. The story I meant to tell is about a fight I was in.

After the same beer bust I have just spoken of, on a six-by truck, one of my troops pushed a lieutenant. He didn't push hard but as the beer bust was over, the boot just out of infantry training was in the serious wrong. I saw the push, and the Gunny Sergeant saw the push. After we had come back to the barracks area, we formed up and were formally dismissed. I headed for Hesberger, his real name, and began to chew out Hesberger in fine Marine sergeant form as I remember. Hesberger turned to hit me, but he started to draw back his right hand to hit with—a big mistake. As he was pulling his right hand back, I hit him with a serious and fine left jab. He fell forward on his face, but he climbed up my leg, and I hit him again and again. He was tough, but he had little idea how to fight. He was carried to his rack (bed), and I went on duty. I was worried because sergeants aren't supposed to hit privates. However, the fight had been watched by the Gunny, and Hesberger had tried to swing first.

The fight was not over. As I toured the barracks with Hesberger in it, he came off his top rack and came at me again. Again I knocked him out. I had fought in the Golden Gloves and the Texas Amateur Athletic Association for four years where I had knocked out a few others, but this was the first fight out of a ring where I actually knocked someone out. It is not common to do so because bones break on hands and on faces and that usually ends the street fight. I never remembered much about these fights with Hesberger because I was overloaded on adrenaline. I only clearly remember a few moments. I remember standing over him after he was down, and I remember his being carried to his rack again.

One of the "Duty" jobs was to tour barracks. The second time I entered Hesberger's barrack, he attacked me again. Same result.

The next morning I seriously considered deserting and heading to Canada. I thought that Hesberger might die. His face turned several different colors during the night. His nose seemed to be missing under all the swelling. I shined my flashlight on him a few times as I toured the barracks I was responsible for. His colors and contoures from the swelling were hideous. The Duty post is for twelve hours. I remember I took the Corporal of the Guard with me on a few occasions. The Corporal of the guard is a four-hour post.

The next morning my platoon commander, Lieutenant Gordon D. Gore sent the company runner for me and Hesberger. I had calmed slightly because Hesberger could hardly see, but he was not dying. His nose had a knuckle hole in it and one part of his face was caved in. His entire head was swollen beyond what I thought possible, but this tough, son-of a-bitch was alive.

As the tough guy and I walked in to the Lieutenant office, the Lieutenant smiled at me and asked to see my hand. He felt my knuckles, which were not bruised. I remember I explained that I never hit anyone in the forehead because in my first real fight I broke my hand by making that mistake, and I was the one who took a beating that day.

The Lieutenant turned his attention to Hesberger and said something to effect that he had seen Hesberger fall over his locker box last night and if he told those Navy doctors anything else, he would run Hesberger up with morning colors. In other words, he would file charges against Hesberger for a number of reasons, one of which would be for making a false official statement. I already liked Lieutenant Gore very much, but now he entered the growing list of men I would follow to hell. Hesberger was gone for three months and when he returned his voice was not the same. He did not sound as he had before. I understand that persons in car wrecks and serious fights often have a sound change. Something about moving the facial cavity, I understand. A few months after that incident Lieutenant Gore and the new company commander Captain Ledin recommended me for officer training—OTC in the Corps. Officers Training Class.

Episode Three:

Two months before my enlistment was to be up, I reenlisted to go the OTC, but before that ordeal was to begin I took a thirty-days leave. On leave I did nothing more strenuous than walk from the bar to the bathroom in the Kilarney lounge on Greenville Avenue in Dallas near the SMU campus. (I know Killarney is spelled with two Ls, but the owner of the bar, a fine man and a friend of mine during my years at SMU would not pay for the second L on the green neon sign on top of the bar.)

After thirty days of as much debauchery as I could find, I reported back to my company. The first morning back reveille sounded at 5:00. We were to run a five mile jaunt over tall hills, running often in sand, singing as loud as we could. I made the run until we had come up the hill into Camp Margarita and were about two hundred yards from the Fifth Marine grinder, marching area, which was our intended stopping place. We were running in column, and I was in the first four men. I did not feel bad or even tired as I remember, but I saw myself sliding off to the left of the column. I tilted myself to the right to get back in place and the next thing I remember I was lying on my side with the dry heaves.

The Gunny Sergeant was standing over me, and he was solicitous—not normally a Marine trait. He walked with me to my barracks and stood with me as I changed clothes to a kind of dress utilities, which the army calls fatigues.

As bad luck would have it, I was to deliver a lecture to the entire company on cold weather packs. I had known I was to give this lecture, and I prepared for it for a month as I was quaffing beer, but I was on the edge of tears. I like so very many Marines, had long bragged that I had never fallen out of anything. Now I had fallen out with the entire company running past me. Hard for me to relate how embarrassed I was. The Gunny, a man in his late thirties, had made the run, and I had not, but he continued to ask if I were okay, and I dropped my eyes and told him I was fine, which I was. We walked to the large building where I was to address the company. The CO introduced me, but before I could make my way to the lectern, the Gunny pushed me aside and told the company that he knew they had seen me fall out of formation a few yards from the finish of our morning run, and then he said something about thirty days leave, but he said that Sergeant Rattan had not gotten tired and sat down, but rather that he ran until he dropped. In a strong voice filled with emotion, he told them that I was a Marine. No finer compliment possible. "That man is a Marine," he told them. No one ever disputed the Gunny about anything.

My chest swelled and I gave a lecture I can't remember a word of. The Gunny displayed leadership, and in the Marine Corps where the higher the rank, the more Marines we have to take care of, be responsible for, protect as best we can. When a water truck arrives out in the bush or boondocks, the captain or the highest rank drinks last. The leaders eat last. Take care of your men is what leadership is about. The Gunny, Captain Reich, and Lieutenant Gore were leaders and true Marines whom I love until this day.

MY FINEST MOMENT

———————————■———————————

*M*y hesitance in calling this piece "My Finest Moment" is that the reader will see how dull and uneventful my life has been. I believe one reason for us old guys to lie about our pasts is that we don't want to admit to ourselves we have missed something important in our lives. Now at the tag end of my life, I find myself proclaiming how dull I am. By this memoir, what I have to fully admit is that I have been a Casper Milquetoast, a Mr. Peepers, and a Dull Jon. So be it.

Most of us have had some recurring dream, usually not a serious, sad, or frightening dream, but for me one pestering dream came around on rare occasions that I would smile at after I awakened because it had bothered me only slightly when I was asleep.

My wife tells me that she had a recurring dream of not being able to find the classroom when she was in the public schools. That dream while not a nightmare was slightly trying for her because she was a hard-charger and scared of her teachers. She always wanted to please them. It is one of her most endearing qualities, this wanting to please. So I had only a little sympathy for this dream of hers, and my dream had grown familiar, and it bothers me almost not at all.

My dream was that I was on stage waiting for the curtain to come up, and I did not know the name of the play we were about to do. Most actors know this dream, and I suppose many persons have their own similar kind of dream to the extent that it reflects their constant activities.

I had given up acting in my twenties mostly because it bored me. Too much rehearsal, and while working frequently, I was not getting rich and famous, so I left the stage for the classroom, not that I ever set out to be rich, but it would have been nice. If I had made a lot of money acting, I am sure I would have quit when I had enough money, and that would be less than most people believe they need to be content. In other words my dream did not drive me away from acting.

I went back to school after about five years of acting, and I earned a doctoral degree and began to write poetry. No one reads poetry, but it is a satisfying endeavor to create a world that I control, except controlling my world in my poems pays less than acting.

Push ahead a few years to a time when I was teaching in a small university. We had a new president whom I did not know well. He called me one morning as I was preparing for the day, and he asked me if I would like to accompany him to visit a university where a friend of his—a friend of long standing I learned—was the new president.

I thought that morning that the request was odd but interesting. I think I had ideas about becoming one of the important people on campus like a Dean. Deans make a lot more money than professors, but they have a tedious job that is not interesting. To take care of parking problems, and to be sure the broken windows are replaced and that the restrooms are always clean is not an academic job, and I was wondering if the job he might be about to offer me would pay enough more to entice me. Then too, I reasoned that I could never become a university president unless I had spent some time as a Dean, and University Presidents make a ton of money. These were my thoughts.

The drive to the other university took about three hours, and my new president and I had a pleasant chance to come to know each other, and I found that I liked him— nice, interesting guy. I forgot about the job offer I hoped for—for a while.

When we arrived I was pleased to note that my president and the other president were old friends and more bonhomie occurred among us all. Soon, however, we got up to go to a meeting of the faculty. The meeting was in a large auditorium, and I was seated next to my new friend on the first row. I had no idea as to the purpose of the meeting.

My president's friend was on stage, and he politely introduced his old friend, my new president. Nice, I thought. Everything was especially nice. I expected my new friend and president to speak to the faculty of this university. I had no idea as to the subject of his speech, the speech I expected to hear.

My president spoke briefly of his host and how he long admired his old friend and this particular university. All was well until my president / buddy began to speak about the Southern Association Visit that was to begin next year at this university. My university had just completed our ten-year ordeal of close scrutiny from the only accrediting agency that matters. In our visit by several faculty members and accountants from other universities to see if we were fit to keep our absolutely essential accreditation is painful, very painful. For me the job was like writing a dissertation. If the Southern Association doesn't renew accreditation for a university, courses won't transfer and graduates would not be qualified to enter professional schools or to attend graduate schools. Admittedly this happens only rarely because universities have eight years to prepare for the self-study and the visitation to check on the self-study. But one can see the importance of the ten-year visit.

My president, fast becoming a non-friend, introduced me as one who had survived the study and told that faculty I would be well prepared to help them know what to expect and how to prepare for their upcoming visit. I sat there for a moment and thought not of what I would say, but rather I thought that this was my recurring dream, now a nightmare come true.

I had written one of ten chapters required by the Southern Association. My chapter was on the subject of the faculty. I talked about hiring, about classroom preparedness. I discussed the percentage of professors with terminal degrees, and the number of adjunct instructors we had to have to fulfill our mission on ever decreasing budgets. These things I knew and spoke of them with authority. With so much authority I began to believe myself and proceeded to extrapolate to the other required studies I knew nothing about. In short I lied, hoping to run out of time. I wanted to leave the stage apparently reluctantly, wishing I could help them more. I looked at my watch and realized and mentioned my hour was up and began to make my apologies for not being more economical with my time, but they had seen, I said, how attentive to details the inspectors are.

The president of their university stood up and said that I could have as much time as I needed because what I was telling them was what they needed to hear, at least the young faculty who had not been run through this gauntlet before needed for me to continue talking. I winced.

At this time I remembered that some visiting professors acting as our judges visited many classes. My class had not been one that was visited, but I said it was my frightening experience to have a lady professor spend the entire hour with me. In my earlier talk I had already told their faculty that classroom visits were usually perfunctory and usually short, which was and is true, but the lady remained with me for the entire hour, I lied again. I was not sure, I said, if I were to be flattered or if I was falling far short of my duty.

I made up a story about a class I was teaching. It was a sophomore survey class dealing with a story, "The Jilting of Granny Weatherall" by Katherine Ann Porter. I made up a story about, was a sophomore survey literature course, and I had discussed, I said, was the Katherine Ann Porter story, "The Jilting of Granny Weatherall." The story is a fine one, and it is largely naturalism filled with religious overtones. Kathryn Ann Porter was a Catholic and the story comes close to proselytizing for the Catholic branch of Christianity.

After class, as I continued lying, the lady had approached me, I said, and asked why I chose the story. She seemed to accept my standard sort of answer for a moment, and then she asked me if I were Catholic. I heard myself tell this faculty that I said that I didn't know. Not know if I were a Catholic? Only an imbecile would say such a thing. Silence descended on my audience as I bit my lip. Then without having any idea as to what I was about to say I said, "I'm an Episcopalian, and we haven't decided yet."

The audience roared and applauded until the president shushed them and told me what an excellent morning I had provided for them. After the talk, I was swamped with faculty members who wanted to know where I had earned my doctorate and many other pointless questions. I was a hit, a big hit, and then while I was on the floor, making my way slowly to the front door, their president came up to the microphone on stage and said that if I wanted to change jobs they would have a place for me. More applause.

On the way home my president was elated and told me that I had said just what I needed to. He never offered me a job as Dean, though, and I never told him I had told an enormously long complicated lie that could have finished the afternoon with both looking of us like fools. It would have been more his fault, I told myself, than mine, though I knew I would never have been able to sleep comfortably again. One little Episcopalian moment saved me.

ONE NIGHT AT WAR (A MEMOIR OF M/SGT. JOSE M. RAMIREZ, USMC)

—————————■—————————

Among the personal effects of retired Master Sergeant (Sarge) Jose M. Ramirez, USMC was a small entrenching tool used for the quick digging of fox holes. It was the tool he used in Korea. Each of the Pall Bearers, members of the English Department at the university, including Dr. Dasa Brown used the shovel to begin the process of returning Sarge to the earth. Dasa was a small woman who insisted she be allowed to carry part of the weight of her good friend, fellow horticulturist, and fellow member of the Presbyterian Church where she was the organist.

Each one of us knew something about the shovel, but not the important part. We just knew that Sarge carried it every day, and that sometimes he used it to dig up weeds, though that was not part of his job at the university, but we buried it on top of his casket.

After retiring from a 30 year career in the Marine Corps in 1982, Sarge worked in maintenance until he retired in 2003. He spent the last 14 years at the university working in the English and Foreign language departments building, The Hall of Languages where he made innumerable friends.

Details of Sarge's life are not easily quantifiable. There are no little nuggets of information about a man who was not married, had never been married, and who belonged to no clubs or organizations, the things we usually mention in obituaries. Sarge once told me that most career Marines couldn't have successful marriages because they traveled frequently to places where their wives could not follow, but Sarge didn't feel as he had been cheated out of anything. He made the university his life.

He was truly a kind man, sensitive to everyone. Had he not been referred to as Sarge, no one would have known that he was a retired Marine Master Sergeant. No one could ever remember his talking or mentioning his life in the Marine Corps, and certainly no one knew of his war record until his death.

Sarge made the university his life, his hobby, his true occupation. He attended all football games, basketball games, and track meets that were conducted on the campus. He also attended all the plays put on by the drama department and attended almost everything put on by the music department. Some of the activities of the music department were only during the day, and sometimes he slipped off to listen to those. Everyone knew when Sarge was not in the building, and we all knew where he had gone, and we all approved. Sarge was found on the campus most Saturdays, but after his death we found that we knew very little about him. I suppose I knew more about him than anyone, but only because he asked me to read his account of his first battle in Korea.

I read it, and I told him truthfully that it was perfect, nothing to change. I also promised that I would never mention the account to anyone. I'm not sure why he wrote it. He never wanted anyone, but me to read it, and

I was to tell no one about it. After his death, he cannot be embarrassed. Everybody has something to say about his life and perhaps his purpose was a catharsis. Or maybe he wanted to teach somebody something. No matter. One does not write of his life for no one to read.

The following is his story in his words. I changed nothing, except I indented now and then and added a comma or a period on occasion. I deleted nothing, and of course, I added nothing of substance. I'm not sure why I send this to anyone to read, but many reasons are possible. Maybe I need a vicarious catharsis, and I would hate for such a life not to be noticed.

"After I left high school in San Antonio, Texas in 1951, I worked around San Antonio where my brother, Rafael got me a job as a carpenter's helper. The pay was not too good, and after about a year of this work, I was about to be drafted in the army, so I joined the Marine Corps. I wanted to be a part of the best.

I enlisted on March 10th 1952. I was seventeen years old. I went to San Diego, California where I went to Boot Camp. My drill instructor was a Gunny Sergeant named Goodeagle, a hard but fair man. He did not sit down during the day because he did not want to wrinkle his uniform. You got to admire a man like that, and he had ribbons all over his chest with battle clusters, so you could believe what he told you.

He had been at the Chosen Reservoir where he earned a Bronze Star. Only 13 men in his company walked out of there, but they carried their dead, their wounded, and most of their equipment. Not like the ROKs or the Army outfit on the First Marine Division's right flank. The reservoir was where Chesty Puller said, so I heard, "We got gooks in front of us, in back of us and on both sides. They can't get away now." He and Goodeagle were Marines.

After Boot Camp and Infantry Training Regiment, I was sent as a replacement to K co. 3rd Battalion, Fifth Marines. The 5th Marines were on the MLR, the Main Line of Resistance. The Ist Marines were in reserve at that time. One of three regiments was always on reserve. The 7th Marines were also on line then. I arrived at 5th Marine Regimental Headquarters on Seven November, 1952. All the replacements got off the six-bys three miles behind the MLR and walked the rest of the way to Regimental Headquarters. We were led to Battalion Headquarters by a Lieutenant who got killed that night. I never knew his name. He was tall and very clean for a man who was on the front lines, I thought. I saw him die the next day in the Battalion Aid Station, waiting to be evacuated. He seemed to be asleep or on some pain killers, so no one expected anything from him more than a few moans, and everyone, even the nurses were surprised when he sat up and said, "Why?" He died and fell off the cot. I couldn't tell where he was wounded.

The MLR was a sight to see. It was a big trench that ran all the way across Korea, I was told. And it was well planned and everyone was dug in good. On the tops of the fighting holes, what the army calls fox holes, there was lots of sand bags, so they could take a hit from a 60mm mortar and not get nobody killed. In between the holes was the trenches.

In the front of the MLR, there were many strands of concertina, barbed wire. Out front of the concertina were the mines, personnel and tank mines, but there wasn't going to be any tanks because we had air superiority. The last two years of the war, we called it a conflict in those days, was what the papers called static warfare. That meant nobody moved. It was all real simple: anybody goes out in front of the wire was likely to get killed. The Marines, of course, sent out patrols all the time we were told back in Boot Camp. I didn't doubt it. The days were not bad, but it was a night war those last two years.

I mean anybody sticks his head up during the day was likely to get it blown off. Sometimes though, the gooks came in big numbers. They didn't care how many of them we killed. I mean we had all the companies' mortars and the 11th. Marines, the artillery, zeroed in on the areas in front of the wire, so you know they knew they were going to take heavy losses if they assaulted us, but they did it anyway, sometimes.

They didn't have no artillery barrages to let us know they were coming, they just came by the thousands. Many had no rifles, I heard. Just clubs and sharp sticks was all that some of them carried. They could create some trouble though. The MLR went all across Korea, and us with the Gooks about 800 yards to a 1000 yards apart, and everybody dug in good for those last two years. The war made a kind of sense because whoever was out in no man's land stood a good chance of being killed. If you just stayed put, your chances were good for living. And we didn't make no all-out charges like the gooks. But the Marines patrolled almost every night and took the most casualties, more than the ROKS (Republic of Korea, meaning South Korea) and the army, I mean. We patrolled more than the gooks too. I never knew why. It seemed silly. I mean if they came, they came. I never could figure what good we was doing by all that patrolling, but as things turned out, I never made no patrols myself.

But after the war, we talked about that all the time. One sergeant I knew thought that we were afraid that they might tunnel under us and attack us from the rear. Maybe, but it still seems unlikely to me. Most of that static war was fought at night. Some Marines I heard talking knew that no man's land in front of them better than they knew their mother's cooking, they said. But war stories, like most stories, grow from time. The slop chute wars got better all the time. (The Slop Chute means bars and lounges.)

Five guys got off the truck with me, and we all hiked the three miles to the MLR carrying all our gear, everything we owned, although the Marine Corps really owned everything, including us. We had rifles, full packs and seabags. We was used to walking much farther, but with less to carry. I still remember how heavy that seabag was, and how tired I was even after a little hike of three miles. We made it okay, though. Coming closer to the war made us less tired. All six of us was assigned to K company. We had to walk down the trench to get to K Co. Headquarters, may be another mile, hard to say, but it was a long way for some reason. We came in the back of the Company commander's hooch, really just a big hole in the ground, fortified with sandbags and wooden beams. We expected to come to attention or something but it never happened. Maybe at war all the other stuff isn't so important.

We just stood around and getting in everyone's way until the company commander, Captain DeAteley told a radio man to get on the horn to the 1st. platoon and tell Lieutenant Broderick to send somebody to get two of us. I was ready to get out of there, so I said I wanted to go to 1st. platoon. Nobody cared, so I went with the sergeant from 1st. platoon down the trench line maybe another mile or so, maybe, to the 1st. platoon area. Every hooch or hole we went through told us something different to expect. I expect they was all shittin us. The sergeant said not to pay them any mind, so I didn't. Lieutenant Broderick, everybody called him whale neck behind his back, sent me to the left flank of the platoon area and put me in a two man hole with a Corporal Dyer from Sacramento.

It was getting dark, so Dyer asked me if I had anything to eat, and I told him In had C rations in my pack. He told me to eat what I wanted before it got dark because after dark there was no way to light one of the little stoves they give you to heat anything. The heat makes the c rations better. The light would draw enemy fire Corporal Dyer said. I cooked some beef stew and ate some fruit and talked to Dyer, a good guy, not like the corporals in the Infantry Training Regiment. I was glad for that.

I remember I asked him what it was like on the MLR at night and he said that the thing to do was to keep your head and not report to the company headquarters that we were getting probed or hit by the gooks until you could actually see them in the wire. He said we could call in for lots of flares though. I was glad for that.

We were on 100 percent security that night because intelligence was expecting a probe in our sector. That meant we both had to stay awake. I should have been awfully tired, but I wasn't. Dyer said not to worry too much because Intelligence always expected a probe and not to worry too much about it, so I tried not to. I liked it better that it was 100 percent because I didn't want to be the only one in that hole awake, and I didn't think I could sleep when it was my turn anyway. Dyer didn't seem to care much that we might get hit that night because he said intelligence was rarely ever right. So we stood there, whispering about where we were from and telling private stuff about our girlfriends. The married men never talked about their wives, but the rest of us probably lied a great deal. A good story is worth a lot in a boring situation, and it is boring standing in the dark without being able to see anything, and we didn't hear much. Anything to make the night less scary is okay, even good.

I remember Dyer saying, 'The only thing you got to worry about is being out in front of that wire, but the Lieutenant won't put you on any kind of patrol for a week or so. Until you get used to it here and get over the jitters, you can relax.' That made me feel better for a while, but that was damn near the last thing he ever said.

We were standing about six feet apart, both of us trying to look out over the parapet, but it was cold and dark as night can get, no moon. It had been a full moon, but it was covered by lots and lots of clouds. Dyer said no moon was the time the enemy might hit us, and he began to act as though he was nervous, looking harder with his head straining to see. His whispered words sounded like they was in front of us. Maybe the wind, which was getting stronger, was blowing his words back at us. I was standing on my tip toes, but I really didn't have to. I don't know what I could help by standing on tip toes.

It was about 1:00 in the morning when Easy Company on our left began to open up. Soon they were firing all their machine guns and we had lots of flares on our left. We could see them, but Dyer didn't shoot. Suddenly it was light as day and all those trees out in front of turned into gooks. Dyer yelled into the phone: 'Gooks in the wire.' I could hear the command post telling Dyer not to get shook, mortars were on the way. They were on the way, but they were hitting behind the ones in the wire. Dyer opened up with his BAR. I watched for a minute, but then

I remembered I was in this fight too, so I began to shoot as fast as I could. It didn't seem fast enough and when I emptied a clip, it took a long, long time before I got another one in. Time hurried and slowed down like that for a long, long time too, minutes I guess. I never knew how many bandoleers I went through, but it was many.

I heard Dyer yelling into the phone telling the Lieutenant to bring the mortars back almost on us, I think. He yelled to me to keep my head down. I just kept on shooting and so did he, I think. It was getting awful hard to hear. Mortar hitting, machine guns and Bars going crazy and then there were those damn bugles, I had heard about in Boot Camp and Infantry Training Regiment. The training was good. The whole company was under attack and Easy Company too, and I don't know who else. It wasn't no probe, it was a full scale attack. The flares kept coming down, and we kept shooting. The three 30 caliber machine guns each company has was firing less. They had to slow down or overheat the barrels. Sometimes when the 50 calibers were reloading we counted out loud, though no one could have heard us. I looked at Dyer some times when a flare was really close to us. The whole MLR as far as we could see was lit up sometimes.

The bodies out in front of us, in the wire and behind it, were stacking up, and we could see as far as we could during the day. I figured the whole Chinese army was after us. And I wasn't too sure they couldn't get us. After about ten minutes that seemed to be hours and hours, and we looked out and there no gooks to be seen, but the dead ones. We got an order to cease fire at about that time, but we already had. I noticed that both Dyer and me were breathing hard, though we had not been doing anything but shooting. Dyer said, thank God, that if I saw feet coming in the hole to shoot. Marines came in head and rifle first. That was good to know for a couple of reasons because about that time we hear Charlie Company close to the Command Post start firing again. We been sucking some air, but when we heard firing again, Dyer, he stood up to look over the parapet. He didn't say nothing, but he started firing again the minute he looked up.

I stood up and see Gooks with ladders they were laying over the wire and walking on them. I started firing too, but this time I noticed what I was doing because I remember it. I was thinking about what I was shooting at where before I was just firing in their direction fast as I could. I noticed what I was doing, and I didn't fumble so much with the new clips, and I took more time to aim at what I was shooting at. I saw gooks falling, and I realized I was the one doing the shooting them. It was like a picture I was a part of and watching too.

We was firing so much Dyer said we better just shoot when we could see, when the flares showed them. The flares always showed them. They were never fewer. Dyer said that there was nothing like this happened in the whole year he had been in Korea. In a minute of lull, somebody on the radio told us that Lieutenant Broderick was on his way up to the C-P, and he would be coming in our hole in a minute. The point was that we were not to shoot him.

I think it was good we were told. When the Lieutenant came in, he was head first with his 45 in his hand. He told us that he thought C Company had been overrun, and he was going to see before we called up the 1st Marines in reserve. The radios were out. That scared me. He told us to fix bayonets. I was mighty scared, but I was glad Gunny Goodeagle taught us to sharpen our bayonets right. You never sharpen the tips, only the sides. The tip hits a bone, it should slip off and cut through, so you just sharpen the sides of bayonets. Goodeagle also said a man's belly will convulse around the bayonet, so you may need to squeeze off a round or two to get your bayonet back. Even then you might have to put your boondocker (shoe) on his chest and pull hard to get the bayonet back. If you got no rounds, disconnect the bayonet and leave it in him, then look for another bayonet in a hurry. I remember wondering how to do all that and remember it when you needed to, but it was all coming back clear to me now. I remember that we all said in Boot Camp that if we had any rounds left we wouldn't need no bayonet.

Right after Broderick left, while a flare was burning close, we heard a thump. Dyer yelled something and went out the left side of the hole. I just started out the right side when the grenade went off. My back was twisted so I was looking at the sky, not the dirt, and I wondered why. My back was twisted pretty good. I thought that I would die in a minute because I figured I didn't have no legs or anything left much, but that wasn't the way it was because they had thrown a concussion grenade, looking for prisoners.

My back was sure enough twisted, and I couldn't feel nothing below the waist, but I thought that I was in pieces, and I felt for blood, but I couldn't find any. It had gotten quiet for a minute, and I thought I couldn't hear either then another flare went off, and I heard it detonate. Then I saw two feet coming in. I tried to shoot, but I didn't have no clip in my rifle. I lunged forward, falling because my legs wouldn't hold me. I remember I was surprised that I had remained standing as I slid back into the hole after the grenade went off, but I couldn't take no step, so I stretched as far as I could as I was falling with my right arm holding my rifle in front of me, and I caught him with his belly exposed . I guess he was holding on to the roof of the hooch as he was sliding in, his quilt-like coat was up when I hit him. He grunted loud, louder than I ever heard anything before. I still hear it sometimes. He fell against the back wall, jerking my rifle and bayonet out of my hands. He lay there flopping back and forth moaning, shouting something I didn't know what. He looked like a fish trying to get off a hook, cutting his hands bad on the sides of the bayonet as he tried to pull or push it out.

He was laying at the back wall and my face was almost in his belly. Somehow I rolled back against the front wall just under the parapet, trying to get away from him. As he was flopping around, it seemed to me I had done something bad wrong. I prayed to God to forgive me then I prayed that he would kill all the gooks so I would be safe. I could hear fighting going on all around me, hand to hand stuff, not much shooting, just a lot of yelling in both languages and a lot of screaming. I didn't have no idea what was happening. I didn't know who was winning. I thought maybe everybody was dying.

On one of the Chinese guy's flops, the rifle came close to me, and I tried to pull it out of him. He yelled so loud and was in so much pain, I let go. He took hours to die, maybe all night, and he made gurgling sounds like air coming up out of water. Once or twice more I crawled over to him and tried to get him quiet, but when he made that gurgling God-awful wheezing sound, I let him go. I asked him to forgive me, I prayed in Spanish so maybe he could understand me and maybe so God too might understand better.

When I saw I was never going to get that rifle back, I crawled over to my pack, my legs and back were hurting now, and it was a pack I had never even started to unpack, and I got my entrenching tool, a small green shovel that all Marines carry. Like Gunny Goodeagle had said, I sharpened the edges to a fine point. I unfolded it and put it together and lay there listening to the sounds of the fighting and listening to the Chinese boy (I never knew if he was Chinese or a North Korean, and it made no difference, him making all those sounds.) I remember I wanted him to die, but I didn't want to kill him no more. I remember I wondered where Dyer was.

I had crawled away from my side, the side of the hooch where the Dying man was, towards Dyer's side, when I heard Gook talk. I pulled myself up by putting my hands on the parapet, and I had the entrenching tool under my neck with my chin holding it against my chest. When I was up and leaning with my back to what we used to call the front (who knew where the front was now), I let the entrenching tool roll down my arms to my hands with the back of my neck kind of hooked on the parapet to help keep me up. I held the tool in my right hand, and I used my left had to brace myself. Then I saw two more feet coming in the hooch. This time I waited and took my time like an executioner. I swung my entrenching tool like it was a baseball bat. I hit this kid just under his chin before he was standing firm. His head almost came off. It fell down like you knew he couldn't be alive with his head dangling like that. His head was at an angle like you knew nothing alive could do that. He never made no sound either. I guess I cut his vocal chords, but he bled and bled until there was no more blood in him. The blood spurted a while and soaked me. The whole floor of the hooch was maybe an inch or so deep in his blood, and he didn't die right away either, but he couldn't make no sound like the other guy, and he died pretty quick. He flopped around like a chicken, but I think he had died before he stopped flopping around. Maybe a minute or two.

It was awful cold, and I was wet with blood that made me warm for a little while then it froze on me. The fighting had stopped, and I heard Marines calling for Corpsmen. I needed one too, but I couldn't make myself say anything. I heard the CP asking for Dyer all the rest of the night. I don't know how long that was, but I never made no move to get that phone. When the bayoneted guy died, I was ready to die too. I remember I didn't care.

When it started to get light, I could see both of the men I had killed, just boys really, and I didn't see no weapon for either one of them. I never saw the face of the boy whose I head I had almost cut off, but he was just a kid too. I knew. Not long after the sun came up, Captain DeAtely stuck his head in. I knew it was a Marine and not a Gook when I saw the head and not feet, but it would have made no difference who it was, I had no more fight in me. Dyer had been killed when he got out of the hole. They found five burp gun holes in his back, and saw almost no front of him at all. If he was not wounded, I guess they didn't want him. Everybody in the company was accounted for, so they got no prisoners. I was glad for that a few days later. At the time I didn't care much about anything.

They carried me back to battalion aid, and I didn't see K Company again until I was out of the hospital and me and the First Marine Division was back at Camp Pendleton about a year later when the "conflict" was over. The Captain came to see me in the Hospital before I went back to the states. I got the Bronze Star like Goodeagle. I don't know why. I just tried to stay alive.

I never shot nobody again or even went hunting again until Vietnam in '65 and again, in '68. I shot at people in that war, but I don't know if I ever hit anyone. I'm glad. I hope I never hit nobody. I just wanted to scare them away. I bet they just wanted to make me go away too. I took no pleasure in either war. I guess the Marine Corps is a good place to be, and the Corps does what it has to. The Corps taught me all I know about courage and war, but I wouldn't let my son, if I had one, go to war."

Respectively Submitted,

Jose M. Ramirez, M/Sgt U.S.M.C. (Ret)

About four or five years after I came to the university, and not long after Sarge came to work in the Hall of Languages. Two other professors and I asked the Sarge if he would like to go hunting with us. He politely declined. That he was unwilling to go with us surprised me slightly, and I thought that the expense of a gun or perhaps the thought of paying for a lease was the reason he didn't want to go, so I assured him that we had a gun for him and that he would be nothing out of pocket but for the expense of the shells. He was patient with me and told me that he hoped the three of us would have a good time, but that he didn't hunt. He said he had made peace with the world and if something didn't attack him he would not attack it.

I thought that was a good idea, but like a smart alec, I asked about his conviction further. He told me that he wore no leather and was a vegan. He said that he saw nothing wrong with hunting, but the enjoyment of it. That he lectured me might be wrong.

I never enjoyed hunting so much after that or fishing either, but then I never enjoyed fishing, and I am almost a vegetarian today. When friends invite me to dinner, I will eat a small portion their offerings, but I would rather the Sarge did not know about it. His reasoning was good for me.

We, all of Sarge's friends, wish we had read his account of his one day at war in Korea while he was still with us. We wrote to his brother Rafael in San Antonio to see if there was a diary of his experiences in Vietnam, but the brother said that there was no record of Sarge's thirty years in the Corps—no diary, no uniforms, no record of his awards. Rafael did not even know where Sarge's discharge papers were. He had one picture of Sarge holding a young Vietnamese boy and feeding him something, maybe candy, the brother said.

THE ART OF GOPHER PRAIRIE-HADLEYVILLE-DRISCO, TEXAS

(Read *Main Street* or seen *High Noon?*)

*R*ecently I became engaged in a slightly unpleasant argument with a young man who lives in the same town I do. I foolishly spoke my mind about this foolish, fetid, fecal matter-full town because I forgot he is a native of Fecalville. I thought because he had been to two universities and earned two degrees he was able to be analytical, unbiased, and able to render judgment beyond the indigenous scope that afflicts his local contemporaries. Since my talk with him, I have investigated other MBAs and found that most of them have not read much. Pity. Of course, George Bush and Bill O'Reilly are MBAs, too, so I should have been suspicious. I can only say in my defense that possessing the MBA is a big step for the natives of Gopher Prairie, and I expected more. How foolish.

All I originally said to him was that Gopher Prairie (pseudonym for Disco, Texas) was a dying, mismanaged, hideously ugly little town of approximately 3000 souls cinched by the Bible Belt. Hideously ugly is much worse than plain ugly. At any rate, he took offense. He is a cheerleader who believes that cheering helps. Cheering not only doesn't help anyone, especially football players, but also the noise hurts. I know that benefactors are frequently crucified, but I am willing to make the sacrifice. I am quite brave, apparently, which surprises me.

Hometown boy took offense and asked me why I continued to live here. I told him the truth as I knew and know it, I would prefer to live in Colorado Springs or San Francisco, or Ft. Worth or Abilene, but the only job I could find where I could afford a small ranch, was at Drisco Jr. College. Drisco is fifty miles east of Abilene, the closest city of any size worth mentioning. Abilene advertises a population of 115 thousand folks.

Since my discussion/argument with the MBA cheerleader, my sons have grown and left the ranch, and I have been professing at a nice university about 150 miles from Driscoburg. However, I maintain my home here among the Baptists on weekends and in the summers because I can't afford to move, and no one here can afford my house. Most of the city folk I know recoil at the thought of driving through Vistalessville, much less would they consider living here. I understand.

As I explained to the MBA, I prefer to live here rather than live in Dallas. Dallas, Houston, San Antonio have seceded from Texas. They brag about their growth, and their road repair. I value neither. These three cities are always trying frantically to enlarge so as to have problems they can use the "latest methods" on, largely choo choo trains, to solve their problems. Traffic is ALWAYS diverted for "Road Repairs." For these people growth is a sign of affirmation. The more the wearier. There is something wrong about bragging about living in a city that requires 24 hour traffic reports.

In Drisco, on the other hand, we try never to repair our streets, so we never have traffic jams. No traffic, no jams. Dallas has had three generations of the same families retire from working on what is now laughingly known as The Central Expressway. It is more like a Central Depressway or Compressway. Cars four inches apart bumper to bumper often honking, plodding along at a galloping 35 miles per hour is a blight upon humanity. No thanks, I'll take the Baptists.

By the way, let me explain the Bible belt and the Baptists. All of those sweet people have accepted the idea that we are all fallen, and thud / thus need a redeemer because they know that no matter how good little boys and girls we are, we are not fit for heaven. Okay, I'll buy that, but what these folk want desperately is to find those among us, apparently in great number, are those who have fallen further than they have. Judge not? Bull Shit. Judge constantly should be their motto. Judging their poor earth-born fellow mortals is their favorite passtime. Makes them feel good to find someone who is more depraved than they are. Compassion, love, and forgiveness for their fellows have been lost in their rush to judgment. Thus the Baptists are a pain in the ass to have to contend with, but I prefer them to Dallas, Houston, and San Antonio traffic. I can largely ignore those folks who know what the bible says, but fail to know what it means, but road repair, traffic, I cannot ignore.

In Gopher Prairie Drisco we don't re-route traffic, we bounce frequently, but we are not obligated to seek an alternate route. Our rush hours are compressed to about ten minutes. In this we are efficient. We are to be admired in some other areas of our lives too. For instance, we never have lines in our court house. We never have to queue up for an even a short stay in the Post Office. I must admit, however, with my head hanging low, that we have lines in the grocery store, especially on food stamp day and on Fridays when the working men are paid. Lines in the supermarkets are as ubiquitous as the iniquitous, alas.

Parking is only a slight problem when one of our ilk heads in to a place meant for parallel parking. No one seems to mind much. And as for driving, I have lived here for forty years and I have never received a traffic ticket or parking ticket, and we have no parking meters. I admit to almost always failing to stop at almost every stop sign in the county, but no one has ever complained, and I have certainly never received a ticket. I have been stopped a few times, but the policeman and I just chat. I'm not a danger to anyone and most of us never stop for traffic lights (we have one in town) or stop signs, so no tickets.

With regards to the local constabulary, when I first arrived here in Dreckville, we had one policeman and he was called chief. I never knew his name, but back then our population was about 5000. Now we have only about 3000, and we have 10 policemen. Fewer people with less to do, except now I sometimes see our local police cars out on the interstate ticketing foreigners. The town needs the money to pay the police, I suppose.

Having done justice to my home town (gag) now I shall try to answer the implications of the young man's question about why I live here. His statement was that if I criticize my home town, I am a traitor. I don't know how to be a traitor to a town. What he means to say, yet cannot find the words is that I am a traitor to the merchants of the town. In fact, I am a benefactor of the town by pointing out what might be done to help this hapless, seemingly helpless, little, ugly, dying, mismanaged Merdburg. (I am aware that benefactors are frequently, if not always, crucified or forced to drink a cup of hemlock.)

One big problem is the town stinks, literally. The imbeciles on the city council built the sewage treatment facility right in front of the Jr. College a few years ago. It is no more than about three hundred yards down the hill from the front entrances to the college. The college is the only asset the town has, and the town is too stupid, almost unanimously, to realize its biggest asset is not a hole in the ground.

Luckily the treatment facility is east of the college and the prevailing wind is from the southwest. Only occasionally, but too frequently, do students and faculty have to smell the smell that would cause better places to close until the wind changes. Tacking a wooden sailing ship into the wind is a far easier cross to bear than whiffing the wind of the city sewage. Oddly, it seems to me the place looks like a large pretty lake when the wind is from the southwest. I think, however, the prettiest, most colorful, snakes and spiders are the deadliest. The "Place" as it is known looks like one supposes Walden Pond must have looked to Thoreau, but the appearance is given the lie when the wind is wrong.

As for the town not knowing what an asset the college is, not long ago I read a letter to the editor of the local once-a-week "news" paper (the paper is really no more than a bulletin board with advertisements) stating that the college employs no more than a hundred or so employees, thus the loss of the college is nothing to worry about. Shouldn't it be obvious that the employees of the college send their children to the local school, pay taxes, and help to support the local merchants? Shouldn't it be obvious that the four hundred people (families of the college employees) have their cars repaired, buy their groceries, support the churches, and support the local morticians?

Car repair and casket selling are the town's major businesses after the college. Without the college, the town would dry up from about 3000 to 1,200.

A business course I took in college before I learned I don't like business said that 12 people are supported by one paycheck. I'm not sure how that works, but some business major can explain to me how that works perhaps, but the meaning must be that the college is especially important to a town of this size that has no other industry. Here, the churlish dolts don't know their assets from a treatment plant, and there is no way to tell them. I wish that for one payday the college could, would pay its employees with two-dollar bills. The number of two dollar bills floating around might be of some value in pointing out value. Alas, the townies (the boars to use Matthew Arnold's term) do not want to admit that the college it abhors supports them.

It is common in Texas that the towns and colleges are at war. Austin has had many skirmishes with the students, largely over local politics. The students fought for and consequently earned the right to claim their college towns as their residence. Hence, they earned the vote. The "Old Boy" crowd began to lose power, and they resented and fought the students. Thus far, the students are winning, but apathy may cause students to de facto lose their rights, but so far the battle is joined.

In Texas, it is easier to name the communities and colleges that are at peace with each other than to list the combatants. College Station, home of The Texas Aggies, pees in their collective pants at the exploits of the Aggies. Lubbock has an equal love affair with its Red Raiders, and Commerce is plumb giggly happy, careless defecators with its university. More than these I am uncertain, unable to name love affairs between the "smock frocked boars" (in the words of Matthew Arnold) and the townies / gownies.

But the problem between the towns and the communities is on a different level with respect to the Jr. Colleges. The governing boards of the universities are appointed by the Governor and the Governor is careful to have the members spread all over the state whereas the boards of the Jr. Colleges are elected by the taxing authorities. Thus the boards of the Jr. Colleges misrule with a heavy hand, especially in the small towns. In South America there is a saying that expresses the problem: "Small towns, big troubles."

Novelists often place their stories on board ships or in little towns because the problems bring the troubles sooner and make the troubles more easily understood. One can see the results of his or her actions sooner. The only difference is that in the Jr. College towns we find the often uneducated in charge of the faculty and seemingly intent on destroying the academic freedom. The "Boars" want their children to learn that what the parents have been telling them all their lives is true. However, the idea of teaching is or should be to stimulate students to think, to become analytical so as to make their own decisions uninfluenced by the ideas of those who have been dead for centuries. To accept the status quo is to perpetuate a world that does not improve. The world is never the best of all possible worlds, but those who tell students this to cause them to think are often crucified.

Local boards are a detriment to the colleges. At Gopher Prairie Drisco, there was once a firm, printed policy telling the faculty of the college not to run for office on the governing board of the local public school. Now the college continues to have such a policy printed in the faculty handbook saying, "In the interest of maintaining a harmonious relationship between the Drisco Public Schools and the Jr. College, it is requested (I hate the passive voice) by the Disco Jr. College Board of Regents that college personnel not seek positions on the Disco public school Board of Trustees." It takes seven years to earn tenure, and it would take a brave faculty member to ignore the "request." Reasons to fire a faculty member can be so falsified by the lock step thinking of the "boars" that they come to believe what they want is right and just.

This policy has effectively denied participation in the local schools by a large percentage of the few educated electorate of Smellyville. This is not democracy at its best. It is an "us" and "them" situation with the townies occupying the "us" role to keep "them" from having a say in "our" schools. This situation is not fair, not healthy, and probably not legal. Our situation in Gopher Prairie/ Hadleyville is an illiteracy test. The "townies" on the College Board do not want the "gownies" interfering in their community's local board. Of course, many of the "local" kids are here by way of their college educated parents teaching at the Jr. College. Perhaps we need a tenure situation applicable for membership in the city. You see that in a world I organize not everyone has a right to vote. In this respect I am just exactly like the founding fathers. They thought the "Public is a Great Beast" and wanted and achieved a limited democracy. I concur. In addition, I would like to know what constitutes a "harmonious relationship" and if harmony has a positive value in a world propelled by dialectic.

The big majority of the money to run the college comes from the state, not the local taxes. It would be better for the community if the governing boards were appointed from all over the state like the universities. I once heard one president of the Jr. College say that the money from local taxes would not pay the electric bill for the college. I am sure that is true. The uneducated are almost always suspicious of the educated, and the step from suspicion is not far to hostility. I think the college faculty is fortunate that heresy trials and lynchings have become (somehow) unpopular. I worry that they could happen again. (If the college faculty floats, they are witches or warlocks.)

In the diary of Benjamin Franklin he tells of attending a witch trial where a woman was exonerated because she sunk. The man on trial somehow continued to porpoise-like return to the surface. When he was extricated from the water, Ben heard the man say, "The fact that I am a witch is more than I have known." Perhaps this anecdote helps to explain the timidity of the college faculty. We tend to believe what we read and have been told. However, it is more likely that apathy has set in, and the college faculty spends portions of their evenings telling their children that that which they "learned" at school that day is not true. I know that is what I did. On the other hand, John Ciardi, a well-known poet and English teacher at Harvard, said that college teaching was planned poverty among sheep.

Most of the indigenous personnel who run for positions on the city council and the public school board and the college board run on a platform telling what they will not do, which is raise taxes. A local Realtor recently told me that I live in the nicest house in the city, and believe me I am not bragging, (Shit city is dying) but my point is that I pay only slightly more than a thousand dollars a year for my combined taxes: city, county, schools. I have a son in Dallas who pays more than $7000 a year in taxes, a son in

Los Angeles, who tells me he pays more than that, and a son in Ft. Worth who has never told me about his taxes. I must remember to ask him.

Am I asking for more taxes? Yes, if it helps the city and its schools and hospitals, but of course more taxes will not help a town whose leaders are extremely ignorant.

I attended a board meeting once for some reason I can't remember, but at the meeting the president of the board asked, or rather told one of the deans to write a report of some sort and send it to him at the local bank where he was president there too. The report should have been sent to the president of the college. And the president of the board should have discretely and privately suggested to the college president that he the board president would like to see a copy of the report too, please. At that moment of the demand by the board president, the then president of the college, a man who knew his worth, resigned on the spot. Many younger presidents have come along who have to toady to the board and cannot afford such luxury as rebelling against a board who knows not how to manage. The local board micro-mismanages on a daily basis. And I am convinced that the board judges the administration of the college on the basis of how much money is left over on the budget at the end of the year—another red and blue-black situation in politics, not exactly black and white.

Do you know what qualifications a person must have to serve on the board? Other than place of residence, there are none. One need not be ambulatory or able to detect bat guano. In fact, it must be better not to be able to detect guano. Through the years one notices that some of our board members have been to college, though usually to visit. Not many have been students; more than one

I know of did not graduate from a high school. I expect many did not graduate from anything more important that a mortuary Science school. One of our board members, now the president of the board, has upon occasion listed himself with a MS following his name, meaning for him is mortuary science. Ludicrous.

Speaking of ludicrous, I once suggested to the president of the college that we re-name ourselves Drisco Jr. University. It would be a master stroke of advertising for the college. *Texas Monthly* would not be able not to notice, and we could make a fair argument for the name change.

Most of my suggestions through the years have been dismissed as nonsense from a nut, but some of my ideas have been accepted, though one president took credit for one of my ideas he liked. I would like to list some of my moments of helping the city, but who cares? Not me. I just want the reader to know I have tried to help and become exceedingly unpopular in the process. Well, Sinclair Lewis and William Faulkner were hated by their home towns too. I am in good company, and I could mention some other recent martyrs too. My ideas have cost me, but another time for bragging.

Readers might consider driving through Hadley-Prairie before it collapses like most of the leaning and deserted houses and stores in the town have. The town looks a little like Hadleyville in *High Noon* with Gary Cooper and Princess Grace as they drive off with Gary's badge lying half covered in the dirt with the townspeople staring blankly about.

Did you ever read H.L. Mencken's "The Libido for the Ugly"? In the essay, he complains about the incomparable ugliness in the industrial heartland of America, but he says Texas has its share of ugliness too. I think he must have driven through Gopher Prairie Hadleyville. Mencken says,

I have seen, I believe, all of the most unlovely towns of the world; they are all to be found in the United States.

"I have seen the mill towns of decomposing New England and the desert towns of Utah, Arizona, and Texas."

I believe he was talking about Gopher-Prairie/ Hadleyville and the other truly ugly towns of the area or he should have been. Not far from GPD, a few miles north, there is a windmill that has fallen and is caught and cradled by a tree. The picture is worth seeing; it says a great deal about the rotten civilization, supported by nature.

In GP/ Hadleyville town, one sees toilets used as planters in many yards, and yard art on grassless ground surrounded by a frame of tasteless denizens, roiling rustics reveling in their clever use of the ruse of "art." (Couldn't resist, sorry.) It is all too common to see a wooden woman bending over, showing her red bloomers to the passer by. The pink flamingo just hasn't landed here yet. We may move to that level of "Renaissance Art" someday. The town has its hopes.

The major beauty of the town, however, is the "art" that adorns the downtown buildings. I say downtown, but there is no downtown in the sense that there is no uptown—we only have town. Most of the buildings, most of them deserted and leaning over, bowing to the forces of nature, have large red, yellow and purple flowers and boots painted on them. One lucky building is festooned with large balloons of all colors. White lace curtains are painted on almost all buildings, at least the ones that look to have some hope of continuing to stand for a few more years until the community rises from the ashes of Texas heat and disuse. (That the town will rise again is the litany one hears frequently, just how or why is rarely discussed.)

I received a letter from a friend of my college days who drove through not long ago and took the tour I offered. He commented that he enjoyed seeing the building that had the handprints of the fifth grade kids on one side of a building, and he thought it nice that we had let the children paint the murals on all of the other buildings.

It was the mayor's wife who "decorated" all of the other buildings. Poor thing, she worked hard and long to make the city "more beautiful." Frankly, I think she gives *primitive* a bad name.

Disco GP was always ugly even when it was first built, but we blame old values, hard choices, and new world ignorance on those pioneers now long dead. For the mayor's wife, old ugly is worse than new ugly, so she daubed away with the best intentions to do her civic duty in an attempt to restore the town. The modern horrors of primitive, far too primitive, art reflect on the collective taste of the town, which is to say the ignorance of the town. The young man with whom I had the argument which brought forth into light this obviously illuminating essay had a brochure printed giving directions to tourists so they can find the lacy murals, which are only slightly smaller than the buildings. And we have no tourists to see the buildings. Certainly no directions are needed, except the most expedient method to run from the town. Of course the townies could use some directions in many ways, but they are in charge. This flaw gives democracy a bad name.

God help us, we have seen the enemy and he is us. The yard art, the cesspool, and the mico-mismanaging of the board cannot be overcome. I don't care what Adam did; I don't deserve this.

So I moved on to a university, partly because my sons went to college and did not come back. I don't think they want to fly over GP/ Hadleyville, much less return to the Baptisted, non-compassionate community they graduated from. The citizens missed the message of Jesus. They know what the Bible says, but they fail to understand it. Hence, my second son, who is a veterinarian and the one I thought to see work and improve our little ranch married a French woman, moved to Los Angeles and partakes of all the cuisine of the world except red neck. I cannot blame him, but I miss him. I have moved on to a nice university in a city which at least acts as if it values the life of the mind Whereas in GP /HV schools are thought to be baby sitters until the young become big enough to plow, rope, shoot Indians, ride bulls and other manly stuff for which they were apparently made.

The average IQ in this country is 100, and 100 is stupid. GP'/HV is below average, I'm not even sorry to say. The truth is. And this is the way of the world.

Should you, dear readers drive through GP/ HV, (it is located on I 20 between Ft. Worth and Abilene) do not stop and go to sleep. You will become one of "them." And Dana Wynter does not live in GP Country. Plus, I give you fair warning, short lines, and unrepaired roads are not everything one needs. One also needs air conditioning in a state where summer is at least six months long. General Sherman said that if he owned Texas and Hell, he would rent out Texas and live in Hell. I see his point. Perhaps better than he did, but Merdville seems hotter, the glare from fat heads perhaps.

PONDERING

 ∎

$\mathcal{S}$ocrates doubted his own wisdom, but he firmly
believed that in order to educe ideas, which lie at
the heart of thought, (rather than mindless beliefs) and,
one hopes, at the heart of action by a society, these ideas
must engage in dialectic. The mind of mankind carries on
the enterprise of thought best when the ideas engaged
are discussed, and refined, though they need not necessarily be agreed upon. The trick is to exchange thoughts
without stooping to petty bickering, a lower level of dis-
course than dialectic. However, when sparks fly, the con-
current light produced may be a sign that we are about
to illuminate our minds.

Educational evangelism, whether spurious or informed,
propagated by retired military, or political heroes, or especially instigated by disenchanted taxpayers has value in
that it may excite and thereby inform society of the problems which beset it.

Hence, I propose the following assumptions: First,
prospective active members of a democratic society
must be introduced to the atmosphere of controversy,
which should pervade their conflations, an atmosphere
most often evading the most decorous classrooms; second, potentially literate adults must examine ideas, and

thoughts of philosophers, writers, and critics who have exhibited thoughts, rather than the soporific allegiance to cliché-ridden doctrines; third, prospective members of society must be aware of historical arguments which define and nourish the parameters of debate. These parameters, especially new ones, will ultimately interpret debates. A paradox must be exacerbated and understood to have real value.

"When a true genius appears, you may know him by this sign that all the dunces are in confederacy against him." Jonathan Swift– *Thoughts on Various Subjects, Moral and Diverting*. As an example of Swift's veracity, I point you to the lives of Socrates and Jesus. With modern methods of communication and transportation, I suggest to you that neither of these men would live so long today as they did during their own times. Both of them were convicted of nothing more serious than upsetting the status quo. Socrates was sentenced to death for corrupting the morals of the youth with his teachings. What he taught was that his world as it was then constructed was not the best of all possible worlds, which is always true. Jesus was convicted of invading the inherited rights of the social class that produced the priests. He threw the moneychangers out of the temple. He was upsetting the status quo. Conclusion: Good teachers and good preachers probably ought to be at least fired about every three years. Otherwise we may suspect they aren't performing their jobs.

Has mankind changed for the better in the last two thousand years? Or has there been change? Do we see significant changes in that a more humane quality of mankind exists today? If so, does this new quality exist in great numbers? If it does not, then can we say that Christianity has failed? Or did any respected theologian ever say Christianity was intended to make a better, kinder mankind? We are told: " . . . many are called, but few are chosen." Perhaps two thousand years is not enough time to expect the nature of mankind to change, or perhaps we should consider that the entire world was never expected to make a visible improvement. Consider that two thousand years ago Christians were thrown to the lions, but less than sixty years ago six million Jews were sent to the gas chambers. The Nazis made soap of the bodies and lampshades of their skin. And remember Germany was a so-called Christian nation, and had been a democracy before Hitler took over. Appreciable progress in our humanity and intelligence are hard to see.

What does our government do to make the world better? Is there anything positive that a government can do to improve the nature of mankind? See Shelley's ideas on this subject. When Shelley was very young, he believed that if the method of government by Kings were to be replaced with democracy then many of mankind's problems would disappear. He later decided he was wrong. And he was.

Our government is run largely by professed Christians. May we suppose that a mere two thousand years is not a long enough test to see improvement in the behavior of those who profess to be followers of Christ? Then too, though many are called, few allow themselves to be chosen.

Several years ago when Guy Newman, then president of Howard Payne University, a Baptist affiliated university, was interviewed quite by chance on the streets of New York by a reporter for *The Today Show*, Jack Lescouli. Lescouli asked Dr. Newman if it were true that Baptists thought they were the only ones who would be allowed into heaven. Dr. Newman said, "Oh, we're a great deal more narrow minded than that; we think very few of us are going to make it."

If nation states are not apt to have the ability or the inclination to try to improve the nature of mankind, perhaps no one should expect much from governments. World Wars One and Two were fought mostly by Christian nations. The Muslims have often commented on how Christianity is a failure because Christians kill one another so often; however, since Saddam Hussein invaded another Muslim nation, their arguments and observations have not carried much weight. Then too, Christians, although they seem to have an inclination to want to believe that mankind is improving in humanitarian inclinations, must remember that the advantage to being a Christian is that we have faith that we are forgiven for our sins every day. All we have to do is to try to be better. If we display this faith then we are forgiven for all our many, many sins. However, if all of us are going to fail every day, we should not expect the world to be observably better, more humane, generation after generation. The admittedly brief history of mankind indicates progress of mankind in technology only.

If we can't be better, how then can we expect our government to be better than we are? We are the government. Do you want to impeach the memory of Jack Kennedy because he had affairs in the White House? Did you want Bill Clinton to be convicted for his sins and lies? What about Richard Nixon? Nixon, Henry Kissinger, Lyndon Johnson, George Bush II, Dick Cheney and Donald Rumsfeld have admitted that they broke American and International law by using torture. Kissinger has been indicted as war criminal by a world organization we recognize. Ronald Reagan tried hard to subvert the will of the congress in the Iran-Contra affair. He could have been impeached for that offense, but we didn't want any more of that sort of sordidness after Watergate. Ike Eisenhower had an affair with his driver during world War two. Franklyn Delano Roosevelt had a woman, with whom he was admittedly in love, in the White House overnight often. The list of famous politicians who have sinned is endless, literally endless. If we are all sinners, we should try to forgive those who sin. We will better off when we forgive others. The precedent is beneficial. We have only one role model.

Perhaps we don't deserve any better government than we have. We should not expect too much from our fellow earth-bound mortals. And the idea of heaven is that we can all have something beyond that which we deserve. Our two political parties are now engaged in furious fulminations that tend to take us on the road to becoming factions like those we see in Iraq. The Shiites, the Kurds, and the Sunnis are always at one another's throats. They never forgive. Their animosities and antipathies are centuries old. We have never had that sort of a problem in this country. We have even forgiven one another for a huge civil war, but now we may be on the verge of leader-led hate for one another that we may never get over.

The nation of Iraq is so fractious that it will not in the foreseeable future be the home of a democracy. In order to have one nation united, Muslims must respect one another; otherwise, a dictator will be a necessity. If we, the U.S., somehow oversee the division of Iraq into a three-nation state like India and Pakistan have become two nations, we may see three Muslim nations, each united in common purpose without noticeable internal dissent that may want to engage in atomic war such as now threatens the world in the India, Pakistan manner.

Perhaps some dunces as leaders would be better for us than others, but we should not be depressed by the inability to elect a Saint. Mother Teresa didn't want the job—I doubt that any Saint would want to be a world political leader. Saints are more interested in the next world.

Gore Vidal wrote a fine play circa 1959 entitled *The Best Man*. The theme of this play is that the best man cannot get the job as president of this county because the electoral process would corrupt him. What one must do to be elected is to sell his soul in the manner of all the great tales of man and the Devil. Mankind sells his soul for power believing that he will use this knowledge, money, power to buy back his soul, but alas when people sell their souls, they become too corrupt for redemption. The best man never gets the job because the process is so evil that the Saints are afraid to become corrupted. Hence, we have the government we deserve, and you and I want better than that.

I would vote for almost anybody that Rush Limbaugh dislikes. That person could not be all bad. Dunces more often than not favor other dunces. And Limbaugh stands firmly for all dunces. I see no sense in him; he is a hate-monger of the first order. Hence, he is useless for the common good except as a sort of barometer of idiocy. He and Jerry Springer indicate the road we should not follow.

However, in a country that allows boxing as a sport, the purpose of which is to drive the blood from the brain stem, a country that favors professional wrestling, and pays athletes hundreds and thousands times more than it pays medical researchers, that pays truck drivers more than it pays teachers, that pays actors far more than it pays philosophers and ministers then we live in a country that has a value system gone awry, askew.

Admittedly, in a democracy we have the right to pay for what we want, but if we worry about the uneducated Muslims being taught hate for us, perhaps we ought to worry about what and how we teach our children. Mass Education in this country has failed. Matthew Arnold worried that in a democracy when the masses learn that they have the power, they will use it and education would fail. He was right. Everyone enters the race; everyone wins a ribbon. But the ribbon has little or no worth.

I am afraid that democracy gives us the government, and the schools we deserve.

George Bush is a dunce who has been able to become a multi-millionaire because of privilege that we say that we do not favor in a democracy. In America, students are not intended to be separated academically or socially according to their social class, though the relentless realities of poverty and ethnic bias intervene to preserve most of the class selectivity that our stated educational democratic philosophy purports to repudiate.

How this happens is that the moneyed classes have the power to use the system to put their children in schools such as Andover, Yale, and Harvard—schools from which George I, George I's father, and George 11 have graduated, though the Georges seem to me to be supreme dunces. The University of Texas Law School wouldn't have George Jr., and George I put his library at Texas A&M. That should have shown UT-Austin not to mess with the system of preference that the Bushies want to preserve.

Bush was admitted to Andover and Yale because his grandfather and father were graduates of these institutions. He was a legacy and thus entitled to preference. Privilege got him in, but Bush, the younger says he does not favor quotas, opting for merit, he says. Bush thinks his kind of privilege should not be extended to others not favored by God. God talks to him in ways that the rest of us cannot hear. I doubt that George the younger sees the irony in God anointing him favored. It is all so obvious to him. And in Texas it is obvious to all but a few minor voices out in the wilderness that Obama entered Columbia then Harvard Law School on the basis of privilege of a quota system, and that he is undeserving. No matter he was editor of the Harvard Law Review and thus at the top of his class. Ponder, Please. And try hard to find some way to critize our President other than on the basis of his race and culture.

SUBVERSIVE THOUGHTS

---∎---

*J*esus was somehow touched by God and had true religious experiences. Further, the way to God is through Jesus and some others, but Jesus is best. Every word of the bible is true, though very little could be literally true.

Literalism is a reaction to modern culture. Christian fundamentalism as a religious movement originated early in the 20th century in the United States—the only place on this earth where Puritanism grew unfettered. I could explain the history of this, but it would take far too long. Literalism stressed the infallibility and inerrancy of the Bible in every respect, especially against Darwinism.

The roots of evangelic understanding of the bible are older, going back to the Protestant Reformation of the 16th century. The Reformation replaced the authority of the church with the sole authority of the scripture. John Calvin and Martin Luther, the two most important leaders of the Reformation, both had a strong sense of biblical authority. However, it was in the second and third generations of the Reformation that claims for the infallible truth of the bible were made. It was circa the 1650s on before the idea that the bible was free from error was emphasized by later reformers.

The realization that these developments are relatively recent is important. Ordinary people did not read the bible until relatively recently. The printing press was required. The accessibility of the Bible has been a mixed blessing. The good part is clear, but the elevated status of the Bible by the Protestant Reformation has fragmented Christianity into a multitude of denominations and sectarian movements, each grounded in different interpretations of the Bible. Before the printing press was experienced, the bible was a collection of manuscripts. Once the bible was bound it was easier to think of it as a single book with a single author.

Another difficulty in seeing the bible as being inerrant is that this view is exclusivist. Does it make sense that the Creator of the whole universe would be known in only one religious tradition, which happens fortunately for us to be our own? Another problem is that if a person claiming to be Christian has not asked him or herself about the problem of good and evil and the problem of pain in a world created by a God whom we believe to be Omnibenevolent and omnipotent, he or she should read the Theodicy of St. Augustine. St. Augustine was writing in about the 5th century, C. E. His answers to these questions are commonly called "The Free Will Defense." One must know these answers to understand his or her religion.

For instance, if God is all-powerful, he could keep evil away from us. If he is all-good, he would most likely want to keep evil out of this world. Why he didn't is something to think about. The answer Christianity likes best is the one formulated by St Augustine.

The Christian churches all agree about this. Other theodicies are as reasonable as the Augustine one, but Christianity has declared these works to be heretical. (The only real difference between St Augustine and Bishop Irenaeas, a Greek Bishop, is the good Bishop, writing in about 150 C.E. proclaims that if God is all good then he would not cast anyone into hell forever. (Forever is a long time.) Interestingly, even the redoubtable C.S. Lewis believes that the dead are often "improved" post mortem, which puts him in the Irenaean camp.* Some theologians do not want to hear that part of the subject, but the ocular proof is in *The Problem of Pain*. By the by, if you want to read a much more easily read version of the Augustinian theodicy then read *Paradise Lost* by John Milton. It is the spoonful of sugar that helps the Augustinian Theodicy go down

The alternative to literalism is to see the bible as a human product—the product of two ancient communities. The Hebrew bible, the Old Testament, is the product of ancient Israel. The New Testament is the product of the early Christian communities. What the bible says is the words of those communities, not the word of God.

To see the bible as a human product does not in any way deny the reality of God. Indeed God is real and can be experienced as many have been. See William James' Book, *The Varieties of Religious Experience*. I see the bible as a human response to God. The bible contains responses to God from these two ancient communities.

The bible as all great ancient literature was quite probably carried on through the oral literature tradition that has always been common. The first writer of the bible was Paul writing somewhere between 42 and 50 C.E.

The earliest writings in the New Testament began no later than 50 C.E. with Paul. Most believe that he could not have written before 46 C.E., but what is six years or so among friends? The so– called Apostles, writers of the gospels were not likely to have been the men named Matthew, Mark, Luke and John. These men were dead before they could have written. Probably committees believed that the words and acts of Jesus and the early Apostles should not be lost, so they convened and told what they had heard their fathers and others say about many incidents. This would especially be true after Mark's Gospel, the earliest, was written. Others wanted some words and moments not to be lost, so the committees gathered and wrote the words as *they* remembered how they had been told to them. We are to be glad they did.

The gospels were written from about 70 to 110 C.E. The Gospel committees used the Hebrew bible to provide the language of the sacred imagination, that place in the psyche in which images of God, the God-world relation- ship, the God–human relationship resides. The commit- tees must have referred to the Hebrew bible frequently, sometimes by quoting it, but more often by alluding to its stories and texts dealing with Israel's past. The gospel writ- ers grew up with the Hebrew bible and throughout their lives lived within the symbolic universe constituted by its words, images, and stories. It shaped their identities and their vision, their sense of who they were and their way of understanding as individuals and as communities.

Though we call the gospels *Matthew, Mark, Luke, and John* we are not sure who wrote any of them. The author of Mark did not write, "The Gospel According to Mark" at the top. Names were not assigned to any of these until sometime in the 2nd Century. For us they are anonymous documents.

The gospels show little interest in the early life of Jesus. Two, (Mark and John), do not even mention Jesus' early years. The other two have birth stories, and Luke has a story about Jesus at age 12.

Like the historical documents of the Bible generally, the gospels are the product of a developing tradition which contain earlier and later layers of materials combining history and memory made metaphor. They preserve the movement's memory of Jesus. When, however, the gospels say that he multiplied loaves, walked on water, raised the dead, one who had been dead for 4 days, and called down 12 legions of angels from heaven, this makes this son of man Jesus not one of us. Then Jesus becomes unreal, and we lose track of the truly remarkable person he was.

Jesus was a Jewish mystic (a good word), healer, teacher, of unconventional wisdom, social prophet. I also see Jesus as the Messiah and son of God.

When will the prophesy of Mark happen? Soon, he (or they) thought. The Jesus of Mark says, "Truly I tell you this generation will not pass away until all of these things have taken place." Mark says more much like this. He or they wrote an apocalyptic eschatological gospel. Largely, he talks about "The Way." Repent is his story. The meaning of repent for Mark is rooted in the exile story: to repent is to return from exile. This is the message of Jesus for Mark. It is a metaphor referring directly to the exile of the Jews from Babylon. "Babylon is a word for the Jews that has many meanings. More on this later with John of Patmos. Metaphorically, exile is to be exiled from God, by not paying attention to his adjurations.

As New Testament authors historized prophecy, they often took passages out of ancient context and gave them very different meanings from that which the prophets intended.

Matthew uses Isaiah 7.14 as a prediction of the virginal birth of Jesus, but as the full context makes clear, Isaiah was speaking to the southern Kingdom of Judah in the 8th Century B.C.E. Isaiah 7.10.14 makes clear that Isaiah was speaking to King Ahaz and telling him that God will give him a sign—namely, a young woman already pregnant (a virginal birth for Matthew) Matthew I: 22-23 will give the child the name Immanuel, not a proper name, but a sign that God will be with them and protect them from invasion and his crisis of the moment will be over.

Matthew uses Hosea 11.1 in his story of Mary, Joseph, and Jesus returning from Egypt and illustrates the point. ". . . out of Egypt I called my son." But the full verse makes it clear that the prophet is referring backward in time to the exodus, not forward: "When Israel was a child I loved him, and out of Egypt I called my son." Not only does the passage refer to the exodus, but it is Israel, not Jesus who is called God's son.

Finally, the story of the birth of Jesus in Bethlehem may be an example of prophecy having generated historical narrative. The majority of mainline scholars think Jesus was probably born in Nazareth, not Bethlehem. Why then do both Matthew and Luke both have him born in Bethlehem, probably because of the tradition that the Messiah was to be born in Bethlehem, the son of David. Bethlehem was David's city. A passage from Mica quoted by Matthew expresses this connection: the future and perfect King–a King like David—will be born in Bethlehem, the city of David. Thus the story of the birth of Jesus may not reflect fact, but instead expresses the early Christian movement's conviction that Jesus was the Messiah, son of David and the ideal King. I can cite several oddities in the gospels, but I continue to believe that Jesus was the son of God. I will not bore you with more such information, though much more could be said.

Many prophecies can be read with the activities of Jesus in mind of those of us today that cannot be factually true. Notice that I am not mentioning many, many problems with factual reading of the Hebrew bible. Perhaps a thousand pages might be used for such activities, but now I remain with the New Testament.

I would love to show many contradictions and other problems in the psalms, but I will now get to John of Revelation.

Almost no scholars believe that the Apostle John and the John of Patmos is the same person. I have no way of checking, I don't read Greek, but those who read ancient Greek maintain that the use of the language was so very different that the writer of Patmos could not have been the Apostle, who used the ancient Greek language beautifully, I am told. It was, by the way not uncommon for a writer to use the name of another writer as long as the writers were on the same subject. There is no doubt this happened to the Apostle Paul. The evidence is incontrovertible that Paul did not write the books of 1st and 2nd Timothy or of Titus. In fact, the writer may well have been one of those who is known as a "corrector." He was, he supposed, helping Paul to be clear about homosexuality and a few other things, but this is a little matter. In addition, the gospel of John is quite different from the synoptic gospels. I will mention only a few differences that almost everyone even in the pews knows to be true.

John has the ministry of Jesus lasting for three years whereas the synoptic gospeleers say his ministry was for only one year. Moreover, it is commonly known that the first event in the ministry for John was throwing the money changers out of the temple whereas the other three say that event was the last event in the course of Jesus' ministry. Again, not much difference, but one that puzzles many theologians is that the big three and John disagree about the day and time of the crucifixion of Jesus.

The event of casting out the money changers is more than just consistent with the behavior of Jesus, and all four agree that he did that. Luke, who sees Jesus as a social profit serving the poor, emphasizes this action, but all agree. Remember, in Luke the shepherds were at the birth. Shepherds were at the bottom of the social ladder. (Remember the money changers at the temple were of a higher, inherited caste.) For Matthew, the wise men came although the journey may well have taken three years or so. Remember, Matthew sees Jesus as "the King." Luke sees Jesus as the benefactor of the poor and the gentiles too, although there is no evidence that Luke was a gentile. Luke traces the genealogy of Jesus back to Adam and Eve so as to be more inclusive than Matthew's seeing Jesus as the descendant of David. (Matthew was often anti Jew and in many ways the most Jewish of the Apostles. He was uncertain of much.) Many readers may enjoy reading Matthew again to note this waffling, which no scholars see as a fault of the book *by* Matthew

John's gospel was the last one to be written. (Mark was first.) And John was by far the most poetic and metaphoric of the gospel writers. His language is beautiful and replete with many examples of his devotion and his education.

Revelation, the book, has no universally accepted interpretation, which causes much confusion. Many people just reject it and leave it to others to puzzle over. However, many best-selling authors like Hal Lindsay (*The Late Great Planet Earth*) wrote a best seller that was on the New York

Times list of best sellers for almost a decade (in the 70s). His interpretation was apocalyptic of course. Many TV evangelists use the apocalypse frequently. Fear is a best seller. *Revelation* stands at the end of the New Testament, but it was not the last book to be written.

Revelation almost did not make it into the New Testament. In the 4th century Eusebius listed it as one of the disputed books. Cyril of Jerusalem at about the same time forbade the book to be read and omitted it as one of the canonical books. Much later the leaders of the Reformation especially Martin Luther and John Calvin largely ignored the book. Martin Luther admitted the book to the Bible reluctantly (he wished it thrown into the Elbe river). Zwingli denied it scriptural status, and Calvin largely ignored it, though he wrote commentaries on the other 26 books of the New Testament. The strongest evidence of the almost limitless problems of reading *Revelation* literally is that the seven communities he intended it for, the ones in Asia Minor, would have no way to know what he was talking about. Not much of a prediction.

Much can be said in dispute of this book. The book itself indicates that John was thinking of his own time. Seven times in his prologue and epilogue he tells his audience that he is writing about the near future. His first sentence begins: "The revelation of Jesus Christ, which God gave him to show his servants what **soon** must take place." Later he says, "Blessed is the one who reads the words aloud of the prophecy, and blessed are those who hear and who keep what is written in it, for the time is **near.**"

In the epilogue, the emphasis occurs 5 times, and the author attributes to the risen Christ the words, "I am coming soon." In addition, to John's prologue and epilogue, we find also compelling evidence in the main body of the book that the author was writing about the realities of his own day. This evidence is most visible in chapters 13 and 17. The number 666 is decoded into the name Caesar Nero. The decoding process common is his day was called gematria. Using such rules we read Caesar Nero. For John, the woman seated on 7 mountains is Rome. Remember that if John were writing about events thousands of years in the future, then the communities to whom he was writing would have had no chance of understanding his letter. Thus why write it? The book is important to Christians for many reasons none of which have anything to do with the apocalypse. We can find large themes in this book.

True does not mean literally true. Moreover, to ignore scholarship is detrimental to our learning and consequently to our world community.

After studying, many have come to believe even more that Jesus is the Son of God. Rather like "Jesus wept" we have to take somebody's word.

Addendum: biblical scholars know, but often they do not teach what they know because it is not a good political idea to send students home with that which seems to too many to be blasphemy.

Moses in the wilderness is an odd sort of idea if taken literally. The journey might have taken no more than two weeks (probably less). The 40 years was about life expectancy at that time (it wasn't but about age 42 to 47 in 1900). The "promised land" probably was not a piece of land but rather a heaven, though no Jews used such words or concepts at that time.

The prophets were a bunch of rabble rousers writing to people of their own time, which is a good thing. Jesus was also a rabble rouser, teaching a subversive wisdom. The story of Pilate washing his hands appears in only one gospel, Matthew. He had reasons other than reporting. Matthew was in many ways anti-Jewish, and in many way strongly Jewish.

The *psalms* teach that if one is a good Jew and follows the law, he and she will profit in this world, but read *Job* and *Ecclesiastes* for an opposite view.

An episode in Matthew may be worth mentioning. In presenting the story of the birth of Jesus, Matthew echoes the story of the birth of Moses. Just as the life of Moses was threatened by Pharaoh's command that all male Hebrew babies be killed, so the life of Jesus was threatened by King Herod's command that all male infants in the area of Bethlehem were to be killed. Matthew's meaning is clear. Jesus is like Moses, Herod is like Pharaoh, and what is happening in and through Jesus is like a new exodus.

In addition, Matthew's gospel contains The Sermon on the Mount. "Seeing the crowds, Jesus went up on the mountain and taught them." Matthew is responsible for locating this teaching on the mountain. In Luke, the teaching is "on a level place," and it is commonly called "The "Sermon on the Plain." Why does Matthew use a mountain story? Doing so fits with the Moses story: Moses ascends the mountain to receive the Torah. Matthew's gospel is in 5 blocks and this reminds us of the Pentateuch. This is the way Matthew and his community told and understood the story. Each gospel writer has a slightly different layer of Christology in mind.

The Hebrew word for "compassion" is in its singular form means "womb." Thus, the Hebrew bible speaks frequently of God as compassionate. And so the statement of Jesus: "Be compassionate as God is compassionate" is rooted in the Jewish tradition. God is the one who gives birth to us— the mother who gives birth to us, and as a mother God loves us. To be compassionate is the major message of the bible.—to feel as God feels and act as God acts in a life giving and nourishing way. According to Jesus, compassion is the major, dominate, central quality of God.

For Jesus, compassion was more than a quality of God and an individual quality; it is a paradigm of a social world. Jesus came to relieve the world of the law, though he thought the law a guide for mankind, but not such a guide as to make us forget compassion. Jesus was often in conflict with his critics about the Jewish purity laws.

We see his challenge to the purity laws not only in His teaching but in many of His activities. The stories of His healings shatter purity laws. He touched lepers and bleeding women. He entered a graveyard filled with unclean spirits and animals (pigs). And He cleaned the temples. One of His most characteristic activities is an open and inclusive table— a table of fellowship. Specifically, rules surrounding meals were deeply embedded in the purity laws. The rules governed not only the preparation of food, but also whom one shared a meal with. No decent person would share a meal with an outcast, and there were many outcasts. Ultimately, the meals of Jesus are the ancestor of the Christian Eucharist, communion. The inclusive vision of Jesus' table fellowship reflects the Jesus movement. He ate with women, the poor (who were thought to be poor because they did not follow as many of the "laws" as they should have). He ate with the maimed, the marginalized, (shepherds, among others), and as well as some who found His vision attractive. Jesus' movement was a radical social vision not based on the concept of the purity vision of the Jews.

The Problem of Pain by C.S. Lewis

PREFACE TO
"WORSHIPPING FOOTBALL"

"All beauty is from God no matter where it is found, the artistic creativity of people is God's good gift. . . . Some writers have even developed an esthetic argument for the existence of God, based on the correlation between human creativity in the arts and the adaptability of the world to this creativity, . . . The mathematical genius of an Einstein and the artistic creativity of a Picasso are God's gift to humankind through common grace." Arthur F. Holmes *The Idea of a Christian College.*

"If you get simple beauty and naught else, / you get about the best thing God invents:" Robert Browning "Fra Lippo Lippi" Lines 218-219

The following article about Doak Walker tries to make the point that God touched Walker and made him into a Saturday miracle maker. Let me begin by saying that I believe that every word in the bible is the truth, though I doubt that much of it is the literal truth. Some Indian tribe, the name of which I have forgotten, began every story to the children by saying, "I don't know if what I am about to tell you actually happened, but it is the truth."

The difference between the literal truth and the actual truth is, in my opinion, inconsequential. Whether the earth was made in six twenty-four hour days or in six eons, the miracle seems to me to be the same. If Jacob wrestled with the angel of the Lord physically or if God spoke to him through what we choose to call a conscience, I believe that God spoke to Jacob. How God spoke doesn't seem to be an important question. By the way, as mankind studies the brain we have learned about efferent and afferent pathways, about the locations in the brain of sight, dreams, and myriad other facts. We can and often do crack open skulls during autopsy and investigate, as we do during brain operations, and we place much credence in the value of the corpus-colossoum, but we have yet to discover a conscience. The word conscience means that there is some process that we have no doubt about, except as to where it is, and how it works. The ancient Greeks called the term for this painful "feeling" the Eumendes. Some today laugh at the idea of the Eumendes, but it is as true an idea as it ever was. Only the term has changed. No one doubts that there is a conscience.

If the earth was made in six twenty-four hour days how did anyone know how to measure what the bible calls a day if the sun was not made until the fourth day? Does this matter? I don't think so.

The only unchristian belief that I know I hold is that Jesus is the *only* Son of God ever sent to this world. I believe that there is a great deal of evidence that there is a God. Bach seems to me to be evidence of a mystery made by God (Bach did the impossible everyday.) Bach was probably created in order to convince us that God makes miracles of beauty. In addition, I suspect that God has sent a few thousand others to this world for such a purpose. One messenger was Doak Walker, I believe.

Joseph Campbell, the world famous scholar, studied every culture found on this globe—there is no doubt in my mind that there are many cultures off of this globe too—and he says that in EVERY mythology, in every human's dreams, we see and say and feel the same things. From Plato to Emerson to Jung and Addler, we talk of the Ideal World, the Oversoul, the Collective Unconscious—and that we are, all of us, chips off of the Old Block, that there is a spark of divinity in us. We are, in the words of *Genesis* made in the "image" and the "likeness" of our God. Just what does that mean? I understand image somewhat, but likeness? Maybe Bach and Walker and a few others are examples of "likeness."

Mankind has, and always has had, the same beliefs that are manifested in awe. The question arises *why*, and not so interesting, *how* did mankind come to make the awe we feel for a force the keeper of morals? God is a universally held idea and has been since before history, I have no doubt. Certainly since.

Joseph Campbell put the idea in my mind that Doak Walker is the hero that every culture has. He fills every requirement, including the one that states that the hero comes from the east, unless he journeys to the east to learn then returns to help his people with the truth that the hero has gleaned (Walker's case).

One matter about Walker perplexes me. Why is there not more disagreement about him? No one who knew Walker ever had one thought about him that was not kind to the point of being loving, and, no doubt, all who knew him were in awe of him.

Matthew and Luke disagree more about Jesus than Doak's teammates disagree about Walker. Luke says nothing about Wise men coming from the east. He says that those coming to worship were shepherds. Luke traces the ancestry of Jesus though the prophets; Matthew traces Jesus back to David through the Kings, and, of course, for Matthew those first to worship the baby Jesus were the Wise men from the east.

Matthew and Luke disagree on the matter of Christology, the layers of beliefs of the nature of Christ: one saw him delivering an eschatological message; the other saw him as a social revolutionary. The answer is, of course, that they were both right, but one emphasized the words of Christ before the crucifixion; the other paid homage to His words after His resurrection. But they disagreed, slightly, on these matters and several others. The reason they disagreed is that the words of Matthew and Luke were not written until somewhere between about eighty CE and one hundred-ten CE. All scholars know this, but they have a way of not telling the many what they know to be true. The first, the oldest words of the New Testament were written by the apostle, never a disciple, Paul. He is thought by scholars to have been writing between forty-two CE and about sixty-eight CE.

Thus, the disagreement comes from the committees who were writing the words of the bible as they remembered them, as they had been told through the oral literature tradition. All great literature was preserved by the oral tradition; the bible is not different in this regard. Homer was writing about three to seven hundred years after the war between the present-day Turks and the present-day Greeks was fought "far on the ringing plains of windy Troy."

Those who knew Walker have (all) been quizzed during his stay among us and ever since—there is no disagreement—no oral tradition was needed to enhance or disagree about Doak's nature.

Make no mistake, I'm not about to tell you that Doak Walker is the same as Christ, the son of God, but I believe that God touched Walker in some way that even Walker did not understand, and I think that there have been hundreds, perhaps thousands, like him that God sent to us to make known that this world is mysterious.

A person ought to be open to mystery. It exists; it inheres. You could miss it. You could see and talk to an angel and not know, especially if you are blinded by the white glare as the women at the tomb were.

Worshiping Football

Recently I read a book about Doak Walker by Dan Jenkins, a fine author who knows a great deal about the Doaker. After reading Jenkins' book, *More Than a Hero*, I drug out all my old clippings from the 40s and the 50s and read them all again. Doak was even bigger than I remembered, and Jenkins is right on target throughout his book. Walker was without peer, without even a close runner up.

I remember a Texas Rangers baseball game when Toby Harrah took a sharply hit ball just to the shortstop side of second base, hit it with the back of his gloved hand straight to the throwing hand of Bump Wills, the second baseman, for a beautiful, almost unbelievable double play to preserve the game for the Rangers. That play was "Major League" and almost too fast for a spectator to recognize its beauty. You want to see such things again; they are among the world's rare and beautiful moments of extemporaneous ballet and miracles. Unless you can see those moments again, you may not believe what you saw. Walker was "Major League" like the Harrah-Wills play, and Jenkins' book brought back all those Saturday miracles I saw as a kid.

I began to follow Doak's career in about 1943 when he was in high school. My first remembrance of him is listening to one of his games on the radio. I thought that anyone mentioned on the radio was much larger than life, and when my father told me that Doak Walker went to Highland Park High School in Dallas, only a few blocks from our house, I was impressed the way that eight-year olds can be impressed—completely. That my father was impressed was in some ways jolting too.

After high school, Walker played football at some Army base in the East (remember Joseph Campbell) where he supposedly refined some of his already superb talent. When Walker went to SMU, after his army experiences, I was old enough to walk the six blocks from our house to watch the football practices. Moreover, my father bought us season tickets to the SMU games of 1947, 48, and 49, the years when Walker was at his best. I not only got to see him practice football, but also I saw him play in most of his home games and some out of town games. We always went to the TCU games, Dallas or Ft. Worth, and frequently we went to the Baylor games in Waco.

In the 47, 49 era, SMU games were played not on the campus at the small but nice Ownby stadium (now Ford Stadium), but rather SMU had moved to the Cotton Bowl to make room for the fans that followed Walker and the SMU Mustangs. Walker himself would never have said that SMU games were played at the Cotton Bowl because of him, but they were.

Read Jenkins' book if you want to see how Walker was a decent, modest, humble person. To be magnificent and humble is quite rare, but in the US of A, it is almost impossible. Walker had football in perspective as a game—just a game. I'm not even sure that he was trying to be a role model. He was Doak Walker—human, decent, modest, and something beyond words. God gave him to us.

At any rate, I was one of the fortunate, very fortunate ones, to see Walker play many games as a college boy. I saw a few of his pro games too. The same deal: he dominated there too. In addition, the daily practices or the football "workouts" as they were commonly known then were interesting because at practice Walker was human—great, but human.

On Saturdays he was something more–something God-like. On Saturdays at the Cotton Bowl, a person could see something unbelievable like the Harrah-Wills double play again and again. Unless spectators could see these phenomena happen Saturday after Saturday, they might not believe their eyes. I devoted every Saturday I could to re-establishing my faith in a hero, who always reaffirmed his God-given abilities.

I'm not being irreverent when I speak of Walker being God-like. Genesis speaks of mankind being made in the "Likeness and Image" of God. In Walker, I see some proof. Mozart and Bach were made in the "likeness" of God too. What they did cannot be done. If you know anything at all of music theory, you know how mathematically difficult Bach's contrapuntal music is to write. To have two, three, or more melodies running through the treble and the same number of melodies in the bass, all providing harmonics for the others, is impossible. Bach did the impossible every day, literally. Walker did the impossible and created the beautiful every week on Saturday. And unlike Bach and Mozart, Walker was one of the nicest people God ever made.

I spoke to Walker only once. When I was twelve, I took my football to the campus to the practice field, which was just north of the present day Ford stadium. I think there is a track field or soccer field there today, but I am not sure. All three of my sons live only a few blocks from there, and I should go by and see, but every time I go by the SMU campus, I get lost in time and forget to note differences.

But before the truth of nostalgia broke in, I was saying that I met the venerable Walker just once. He came up to me after his practice was over as I was trying to kick field goals over an imaginary cross bar. In those days kids kicked little indentions in the ground with their heels to hold the ball for kicks. Walker appeared at my shoulder; his glaring white practice jersey blocked out the sun for me, in the late summer afternoon, and scared me. I thought that he would yell at me for the sin of kicking holes in the practice field, but he laughed and told me not to be afraid. He then told me to keep my head over the ball and not to look up at the ball to see where it was going until it had time to get there. I never forgot. He even held the ball for me and let me kick one. I don't remember where the ball went, but I never forgot his presence.

Ah, you say, I met my hero, so I loved him. I was entranced by that moment, yes, but I loved him before and after he talked to me.

I remember in some ways vividly and in some ways foggily the first Doak Walker miracle that I saw and knew to be a miracle. During a game against Rice in 1947, I think, Walker was back to punt when the ball was snapped over his head. Walker turned to run after the ball, and luck-ily, maybe it was luck, the ball leaped up into his arms. He turned toward the sideline, running as fast as he could and punted the ball out of bounds on about the Rice ten-yard line. Do you get the image? He is running full-blast parallel to the Rice goal line and kicks the ball forty to fifty yards in a direction other than the direction he was running. You can't do that. Nobody can. Walker couldn't have done it in practice, but in games he was somehow touched with abilities that go beyond human experience.

My salient remembrance of that moment, however, is not so much the beauty of the kick as a lack of an acceptable method with which to register strong emo-tion. Applause was inadequate, crying was out of the question, though not out of the realm of possibility, and laughter seemed to be un-called for. I had no proper way to record or even understand my emotions. People around me were astonished, and some were not entirely sure what they had seen. They were slapping one another on the back and shouting indecipherable babble in some spirited ecstasy. As I remember, the only thing most people agreed on was that Walker had some authority on that field; he made things happen. I thought that too little was made of that moment. I still do. I read the next day's paper looking for a way of understanding what had happened, but the paper didn't say much—not enough. Moreover, that kick was merely one of several miracle-moments for the Doaker.

He pulled miracles out of the air many times. I probably remember all of them. I always had faith that the Doaker would win. Most of the time he did, and when he didn't, I knew that the forces of this world, good and bad, were formidable.

Jenkins correctly laughs at the cliché, "poetry in motion" when he talks of Walker. Jenkins admits, however, that Walker was poetry in motion. Jenkins is right.

To shout that Walker was a three-year All American and Heisman trophy winner is somehow to do him an injustice. He was those things, but he was more, much more, something indefinable, indescribable. Some of us feel compelled to try to explain him, but we do so for our own self-help, probably.

Walker's teammates try to help explain him, but they do so in open-mouthed wonder too. They expected him to pull games out miraculously, and they were always appreciative of his ability to win, but equally they were in awe of his lack of any affected behavior that might have indicated the hubris that almost all of the world's great people manifest. It is hard for a player to impress many of his teammates, but to impress all of them so that after fifty years they continue to hymn his praises is unprecedented. Their opinions of him indicate a consensus that speaks of something special. The apostles Matthew and Luke disagree more about the nature of Jesus than Walker's teammates disagree about Walker. And Doak's teammates, then and now, agree that somehow he made them better, but they don't know how.

Walker might have been a two time Heisman trophy winner, but for a letter he wrote to some committee (*Collier's* magazine, I think) asking that he not be considered for All-America honors because he was hurt too much of his senior season. Walker was sincere in his belief that he didn't deserve such honors. He never thought he was anything special, which is one reason he was special. In spite of his letter, he was an All-America pick and justly so. The letter no doubt hurt his chances to repeat as a

Heisman winner, but no one should forget the selfless sacrifice of that glorious letter.

I love figure skating. It is one of the world's most beautiful arts, not sports, in which a person can contribute aes-
thetic value. However, figure skating is choreographed,
arranged. The beauty of Doak Walker's movements was
greater than those of any figure skater, and his motions
were spontaneous, not planned. Walker once said, "Shoot,
I just run down the field trying not to get hit." Ah, but what
a way of running.

And he was major-league clutch. Walker was the best
football player who ever lived. I've seen them all. Eric
Dickerson was a better running back and there have been
plenty of others who could perform their specialties better than Walker. Jim Brown, Gale Sayers, Sweetness, O.J.,
Bedenaric, Butkis, Staubach were close to being the best,
but Walker did it all, and he could win, and win he did.
Statistics don't mean much when applied to Walker, no
more than the number of Christians means much about
the truth of what Christ had to say.

But check Walker's stats for the World Champions Detroit
Lions, and SMU, and then remember that the game was
in some ways different then. For one thing Walker played
both ways. Jenkins tells us that Walker averaged 57 minutes
a game at SMU. And Walker caught as many passes as
he threw. He ran, punted, passed, caught passes, kicked
extra points and field goals, received kickoffs, punts, and
he was one of the best defensive backs that anyone has
ever seen. Yet, my favorite picture of Walker is a large one
printed in the *Dallas Morning News* on November 21, 1948,
showing Walker with his fists clenched, his face grimaced,
leading Kyle Rote around end against Baylor. Walker was
an aggressive, determined, perfect blocker. There are

no statistics for blocking. His coach, Matty Bell said that Walker could have been an All-American on his blocking alone.

And before there was a Dallas pro team, Walker played for the Detroit Lions. I watched Walker in the heat of the pre-season as a player on the opposing team (I forget who the Lions were playing) intercepted a pass and two behemoths, fast behemoths, were racing at Walker to block or kill him. Walker backpedaled perhaps about twenty yards or so, faked each blocker into committing himself to a block. Walker played off both attempts at blocking by pros and made the tackle. It was beautiful. Damn near unbelievable.

Furthermore, Walker could think. I once saw, and I think I heard Walker yell to his coach to send in Gil Johnson while Walker was running by the bench avoiding tacklers. Johnson was a veteran of World War Two who was not able to run well because of war injuries, yet he was a pure passer. Bell did send in Johnson, and SMU pulled out an unbelievable tie. Walker, with less than a minute to go in the game, ran a kickoff back 56 yards. As he ran by the bench, he yelled for Johnson. Walker caught Johnson's first pass to take the ball to the TCU nine-yard line. The next pass Walker was well covered, but a wide-open receiver pulled in the touchdown pass.

I believe that there is a spark of divinity in us. We are made in the "Likeness and Image" of our creator. When humans show some creativity, add a little beauty to the world, we are, all of us, in some way, *moved*. It is not so much the beauty that moves us, but rather we are impressed, and shocked, that one of us could do such a thing. If humans can create great beauty, then there must be some spark of divinity in all of us. That one of us made the beauty means that we, all of us, are chips off the old Ultimate Creator's block. We are, in some infinitesimal way, created in the "Likeness" of our Creator. This means that there is a creator; there is a God. God gave us Michelangelo, Bach, Mozart, Einstein, Feynman, and a few thousand more to provide artistic and intellectual delight in showing some of us what all of us are made of. Some people say that Texans worship football. Perhaps we do, and perhaps we do so with good reason.

God gave us Doak Walker. I wish you could have seen him too, but I am a witness. Try hard to find some film of him at SMU or with the Detroit Lions—both if possible. You will come to be a believer too. And remember no one who ever played with Doak Walker ever said anything about him that was not close to the point of being worship. God touched Walker in some way that Walker probably did not understand. Walker was the superb poet in action. There has never been anyone like him in football.

Addendum: Doak Walker was All-District and All-State in high school. He was four times All-Conference in the Southwest Conference and a three-time All-American who also won the Heisman trophy before becoming a four-time All-Pro for the two-time World Champion Detroit Lions. Walker is in the NFL Hall of Fame even though he played only six years of professional football. Walker, now, since the demise of the much-lamented Southwest Conference, will always be the only SWC three-time All-American. Walker is in the college football hall of fame, of course.

The Great Doak Walker

At a point slightly northeast of the goal,
slightly outside the ivy-fed stadium, a circle
where brick walks converge from three paths,
escorted by long wide rows of red bougainvillea,
deep purple pansies, scarlet and blue, the sun,
the sea, created to show the way to the nave,
this Parthenon, this statue of the great Doak Walker,
poet of placement. He leans right, cleats holding,
left knee bent to place his foot on hallowed ground
where would-be tacklers hazard predictions
of its next coming. No one but him can detect
soft breezes sweeping the chalice he caresses.
Helmeted warriors worship, bow, pay homage
to the spondaic substitutions of his rhythmic feet,
as the wind from Olympus whispers his every step.

RESPONSE TO JOB APPLICANT

———————————— ■ ————————————

*J*une 19, '03 mailed this date

Dear Ms. Overman:

I haven't been the chairman of English for three years now, and so I am not sure how I received your application, vita and recommendations, but I will forward them to Mr. Billy Tucker in Abilene. Bless him, he now has that thankless, difficult job.

Your credentials are impressive as are your recommendations. Are you sure you know what you are doing? The chances of our having an opening this year are almost non-existent, but "the difference betwixt a benefit and a injury." Who can tell?

May I suggest that even if you have to borrow money to do so, you should go back to UTPB and earn an MBA in accounting. If you stay with English, you are doomed to teach in a high school for an ex-coach principal who will most likely treat you as if you were not smart enough to be a coach. Ah, and how that rankles.

You know, I am sure, that Texas is the next to the lowest-paying state for Jr. College teachers, and Cisco is the next to lowest paying JC in the this state. Only Ranger JC pays less than we do. I have been teaching for thirty-five years and I have five degrees (three masters and a doctorate), beaucoup (more than 350) publications (I was the State of Texas Poet Laureate for 2004), a formally cited Distinguished Alumnus of a fine university, and I will receive the grand sum of $ 47, 000 something this year. In addition, I have been the highest paid faculty member here for more than twenty years. This year marks my thirty-fifth year here. One lady here who has been with us for nine years tells me that she has just this year gone over the thirty-thousand mark.

The faculty is nice, the town is awful, and the students are now usually inner-city kids who come here to play games for us. If you have to go into debt to stay in school, do it. You cannot pay off your debts on what we will pay you. Anything to do with computers and accounting or with the health professions are sure money makers for the next twenty years. Today's middle classes are headed to the lower classes. We are in the process of losing the middle classes and their value system. Pity. Teachers have always come from the lower middle classes. Now we are "outsourcing" jobs to India and China and raising an enormous number of citizens of those countries to the middle classes. You understand that the amount of the world's resources–steel, fossil fuel, in particular—are limited and as citizens of those countries become middle class and compete with us for their fair share of the world's limited resources, our living standard comes down as theirs rises. Nothing wrong or immoral in this situation, quite the contrary, but we are losing the middle classes whose values have been measure of our country and its source of largess and noblisse oblige. We may become a country filled with Jerry Springer shows as we pander to the values of our lower classes. No middle classes means no teachers from the middle classes. Teachers are headed down, and that will be a disaster for the entire country, but you do not have to become one of the lower classes.

The future for teachers on all levels could not be more bleak. For instance, Governor Good Hair has recently recommended that all Jr. College teachers pay for all of their health care benefits—pay our own insurance premiums. This recommendation could cost me several hundred a month. The co-pays have as of June first risen considerably and the forecast is that the hiking will again increase September first. Next year will be worse yet. Run, run, run, fly while you can. When you become my age, you are trapped. No one will hire you.

With the MBA in accounting, you can expect to make more than $200,000 a year in ten years, adjusted for normal inflation, perhaps $300, 000.

I could not live with myself if I did not tell you what is going on in our so-called profession. And more are clamoring to get into this thankless, lower and lower paying job every year. I see in the *Chronicle of Higher Ed.* that many Ivy-league PhDs, even those with many publications, are giving up on trying to make claims on some small pieces of academic turf—middling colleges, I tell you, not Old Ivy. Well-qualified people cannot find jobs at small colleges.

During the Reagan years with the inflation rate in the teens for several years we received seven and eight percent raises a year. With the inflation rate in the teens, we lost six, seven, eight percent purchasing power a year. When the inflation rate came down to four and five percent a year, we (teachers) received one to two-percent raise for years. When inflation hit, we were told that we had to tighten our belts because everything cost more. When the inflation rate declined, we were told that the state's income from oil had declined, so we would have to tighten our belts. When can a teacher win? Never, that's when. My purchasing power is now lower than it was thirty-five years ago. No one expects to teach, or do any sort of work to make less year after year.

Example: when I first arrived in Ciscoburg, I was making seven thousand, three hundred a year. That pay was an increase for me of a two thousand, three hundred a year, and I had been teaching in one of the best-paying public school systems in Texas. In the year I came to Cisco, I bought a new Chevy pick-up for $2300—approximately one third of my annual income. The same moderately priced new pick up today will cost me more than half of my annual salary. And economic indicators are now worse than then.

When I entered the so-called teaching profession (trade, craft?), Sputnik had not been floating in space for long and there was a general feeling of unease among the electorate because we thought we were, and indeed we were, behind in the space race. Teaching salaries were rising. Students were offered strong monetary encouragement to go to school and then teach. The door slammed shut in about 1969. Since then my salary has continued to decline, and as John Ciardi once said, "College teaching is planned poverty among sheep."

Sheep we are and that is the reason we have no hope in the state house or senate. Teachers are, make no mistake about it, passive folks. There is no basis for hope about the teaching profession. Come to think of it, let me attempt to explain to you that by any definition teaching is not a profession. Can you imagine a would-be patient coming to a doctor, announcing: "I need an appendectomy cut here at my shoulder. I'm paying the bill, and I will tell you where to cut." But this is what happens more and more all the time. The TEA and the Southern Association are telling us what to teach, and soon they will be telling us exactly how to teach it.

In order to keep the public off of the collective backs of the legislators, the legislators have devised methods to allow themselves to continue in their collective houses of government till they can retire. Did you know that if one retires with ten year's service in the house or senate (state), the lucky legislator receives the same retirement pay as a District Judge? Not too oddly, judges' salaries go up regularly. The legislators tell one half of their constituents that they are making the schools more "accountable." The other half they tell that their kids had a chance because the state has built Jr. Colleges rapidly, and that they are open-door colleges. By the time results are in from experiments of making colleges accountable, the legislators will have retired, comfortably.

When the TASP first came into being there was a one page, less than a page, actually, telling of exemptions. We were going to rid the state of the expense of trying to educate the uneducable. Now, several years later, the instruction booklet for the TASP is several pages, and the instructions as to who is exempt and who is able to become exempt would make a nice episode on Monty Python, the lamentably late TV show. TASP has become so absurd that we are doing away with it. It served its purpose. The legislators could look at half their constituents and tell them that their kids had a chance—they were admitted to college. On the other hand, the legislators could tell the would-be reformers: "Look, we have made colleges accountable." All the attempts to make colleges accountable have done is to add pointless red tape to show how the legislators can document their success in improving our schools. The schools are not better; they are worse. Red tape, restricting, all-too-sticky, red tape, piles up from the desks of the *educationists*, and I use that term in its most pejorative sense, till we can hardly move. This purposeful obfuscation will grow worse.

By the way, I once read of a dissertation in education that dealt with the values of the plastic tray over the steel ones in public school cafeterias. You realize that writer is now probably a principal or school superintendent somewhere, earning five times the salary of a teacher with a real academic degree, like an MA in English.

Matthew Arnold once said that he thought it impossible to educate the masses because when they learn they have power in a democracy, they will use it. Everybody will enter the race, and everybody will win a ribbon of no value..

I know it is fun to be on the edge of good minds in a university and to get the feeling that we are all linking arms to roll back ignorance, but the dream and good feeling will not help your retirement or difficulty in helping your kids through college, or help pay for your parents' operations that the government won't fund much longer, and health cost can now literally break us. Nursing homes can take your kids' inheritance, if any.

Well, now I feel much better. Perhaps I won't have to go to my psychiatrist or bartender this week. As I said much earlier, I will forward your application and supporting materials to Mr. Tucker. By the way, accounting is not tough, it is only boring. Many would say Victorian novels are boring. A matter of taste, which can be cultivated.

Oh, by the way, I told all my sons what I have just told you, and they are all three doctors. Not one makes less than three hundred thousand a year. An MS in nursing, just two years after a BS, can make the student into a Licensed Practioner at about eighty- to one hundred-twenty thou a year. A nurse anesthetist can make twice that, and the degree is only two years after the BS in nursing. With those kinds of earnings, one can pay back the debts one incurred in earning the degrees.

Addendum: I have long known that the folks among us who have whatever quality it takes to earn an MA in English are almost always nice, very nice, dedicated persons. The world should be better than it is, and teachers should be, in a better world, among the best paid in our culture as they are in many European and third world countries. But, we are anti-intellectual in the U.S. We think schools are fine places to confirm for students what their parents have always told them to be true. Schools are a nice way to entertain ourselves on Friday nights and nice places to use for baby sitters until the kids are old enough to shoot Indians (of any country), ride bulls, or sell insurance, or plow fields.

Look at the one we have elected president. He is not smart. C students run the world, and they don't care much for teachers, and that is the way the world is, and it isn't about to change for a long, long time. Don't try to be a missionary to the anti-intellectual world unless you have a prestigious PhD and several award-winning books in you so that you won't have to "deal with," a strange term, the anti-intellectuals. "Put money in thy purse."

Sincerely,

The Making of One More Lawyer

Watching "Demons" day after MWF day,
far more than six,
he saw them wave
speak to other gladiators in the hall during class,
scratch, amble out to the bathroom
every time they were bored
which was once an hour.
They farted, giggled like fourth graders,
brought no notebooks, no textbooks,
but roared indignantly that they had come to class.
Hadn't they been there?
what did he have against athaaletees?
The new M of A climbed on his desk,
shouted, "You are all in the lowest
of three non-transferable, remedial classes
at a non-selective, open-door college."
"Remediate, remediate," he commanded.
Spittle slid down his cheeks
they carried him out past the stadium
toward the law school.

INEFFECTIVE EDUCATION AND
EFFECTIVELY CORRUPT GOVERNMENT

———————————■———————————

Parts One and Two

*T*he Greek slave and historian Polybius (circa 208-122BC) wrote: "Since the masses of people are inconsistent, full of unruly desires, passionate, and reckless of consequence, they must be filled with fears to keep them in order."

"Shall I tell you what I believe to be wrong? What I consider to be wrong is that most of the people in the western hemisphere are stark, staring mad and the few people who recognize this are regarded as lunatics by those stark, staring mad people." Ashley Montague from remarks made at The University of Wisconsin Symposium "Alternatives Futures for America." 1971

"As democracy is perfected, the office of president represents, more and more clearly, the inner soul of the people. On some great and glorious day the plain folk of the land will reach their hearts desire at last and the White House will be adorned by a downright moron." H.L. Mencken 1880-1956

If Students Never Fail, Education Does
Part I

In America, students are not meant to be separated academically or socially according to their social class, though the relentless realities of poverty and ethnic bias intervene to preserve most of the class selectivity that our stated educational, democratic philosophy repudiates.

American education, unlike its European counterparts, serves larger numbers for a longer period of time. The American way is more universal, more leisurely, and less rigorous. It is also more wasteful. European class-oriented systems are prodigal of the talents of the underprivileged whereas American education tends to be more prodigal of talents of all classes. American prisons are filled with school failures, and welfare recipients are usually not beneficiaries of a so-called universal educational system.

"California has roughly 2.7 million illegal residents, according to an April report from the authoritative Pew Hispanic Center, accounting for about 7% of the state's population. State officials estimate that they add between 4 billion and 6 billion in costs, primarily for prisons, jails, schools and emergency rooms. Beyond those services, the illegal population adds to the costs of other departments of local government, from police and fire protection to highway maintenance and libraries."

Anna Gorman and Teresa Watanabein in *the Los Angeles Times* July 10, 2009

Think how much more our legal, non-alien poor, homeless, and prisoners add to these costs.

Prisons in this country are an enormous drain on taxpayer dollars, as is higher education, (state universities). The public schools are publically funded too. Then we must not forget the medical services that we in the U.S. decree that our poor should have paid for them. No one is locked out of all hospitals much in the same manner that we have project housing scaled down in rent paid (if any) to the government. Government housing is often subsidized also in the manner of shelters made available for the homeless. Food stamps are not only an expense in themselves but also in the attendant bureaucracy. Prisons or education, which do we want? Both? Not possible at the rate we are going. Something must change, and we don't want an uneducated electorate.

We are not going to change our minds about welfare. That expense for the taxpayer is going to remain constant if it does not grow. Not because we are so very kind, but somehow, I know not how, we have learned the difficult lesson that if we don't give the poor something, they take it. We apprehended the lessons of largess slowly, and believed we had solved some social problems. The problem of the poor in our wealthy country festered. It had only been postponed until the poor and under-privileged learned how much better the middle classes lived.

Of course, many of us are simply kind and concerned with the literal welfare of others, no matter if we think them deserving. The expense of the poor will quite probably always remain with us unless we act soon. Society is only now arriving at the difficult realization, however, that no matter if our poor here in the U.S. are the best fed, best transported, best entertained, best housed and cared for poor in history, they are still a big problem because they are mad, upset, torqued that they are on the bottom rung. Somebody is always on the bottom of the totem pole, but now with television and transportation our poor see how others live much better than they do, but they fail to see how some people have worked hard in school, and in the work place in order to earn their places in the hierarchy of society. And when the poor see themselves as victims, not beneficiaries, they cause trouble and even more expense in the enormous and growing numbers of prisons and in their sense of welfare entitlement.

Possible solutions: Perhaps our public schools should select students for vocational schools and make vocational education available that will actually prepare the graduates of such schools to enter the work force. Only rarely do students in our country learn how to earn a living in our public schools. By age fourteen, most of the well-educated recognize the students who will not profit from higher education. Should these students be sent to real vocational schools? If graduates of work schools are able to make a good living from well-paying artisan and labor jobs, many of them will leap at the chance, though some will feel cheated by not being allowed to enter colleges. Some students will not be able to profit from any schools. This we know, but we are hesitant to proclaim judgment on this matter. Our egalitarian impulse in the U.S. is a part of our heritage. Though not always a qualitative good, our impulses in these matters do us credit, but the method of compulsory work education is one that most European countries employ successfully. We could do the same although we would have a generation of some vocal vehemence that would abate when parents notice their children making good money at good jobs.

Large necessary expenses make us wonder about community colleges. Should we add the burden of community colleges to all the necessary expenditures? Community colleges do not require much by way of entry standards. If any community college requires SAT scores, I am unaware of such selectivity. Community colleges brag that they "Take students where they find them" and lead them to the path of academic achievement. Perhaps they do, but do they remediate enough students to justify the expense? Should we add to all the necessary expenses the cost of remedial colleges for students who did not do well in the free public schools? I say we should find the few who can learn and who want to learn and support them in all ways. The investment like the GI bill will be of benefit to us all. The gross national product will rise.

One argument to be made for community colleges is that the taxpayer gets a good deal because the cost to the state for the same student at a university is much greater because of the funding method. The state of Texas sends money to the community college on the basis of registered contact hours. For instance, not long ago courses in English paid about $2.00 an hour to community colleges whereas the cost to the state for the same hour at a state university was about $5.00 a contact hour. Science and engineering courses are more costly per hour at both types of institutions, but less at a community college.

However, many community college students would not be allowed to enter universities; thus, the cost to the taxpayer would be lessened. Think of the replication of buildings, the cost of maintenance, the number of highly paid administrators, and significantly fewer teachers to pay when calculating how much money will be saved in a state like Texas, which has about fifty state-supported community colleges, and about fifty state-supported universities. We cannot be all things to all people, and we cannot afford their mantra to "take [students] them where we find them." Without community college to fall back on, the public schools might be able to do a better job with better motivated students. All high school students know they can attend community colleges. Thus, they believe community colleges are no different from high schools. They do not anticipate universities being different and flunk out in great numbers. Their school experiences before university level teach them that no matter what one says about universities, study at the university will require no more effort than usual. After public schools and community college experiences, many students believe universities will be no different and fail: an unnecessary expense for the taxpayer.

All public school students know or learn schools lie all the time. Schools constantly lie about the level of education equaling earning power. Statistics seem to back up what is only an inference about causation. Education is a superb idea, but the better argument for making money is that those who finish what they start are the people who work hard and do well. One must never infer causation from statistics. Only good guesses are possible, nothing more. That the level of education is of benefit to workers is not in doubt, but other benefits accrue that are in the affective domain and are not objectively verifiable. Earning power may be helped by education, but no one can say with certainty that which the schools continually proclaim loudly: years of learning equal money earned. The studies of literature, history, and philosophy help persons to understand the world they live in, but such knowledge is not usually marketable.

Perhaps we forestall revolution by saying to the taxpayer that we gave his or her child an opportunity to go to college. In a democracy it is usually not a good idea to have any segments of the society feeling and believing that they have not had a chance, though free public schools offer a pretty good chance or opportunity. Attitudes and "feelings" of the public can be changed or Madison Avenue advertising never existed.

Many, perhaps most, of our citizens see public schools as places that might actually be unfair to their children. Often parents who have not profited from the public schools see our compulsory schools as the enemy. The attitudes of these parents are easily conveyed to their children who have no respect for education and schools. In even small numbers, disaffected "students" make education for other students difficult and in many cases impossible. In large numbers when many students see the school as the enemy, other students have a difficult job in learning. Then too, these "students" make good education for anyone unlikely.

Many citizens believe that the schools are designed to be baby sitters. Also, many people see the public schools as places for our children to entertain us inexpensively. "Friday Night Lights." But many students at many secondary schools are now required to pay for the opportunity to participate in extra-curricular activities, including football, so we can see the public is willing to pony-up for school-based entertainment.

However, like the British, we can devise methods of entertainment pitting residents of one area in competition with residents of other areas and other states with a minimum expense that should satisfy these urges to see our young succeed or fail at games. The expense would be considerably less than sending the uneducable or uninterested to public schools and public colleges.

No thinking person in the United States believes the U.S. is an intellectual country. We want to see our children graduate, but our culture's respect for intellectual achievement is minimal. Most parents send their children to the public schools and universities to learn that what they (the parents) have told them is true. If, however, education is to excel, it must challenge the students to think, (not many people do), and not to accept all or even many ideas held by society. Students must learn to think, to scrutinize, and to challenge commonly held ideas for veracity, which requires thinking. No place, at any time has been the best of all possible worlds and the power figures of all societies resent anyone pointing out problems.

Bright students must learn to be brave enough to try the patience of the power structure, or we stagnate in waters that are already darkening. We need many saviors in order to have far fewer detractors. Jesus and Socrates were and are whistleblower saviors. Look what happened to them. We will have more saviors when we educate the educable better by not putting them in classrooms where they are dragged down and bored by the malcontents.

The day the majority in a democracy learns that it has power, it exerts that power through the legislators and elected governing school boards and the public schools fail. Every student passes if he or she does not drop out even if he or she has the I Q of an earthworm. Everybody enters the race and everybody receives a ribbon that is of no value. Keep them quiet, don't let them breed in the back rows and for goodness sake pass them is a *de facto* educational creed however unspoken, un-admitted, and even unrecognized by the schools.

Public schools want no one to leave or drop out of school because the schools lose money for the students from the states, and public schools are seen as failures. The method of funding by sending money to schools for bodies amassed in large buildings is silly and far too expensive.

The special power of university alumni who want "good" football teams is another problem difficult to understand. Our system leads to corruption such as

"Special Admittances." How does the system control those persons who are not actually in the system? No one knows, but my close and frequently personal experiences with many universities over a long number of years indicate to me that the corruption of intercollegiate athletics is not controllable under the hypocritical system now in place. Remember too that the problems have long been identified. The first novel and later the first movie on the corruption in higher education athletics appeared in 1948 and1950, though the problem had been long been known. Millard Lampell's novel, *The Hero* (C. 1948) became the first novel on this subject. His novel became the movie, *Saturday's Hero* in 1950 with John Derek. This book and its movie incarnation enunciate the problems. Most of us know our problems, but few of us understand the seriousness of such problems or have knowledge of the precipice on which we stand as a nation and as a species.

Our species and our country need more help from the intellectual elite, but money problem solutions, arriving on the path of athletics are corrupting our schools and our culture. Universities recruit good athletes with little or no scholastic ability with public approval. Ivy League athletics are better done than by the minor league platforms that Division 1 and Division 2 athletes on "scholarships" leap from to the pros. The Ivy leaguers are better because their athletes do not receive scholarships except for scholarship. Non-scholarship athletes play because they want to, not because they must play in order to afford a college education, or because the next step possible is professional athletics. At the big state universities football players and basketball players and many other types of athletes are recruited and receive "Special Admittances." If the University of Texas system requires a 1200 SAT for entrance, the athletes may be required to achieve only a fraction of that score in order to play games. Most universities have "Special Admittances" and when television audiences see and hear interviews of players after games shown on television, they have their suspicions confirmed about higher education. In other words, uneducable athletes make higher education appear to be a farce. Very few universities on the division one and two levels require their athletes to be real students. Exceptions include Stanford University and Southern Methodist University who play games with real students. But for most D-1 universities to hire their athletes says to all sports enthusiasts that higher education is as corrupt as the rest of the world.

In one category, The University of Texas at Austin ranked last in the Big 12 recently because only about 40% of the "scholarship" athletes graduated in five years. The percentage that maintains eligibility and receives any degree is not a statistic published where it can easily be perused.

Even in fairly honest schools, the best players frequently receive cash from "friends" of the athletic programs. And do not think that these problems are greater now than ever. When college football began to draw 50, 60, thousands of fans back in the 1920s, the corruption began, and it has not decreased today. Only in the amount of money college athletes receive these days is the difference observable. Well documented cases are recently on record where alumni paid athletes hundreds of thousands of dollars a year to play football and basketball at "their" universities. I have no idea as to the motivation of such alumni.

At Southern Methodist University in the early eighties, a 2nd team linebacker, mad because he was second team, ratted on SMU and proved that he had received $25,000 a year. One running back, Erick Dickerson, is said by many SMU Alumni to have been paid $250,000 a year to play at SMU. That may be a lie, but I doubt it and Dickerson certainly received more than a 2nd team linebacker. Of what value is it to wealthy alumni to have their alma maters proclaimed the best or one of the almost best in the land at a game?

SMU received the death penalty for its infractions of NCAA rules–no football for a year and a reduction in the number of scholarships to award. SMU has not had but one winning season since 1987 and that one was 6-5. The big problem for SMU' football program was that the Alums continually bragged how much they had paid for a team that was second in the nation. Apparently, most universities pay some of their players through alumni with jobs where they are not required to work as in the case of the Oklahoma quarterback, Rhett Bomar. Few, if any, publicly proclaim their rich sins as SMU alumni. Several cases are known at other universities and should be public knowledge, but the NCAA now knows college football might die, and no university will ever again receive the "Death Penalty."* Most people know of the winking corruption in higher education, thus the public has little inclination to support the only institutions which might save the species. In the 2009 U.S. economy, with all the hurt pocketbooks everywhere, we need to send more money to the thinkers at universities, not less.

*In 1987, SMU became the first and no doubt the only program in collegiate athletic history to receive the NCAA's "Death Penalty. "SMU's football was terminated for the 1987 season because the allegedly making approximately $61, 000 in "booster" payments from 1985 through 1986. It later emerged that a "slush fund" had been used to pay players from as early as the mid 1970's and the athletic officials from SMU knew of the payments as early as 1981."

Wikipedia.org/wiki/SMU Mustangs football

The above information comes from Wikipedia but as often the case in Wikipedia the information is woefully inadequate. Read *College Football* by John Watterson, chapter 18, to see that the SMU board of governors knew of the payments and approved of them continuing through the period SMU was on probation. Bill Clements, twice former governor of Texas, was president of the board and far more money than $61, 000 went to players for many years. Clements has been quoted as saying to the then SMU president, Donald Shields "Keep out of this and we will handle it." But the point here is not so much to wag a finger at SMU, but to point to many other schools who have been found guilty of such offenses and received lesser penalties with far less publicity from the NCAA, because the NCAA, mostly former coaches, now realize that they might kill the golden goose of football altogether. Thus, today many universities are allowed to investigate themselves and assess their own penalties. Corruption continues, and voters know it.

College football and basketball teams are minor league professional teams now. Let us be honest crooks and change the system to acknowledge that what we do now is slimy. Let us air our dirty doings so that sunlight can kill some of the germs, and the hypocrisy will not contaminate us further. We should pay our college players some of the huge amounts of money they generate or better yet send these non-academic "students" to vocational schools. Young men and women will easily find other ways to enter professional sports. The NFL and the NBA will create paths for excellent athletes. They must. Players can find other ways to make the big bucks in professional sports without being supported by the taxpayers.

What are we teaching in our universities when the universities are corrupted by big money? When we hire athletes who are not acceptable university students, we are teaching corruption is acceptable, if not a clever and practical solution. Our thinkers should be better. No one expects coaches to be better because their success and their pocket books depend on athletic success. Administrators, however, we want to jump off the cliff lemming-like for us and keep the system clean. They will not until public opinion changes. The decision to stop the corruption of institutions of higher education may cost many administrators their jobs and will be a sacrifice on their parts, but we want people who have read books to be the best among us, and when they aren't, we accept the status quo because that is easier, and trouble makers are often seriously punished. Again, note Socrates and Jesus as prime examples of what happens to those who are the whistleblowers who sacrifice themselves for us.

Polybius said 2000 years ago that all democracies will fall as will all monarchies and oligarchies. Thus, we have what is known as the Polybian cycle. Monarchies become corrupt and lose their power to the aristocrats and the oligarchies rise, followed by the fall of the aristocratic rule, to be replaced by democracies. However, Polybius said that democracies will fail because they will be pulled apart trying to please everyone by the way the legislators try to keep themselves in power, which is by spreading the collective wealth (taxes) around so that the necessary governmental functions, exist poorly (now), then not at all.

Hence, a cycle. Out of the chaos monarchies arise. Monarchies are easily corruptible, but they are capable of being far more efficient than democracies. Make no mistake, I am not advocating a monarchy, but a way should be found to educate our young that will not lead to the fall of democracies. We must teach value systems that are not as easily corrupted as today's values. We must have far fewer Ken Lays and Dick Cheneys.

The major message of Nobel Prize winning author William Faulkner is that after the Civil War, the wrong class of people came to power. Sharecroppers became shop owners, and it is their children and grandchildren who have become the CEOs, CPAs, lawyers, doctors, and politicians of today. According to the German Nobel prize-winning author Herman Hesse, these people are ones who are without values and have no sense of *noblesse oblige*, the obligation of the nobility to take care of those less fortunate than themselves. This idea is the Christian one of stewardship. The lack of this quality in society's leaders is a disaster.

Science may somewhere not too far in the future teach us how to render the unborn children of some parents incapable of reproducing. Parents whose IQs may be too low to assure the majority that their children will not go to prison or be on welfare may be made incapable of reproduction. The IQs of children do not "Blend." If a person with an IQ of 120 marries a person of a lower IQ, the children, three out of four times, is that of the lower-scoring parent. Fortunately, one in four is likely to surpass both parents in IQ. Retardation is, however, inherited.

We have had compulsory education for a long time in this country and even when smallpox vaccinations were killing a noticeable portion of those vaccinated with live bacilli, we were forced to submit our children to the needle for the "greater good of the majority." The idea is that to protect the majority some of us have to die. And most of us agreed. Somewhat like the draft for war. Remember, the government forced our citizens to be vaccinated to go to school, and school was and continues to be compulsory. The step to forced impairment of reproductive organs is not a long one. The government has violated the integrity of our sacred bodies for a long time. The government most often can do as it wishes. Never forget our rights are not those things we can stop the government from doing, but rather those things the government cannot stop us from doing, which is very little. Prohibition and the 55 miles per hour speed limit laws come leaping to mind of ways the government could not bend the people to its will. The fight for values change will be hard, but it must be soon.

Not possible you say in a democracy to control citizens in the manner of breeding. I ask you to consider that many retarded people have had their fallopian tubes tied or had involuntary vasectomies before now. Justice Oliver Wendell Homes in the notorious Buck v Bell case rendered his opinion on this subject in his famous 1927 decision: "Three generations of imbeciles are enough." That was the beginning. More than 60,000 persons, mostly female were "sterilized" in 30 states over the next 40 years. Few patients knew what was happening to them; very few gave consent. Remember, the average I Q is 100 and retardation is thought to be close to 70. Thus, about half of the people we meet are below 100. Should we spend our shrinking resources to send the -100 crowd to academic schools?

In *The Abilene Reporter News* August 2, 2009, Celinda Emerson reports in a profile of the Texas Youth Commission incarcerations for 2008 that 83% of those confined had IQs of less than 100. The same profile noted 49% of these youngsters between the ages of 10 and 19 had family histories of criminal behavior. Infer what you will.

It soon may be possible, even easy for those whose intelligence is impaired not to know that they have been used in such a way. Quite soon embryos can be properly be "tinkered" with before birth to make sure some little not-quite-born fetus will be unable to produce more fetuses. These former fetuses can be convinced they are superior not to have children and if not, they will not care after the fact.

My hope is that these thoughts will make all citizens aware of the seriousness of our problems. Creative writing students and all of education must think in such a way as to decide on the needs of mankind as subjects for poems, short stories, and novels that might turn in to movies with a few car chases and loud booms, in order to gain an audience. Students might want to write a series of poems or stories, or perhaps just one short story that deals with questions facing our society. Engineering and science students must have a saving mission for the species beyond making money. The Romantic poets had such a cause, a mission, and they believed they were successful. Shelley once said that "poets were the social legislators of the world." Maybe so, but our causes today lack "universal bones." Many people today do not believe global warming exists. Much less that it is caused by industrialization.

The public will accept these ideas more readily from students than from professors. Remember professors are resented by many if not most Americans. I was once introduced as, "one of the smart guys out at the college." The sarcasm was clear. We don't trust "eggheads." The few PhDs we have had in our governments have had to hide their degrees to be elected. However, when I think of Newt Gingrich, Phil Graham, Dick Armey, and Woodrow Wilson, all PhDs, perhaps PhDs should be limited in their participation in government.

Also consider that the world is over populated, and overpopulation is THE problem. Paul Erlich said during 1960's that the planet cannot support more than 7 billion people. Some statisticians are saying that we have recently gone over this limit. Erlich may be wrong. I doubt he is, but what if he is right? What will mankind do to preserve itself? Think what we would do. We have limited and rapidly depleting oxygen and water supplies. Now water is the most expensive liquid one can buy. Buy a case of bottled water, note the number of ounces in the case and compare water to gasoline. And bottled water is not as well regulated for health purposes as is water coming out of the tap. Bottled water in cases cost on average about $6.00 a gallon, more than beer, more than gasoline. Gallons of water in larger sizes cost less, but the portability of the potable is a large reason for purchases of small bottles in cases.

Texas has recently entered in expensive litigation with the state of Oklahoma over water supplies. Undeclared war over water may be close: between states (Texas against Colorado and Oklahoma when they lower (Dam) our water supply here in Texas). But when we do the same to Mexico, the war will be on a larger scale–country against country–perhaps declared war. Zooks, this is the gray beginning. I hope to see writers, scientists, engineers, influencing movies on these subjects while governments continue to exist. The public must be educated to recognize the full impact of doing nothing.

Remember, we have no answer but to limit the number of births on this planet or to begin a huge kill off that will have to go largely unnoticed, ("Tinkering"). And remember the costs to the taxpayers between now and Armageddon. We will all be poor when the species gives up its collective ghosts. Depressing, isn't it? Poor and wiped out physically too. Oh, the ignominy.

Also readers might be helped to understand the urgency in these matters because the population may quite easily double in the next 35 years. Not only food and water will be fought for, but parking places in Austin and Los Angeles will be completely unavailable. Maybe we will all live all our lives in one building—no transportation problems in this scenario except in elevators, which is already a big problem in Manhattan. Anyway we are close to going broke before we can spend a way out of the world dilemma caused by overpopulation, caused by a lack of understanding, from a lack of education.

The educated must urge readers and viewers to realize the problems facing society in one or two hundred poems, short stories, novels, screenplays that become loud movies with car crashes. Urge these reader / viewers **to do something** to improve our culture, our county, and our planet in other poems and or short stories. We do or we die; perhaps we do and die. Time has probably run out. The death of our species is close in many ways because of stupidity, understandable ignorance, and immeasurable greed. And I am not sure nature just doesn't like us a la huge boulders from space.

One other matter for consideration: Because the public secondary schools are seen as failures by many, if not most, persons, I suspect changes are coming. My prediction is that the changes will be to have longer school days and school through the summer months. This course of action seems reasonable, but we should not do more of what is not working. The schools days must become shorter not longer. Too much of each school day is spent on extra-curricular activities.

We need fewer writing courses for only one instance. Because we teach so much "English" throughout the 12 years of public schools, we employ too many English teachers. Those teachers we acquire often have not taken a major in English and do not know enough to conduct classes on the many subjects encased in what we call "English"—Latin grammar, prose, poetry, novels, rhetoric, linguistics, short stories, genre studies by centuries, by countries and more. However, fewer teachers mean better teachers. Shorter days means more work out of school, but we will stop boring all students—the good students, who have learned "English" (grammar) at least in the 7th grade, and then we have those students who vowed somewhere around the 7th grade never to learn this "stuff." Less, not more is better.

Lastly, the legislators who have a need to be all things to all people hurt, not help, the schools' problems. When a legislator in Texas becomes "vested," which is to say when the legislator has served 10 years he or she receives retirement pay which is the same amount that District Judges receive. Not surprisingly, District Judges receive pay increases regularly. Hence, it is in the interest of the legislators' pocketbooks to try to be all things to all people. They want those 10 years. Remember the aphorism by Polybius: ". . . the masses of people are inconsistent, full of unruly desires, passionate, and reckless of consequences. . . ." The legislators tell a large numbers of their constituents that they have given their children a chance at college, and community colleges. To the remainder of their constituents they say that they have made schools accountable by having students pass standardized tests. The tests indicate nothing but more red tape for the poor, too often ignorant, schoolteachers.

Standardized tests don't work. You want teachers to have students pass tests? An easy hurdle to negotiate. Tell the teacher the test, and the students will pass, but the truth is no test can indicate what of importance we have taught that students will remember or what will be of most value or interest to them. (Who will not be interested in the end of the species?) A rigid curriculum designed to teach the necessary may not allow the time that is important for educational exploration. Times change, students change, and the curriculum is always behind. It has to be. Leave the teacher freedom for exploration. Most teachers want to teach, and student needs and interests change greatly over a span of years. To teach someone to think should be the goal.

What does not change for mankind is the need for thinkers. What the students must know changes as do their interests. Right now, among other matters, students need to think about the damage the earth is enduring, and they must know the causes. The need for big change is upon us and indeed past due. We have very little time left and the schools are the only faint hope we have.

The Failure of the Democratic Government
Part 11

"Seek not the favor of the multitude: it is seldom acquired by honest means. But seek the testimony of the few; and number not voices, but weigh them." Arthur Schopenhaur, German Philosopher 1788-1860

"The vulgar herd can never understand." Commonly ascribed to Beaudelaire in "Flowers of Evil," but in actuality considered to be the world's oldest aphorism reputably deciphered from hieroglyphics within the pyramids.

In an editorial in the *Abilene Reporter News* October 24, 2008 George Will quotes Willie Sutton, the notorious bank robber who said when asked why he robbed banks, "That's where the money is." A pragmatic answer even though the stasis of the question is not what he responds to.

George Will continues by pointing to Senator Charles Grassley, Republican Iowa, and Representative Peter Welch, Democrat-Vermont because they had recently convened a discussion about where and how universities should be spending their endowments. Will says that the government is reaching for control of private resources. Will and I disapprove.

Will then says, "So government in a Willy Sutton move would target the wealthiest institutions—those that are the foundation of basic research that undergirds American prosperity, and that have the most generous financial aid programs for students." Education creates wealth and the government would restrain the wealth production. If this grab succeeds, the differences between public and private education will diminish and perhaps cease to exist. Egalitarianism can be carried too far for the good of all.

If democracy continues as is, education and perhaps the species, fails. Remember, the average IQ in this country is 100. This means that about half of the population is less than 100, and 100 is not smart. If everyone votes we all lose. Oh Plato, have all that you have said not been heard or understood? Apparently not.

At time of voting many, perhaps most, people suggest, fervently, that everyone should "get out and vote." I think those who don't want to vote, should not. I exhort people not to vote. I tell them that statistics indicate that the chances are better that they will be killed in a car accident either going to, or coming back, from voting than the chance that their vote will have meaning. I think the ones I can convince of this indicates I have convinced the low IQ group.

Most Americans think that the idea of voting is a way to find the will of God. We in the U. S. have substituted the will of the people for the idea of Divine Right of Kings. Once many Anglo Saxons believed that God spoke through those He put on the throne–a silly idea we now say, but is it not almost as silly to say that God speaks through the majority? "Many are called, but few are chosen" I don't want the "many" below 100 I Q bunch to have any say in the future of the planet.

Newly elected Barrack Obama is the best immediate hope we have. However, democracy in the last 75 years has become an oligarchy of corporations controlling us with their money given through their hired lobbyists to the legislators. The legislators, who have no connection to the corporation, the ones not chosen by the corporations to run for office, soon receive campaign contributions from the corporations for re-election campaigns, and much more often than not, they sell their souls for the power (staying in office) and belong to the soul-consuming corporations, the "special interests." They believe they will use their power to buy back their souls. See Marlow's *Faustus* and most of the other Devil stories to see how the soul cannot be regained. About 90 percent of incumbents are re-elected.*

What do these statistics tell us? They infer the president may not have a chance to make significant changes, and the voters may never know who is or was at fault. It is often difficult to discern which or what policy is the faulty one or ones. Each incoming administration explains that difficulties which arise under its reign come from the previous administrations. Probably true. If so, the situation is hopeless because no group is always satisfied, and the unsatisfied howl enough to make the voters want to change leaders before all the votes are in (pun intended), though the less visible members of the House of Representatives return more frequently than swallows.

> The incumbents in the House of Representatives are almost always reelected when they want to be because of gerrymandering by those in office for the benefits of those in office, free travel to and from the districts they represent to campaign, free mailing, and millions of dollars for campaign funds from corporations. In recent years, the reelection rate has been more than 90 percent with often no more than five to ten of the incumbents losing seats. *

Democracy is just not efficient and no president can long be a father-figure to us, especially now in an age when we can see the follies of our leaders made to appear on the evening news, and even the best among us is prone to folly. We desire to cancel them like some sitcom we have grown satiated with.

In approximately 200 years, we have learned how to circumvent the safeguards of our democracy. For instance, we pack the court in a way FDR did not. The presidents now appoint those they know to agree with them, not judges who are brilliant. When the court disagrees with the president or his party, the yelling, wailing, chanting begins: "Legislating from the bench." What about checks

and balances? Judges are **meant** to check the legislators, and to make law, thus, the constitution lives.

Look at the 1954 Brown vs. The Board of Education. If
left to the majority, the United States would have continued with the "Separate but Equal" doctrine. The majority
of Americans wanted segregation. Nine men, no women
on the court at that time, decided segregation was
immoral. The majority is not intended to be able to terror-
ize the minorities in a democracy, and we thank God for
this doctrine of doing what is right, not always following
the will of the majority. The majority is often wrong. Judges
should not be appointed for political purpose, or political
"leanings." However, I see no way to assure ourselves they
are not appointed thusly except to elect statesmen, if any
remain, and I think a few do.

The idea of the corporations, which may be our real
de facto judges, at least in the matters that they are most
interested in, is to throw so much money at the legislators
that the will of the people cannot be ascertained, much
less prevail, frequently because we have been taught by
advertising or bought-off media that what would be best
for us is not best for us. Many in government believe that
the people are too apathetic or too stupid to know what
is best. And they may be right.

The media today are primarily all "leaning" one way.
In other words, propaganda machines teach us what
we think we want, which is what they want. Some TV and
radio, not owned by Murdock, are better than others, but
"fair and balanced" is not on the agenda of anyone.

The enemy is the one who robs us and kills us, no matter the uniform, military or Armani. The cigarette lobby
was for many years effective, the health care lobby has
taken over from the AMA, but also we are controlled by

the insurance lobby, the phone companies' lobby, and the banking or finance lobby, the oil lobby, the gun lobby, and others. National boundaries are crumbling, and democracy is failing all over the world.

We look to government for help, but the government no longer protects us; in fact, the government helps the crooks or is the crook. The government, the lobbies, sends us to look for straw men on the red-herring trail. And often we think we have control again, but we are belching into a vacuum, no sound. We look for ghosts while legislators, the majority of whom are lawyers, overtly, openly help the purposeful obfuscations.

No good reason why we cannot read our phone bill, except for the numbers, but we are not intended to read them; no reason exists why we cannot understand why our drug bills are 10 times or more than Mexicans, or Canadians pay for the same drugs. Why when I have an accident in my car that is not my fault should my insurance rates rise? Both the guilty and the innocent suffer. If we are late by one day on our credit card bills, all our credit card rates increase, even the ones we have not been late on. Why? Because they can. Corporations cheat us because the government lets their employers, the corporations, cheat us.

If corporations of the oil type want to chop down thousands of trees for a pipe line, then the lumber lobby profits too. If oil companies want drilling rigs in the ocean, they get them no matter if the evidence is strong that disasters to the environment will occur. Why do oil profits go high, high, high, when we have been told the expenses for all have risen? The legislators change the subject, shrug, and we moan about other injustices. We have so many injustices we stay busy weeping, complaining, moaning, (we may have to put on an extra man to help us whine) but doing little, thinking (or feeling) nothing we do will help.

We must make the government find alternative power sources. When we learn of previous administrations and legislators who profited from our losses, the perpetrators have retired and moved behind locked gates. The moment to control our government is now, not later. We must be active because we don't have the time to be reactive.

Remember when we were in lower schools saying the pledge of allegiance over and over and we were told that eternal vigilance is the price of freedom? We have not been vigilant.

It is true that when China and India become overrun with middle class folk, our standard of living has to go down proportionate to their rise largely because of the finite resources of the earth. Competition for these resources may bring about disaster. The purpose of competition is to eliminate competition. Consequently, most of us know that we will likely never rise to the high standard of living we once had, but that is not the only reason we suffer.

- Campbell, James E., and Steve J. Jurek. 2003 "The Decline of Competition and Change in Congressional Elections." In *The United States Congress: a Century of Change*, edited by Suni Ahuja and Robert Dewhurst. Ohio State University Press.

"When a true genius appears in the world you may know him by this sign that the dunces are all in confederacy against him." Jonathan Swift 1667—1745 "Thoughts on Various Subjects, Moral and Diverting."

Addendum

The coward is the root of all good; valor is common and a scourge. At least 95% of all people are brave and see where that has gotten us. Best movies: *Zulu, the Americanization of Emily, 12'Oclock High, High Noon.* Best Actors: Ben Johnson, The Hadlevillians. Daffy Duck is the funniest cartoon character. Pete Rose should be in the Hall of Fame. Bush II and his leaders should be tried as war criminals. Best novels: *Catch 22, Good as Gold, Coming Home, God Knows, The Great Gatsby, All The King's Men, The Invisible Man, The Secret of Santa Victoria, A Confederacy of Dunces, Cannery Row, Sweet Thursday, Brideshead Revisited, and Sword of Honor.* Conservatism is frequently inimical to a liberal arts education because conservatism often lacks compassion.

PROBLEMS IN EDUCATION:
PRIVATE AND PUBLIC

───────────────■───────────────

*T*he first rule at SMU is don't drink on campus; the second rule is don't throw your beer cans out of car or dorm windows. North Texas has a bar on campus in its student union, so there is no need for students to show their contempt for the rules. University of North Texas has the more mature, honest environment.

The University of North Texas and Southern Methodist University are both universities on the rise. They differ greatly, but each university has much to offer any serious, or non-serious student. If a person has a choice of which school to attend, he or she has many decisions to make—most of them tough, some easy.

One easy decision is expense. SMU is costly far beyond the cost of any state school. Few can afford SMU because the charge is somewhere above $1000.00 an hour. So what can you get for your money? At SMU, a freshman may get into the class of a distinguished professor. The best faculty members teach freshman as well as graduate students. At state schools, North Texas included, most freshman and sophomore courses are taught by graduate assistants, who are not only teaching, but also are working on their own programs, seeking doctoral degrees. The best, well-known professors at state universities are going to teach only upper level and graduate students.

However, many graduate students are closer to students than major professors, and they sometimes know what students need to know better than the professors. Plus, many famous professors at any school, state or private, have little interest in teaching on any level. They want to research and publish. SMU faculty have slightly more interest than UNT faculty in teaching, but both groups know where their pay raises most often come from, and it is not from teaching. The rich undergraduate kids have a better chance for good teaching than do the state school crowd.

The decision about what professors a student wants to study with has to be made before students matriculate, by students who know what they want to learn. If students are just shopping, don't know where they are going, don't have a plan of study, the decision about professors is not as important.

At North Texas, the choice of courses and majors is wider. North Texas offers many more degree programs than SMU does. And the faculty at NT is as about as good as the faculty at SMU, though one finds many more Ivy Leaguers among the SMU faculty. The research facilities at both schools are equal too. The difference between the schools lies primarily in the students. Southern Methodist has more good students per class than does NT. Freshmen students at SMU average about 200 points better on the SAT than NT students, but by the junior and senior years NT has closed the gap. The poor students have gone away by the third year at NT. The attrition rate at SMU is less, but SMU offers generous academic scholarships for students who score especially well on the SAT and ACT. Pony land students sometimes just scrape by, but few are going to flunk out at those prices. The so-called Methodists want the good students, and they have the funds to attract these bright kids. The worst aspect of education at UNT is that good students may find themselves in a class of dunderheads anytime in the freshman and sophomore years.

Surprisingly to many parents and students, the abilities of the students control much of the teaching in a class. One would hope that the class would be the class, but that is just not so. All of the professorate become reluctant to fail the majority of any class, and the professors actually begin, sometimes, to doubt themselves, if many students are not doing what the professors consider to be adequate or average work. The progress of a class usually depends on the average students in the class.

The difference in SAT scores is a considerable difference, however. Students learn from one another, and SMU students have more to learn from other students, at least for the first two years. The progress of the classes increases with better students so that students cover more material in lower level SMU classes frequently, though not always. Junior and senior NT classes are as good as the average classes at SMU, but the likelihood of equal quality for freshman and sophomore doings is not so good.

In many cases, in many ways SMU seeks only achievement and praise—these are childlike, not mature, searches. Achievement is required, and praise is fine, but SMU often offers itself praise. One does not see such self-backslapping at good state schools. For instance, SMU confers Distinguished Alumni status on business folk who have done little but inherit (and make) money and give some of it (in many cases a great deal of it) to SMU. In addition, an SMU former football player, Paul Page received a Distinguished Alumnus award because a rich alum wanted the award to go to the ex-jock. Page admitted this at his formal Distinguished Alumnus ceremony. Shame on SMU. One should distinguish himself or herself by using knowledge and thought processes honorably gained at the university, not because he or she has inherited or made a great deal of money to be generous with. Rich folks should not, but almost always do, have such power at private universities.

To be the equal of the Ivy League is the prime directive of SMU—not a bad ambition for a young school, but difficult. Much money is required. Good faculty command good salaries and good facilities. More endowment money from benefactors (a nice word) means that SMU can and will court more good students, even if they are not wealthy. More endowment money ultimately means SMU can woo more good students. The problem for SMU is that it is private and expensive, although this is also SMU's strength. All SMU needs to complete its ambition is better students. Universities are judged on the bases of faculty, research facilities, libraries, and students. More excellent students are required to achieve the SMU ambition. A great many rich kids and a strong number of serious students enroll at SMU, and sometimes these groups are not mutually exclusive, but more frequently they are.

Whenever SMU tries to increase its good students, it tends to lose the rich kids who pay the expense of a school trying hard to be great. Southern Methodist has made great strides for a young school. No university has done better quicker except for Brandeis, which scoured the world for great faculty before it opened its doors. The great first-day faculty consisted of retired professors who had already earned their prestige before they came to Brandeis.

North Texas, founded in 1890, is a twenty-five years older school than SMU, but until sometime in the 1920s a student could graduate from North Texas Normal College and enter a university as a freshman. Schools usually grow and improve slowly—not SMU.

Southern Methodist University came into existence in 1911 (classes began in 1915) and began quickly to search for great faculty as soon as it could afford them. And SMU made some good choices of professors who were on their way to academic acclaim. Then too, SMU was clever to profit from economic times of a buyer's market—the depression and then the Sputnik era when research money from the government was plentiful—but perhaps too much the social and academic climber, SMU sometimes seems obvious and silly, and many of its good students resent the rich kids who pay the bills.

The rich kids don't know the good students exist. There is precious little feeling of camaraderie between the two groups. The rich kids think that if they ever need the knowledge of the faculty, they will hire them. The good students understand the indifferent attitude of the rich kids, and the two groups have no rapport—no feeling of working together to unlock the world's secrets and share its great thoughts.

North Texas has a great feel for locking arms to roll back ignorance without much thought of hearing mommy say, "Well done." This is well done of UNT, but one finds places in UNT which are childish.

The PhD program in English at UNT, though somewhat recently improved, is afraid of its reputation and its ability to attract good students so that it is in danger of losing that which it holds too tightly. If UNT would allow *only* especially good students in, then give a thorough examination at the end of a few well-chosen (not innumerable) courses more good students would apply. The UNT English department makes sure that the program has the best students it can find who are willing to work like hell for a UNT degree. However, the degree is not especially marketable because the department's reputation is not especially high, because the students are not the best.

The faculty's response to this dilemma is to make sure that their students are knowledgeable because they have to take every course the faculty can think of. The consequence of this silly program is that the best students want to go somewhere that will award them more marketable and prestigious degrees with less work required. No one can earn a North Texas PhD in English without spending at least five years on the trail of the union-card PhD.

The UNT faculty will have to take a chance that some of its members may have to teach a few undergraduate courses as the number of students in the grad program diminishes for a while as the requirements for entry rise. The grad professorate in English at NT apparently will not take that chance.

The Methodists now, recently, offer the PhD in English. They admit no more than four or five students a year in the doctoral program. The grad students in English are better than the PhD candidates at UNT. TCU offers the PhD, and TCU does not have the faculty that SMU has.

Of course, the subject matter of all English programs suffers from not being able to define itself. No one will ever have any respect for any so-called discipline that lacks agreement on what its adherents do. What does an English instructor do? Teach grammar, if so, what kind? Latin? Transformational? Linguistics? Teach literature? How, by genre, by century? Should it emphasize the history, the culture? (What is culture?) Should literature emphasize social structure, manners, values, visions, especially visions of mankind's relationship to nature? Should English teachers of literature teach the philosophy that preceded the literature, and perhaps brought the lit into being? Or should the English teacher make sure students have read many, many great works and hope that they will all be able to profit in some, although obviously diverse, ways?

The rather recent attempts at rhetoric, especially at TCU appear far too pedagogical to have real intellectual content, but the thinking required for these students produces fine, rigorous thinkers. Those who read learn to write, and there is no helping the incurious. Courses with intellectual content appeal to good students and make them more curious.

North Texas is music, medicine, art and philosophy. Philosophy rings through government, history, psychology, sociology, and science. Oddly, UNT has some rich kids too, but they are almost not noticeable among the hard-striving proletariat students who are scrambling to gather facts. Facts, they believe, will move them up the social ladder. Many of the hard-charging crowd become excellent students, and the academic attitude, ambiance is wonderful in Denton. One need not pay for Starbuck's overrated coffee and the students do not have to sit around in a Dairy Queen atmosphere in Denton. Denton has two wonderful old bookstore buildings that are large and quiet where students can listen to softly played classical music as they sit and read the minds of the world's great thinkers. Compared to SMU's Barnes and Noble, located on the horrendously overcrowded Mockingbird Lane, Denton's bookstores are paradise, filled with real students who have neither interest, nor notice of the attire or the fraternity affiliations of the students seated around them.

North Texas (University of) profits from its close relationship to Dallas because many faculty members have the advantage of finding consulting jobs to augment their teaching salaries. UNT is on its way to becoming an excellent, tier-one school. As the population increases, UNT is raising its standards for entrance. For most of UNT's history, it has scrambled for students. Now the academic worm / world has turned and UNT is moving at last into the position of rivaling UT-Austin and Texas A&M for good students.

North Texas has its profane business courses and degrees as does SMU, but these are necessary, though they have little to do with thought. Business is not an intellectual endeavor– though the philosophy behind some of it could be. And the study of business certainly requires intelligence. The comprehensive college is Charlie Eliot's try, screwed up. Charles Eliot was the president of Harvard who was most responsible for modernizing curricular offerings. Having convinced colleges to teach practical matters like business administration, Charlie can have the credit for omitting the study of the dead languages.

From this modernization came the comprehensive high school with offerings such as auto mechanics and woodshop. Business courses are a fact, and all universities must adapt to them and try to add thought, ethics, and value to the business schools' curricula.

Both North Texas and SMU have their absurd attempts at education courses, but North Texas is far sillier. Southern Methodist holds such courses to a minimum—thank goodness. Universities are far easier defined by what they do than what they try not to do, however.

Education courses neither require intelligence nor are they intellectually stimulating. Again, diplomas would be a far better comment on the world of intellectual pursuit. Teachers should not earn academic degrees in teaching. To have education majors receive degrees cheapens the idea of academia. Let no one purposefully misunderstand and begin to quibble, I realize that the state of Texas has decreed that there are to be no more education majors at state schools, but students who want to teach take as many Ed courses now as they ever did. To call the degree something other than education is a lie, and graduate education courses grow like cancers. Private universities may still offer education degrees, but SMU has recently begun to offer Education degrees again. I am suspicious of the attempt, but the program on the outside looks like the best I have seen; however, I remain dubious. Good on SMU. Note—this year, 2005, SMU has reintroduced the education degree to the curriculum. I suppose the money lying on the table was too much to turn down. I am sorry. Lots of rich kids wanted easy degrees, I guess. SMU will no doubt make noises about the contribution to education that the teachers they turn out will make, but I doubt success in a field that has no intellectual value, and continues to try to teach what it doesn't know and cannot quantify. For instance, how can one professor know how to teach all fields, which is a common course offering, methods, for all education departments. These professors of Education teach how to teach English, math, and biology and all the fields. NOT POSSIBLE. Tsk, tsk. The money in Dallas has had its say, I am sure. An SMU degree for the Highland Park kids that won't be too difficult is now possible again. Sad sigh, sad sigh.

The world needs and requires teachers, and in an ideal world teachers should earn academic degrees then pursue a few, very few, courses in how to teach. Later, some teachers should be bribed to take courses in how to administer, but no one should want to administer all the time. The job is boring and problem-plagued.

Good teachers will never want to administer. Academic courses are fun for the good teachers, or no one would call them "good" teachers. Spread the administering jobs around, and pay the persons who have to spend a two-year period administering a little more because the job is painful. Certainly no one should ever want to leave education in the hands of people who never have time to read a book, and administrators are too busy keeping the broken windows repaired, the parking problems solved, and attending games to have time to read books.

None of what goes on now in education courses is academic. It is vocational at best and not even good vocational. North Texas "teaches" endless courses in education, the great majority of which are a waste of the students' time and the taxpayers' money.

Students should learn that the world is most often not predictable, and that to have faith requires a hefty dose of doubt, but to ignore that the world is mysterious is to trip headlong (a well-chosen word) into the boundless. I am afraid for all those who try, ultimately unsuccessfully, to shut out that which is not rational. Rationalism is required, but mystery is, it exists, it inheres. And the two define each other. Neither can successfully be excluded, and woe to those who try. Education is neither an art nor a science. Dialectic is necessary; the human is body AND spirit, emotional AND rational. Education is a mystery, and it cannot be objectively evaluated.

Somehow students must become convinced that they are not all that they want to be. They must realize that to learn is to change. All one can do to measure education is to measure the students' change—an almost impossible, daunting, and mysterious task for both the students and their professors. The students must want to change. If the students are too dissatisfied with themselves, however, they will be in too much emotional turmoil to learn, and the task will be hopeless. Some change is required of all of those who are curious enough to want to change themselves slightly. Thus far only academic courses speak of change as an important fact of education because the educationists are afraid to suggest that its constituency should change. SMU students rarely become teachers; North Texas students frequently do.

Because life expectancy continues to increase and because the information and thought stimulation required for leading somewhat satisfying and successful (whatever *successful* means) lives becomes more complex, colleges should add another year. There is nothing magical about the number four. Then too, as public schools become less successful every day, and they do, more college work is required to make up for the wasted years of playing games and baby-sitting that the public schools are forced to do. We entertain ourselves by watching our children grow and play games for us, and though playing games is not a bad endeavor, it is often too time consuming.

Perhaps SMU should add a doctor of liberal arts degree to its curriculum instead of its Certificate of Advanced study as it does now. No one could use such a degree today to teach anything; the field is too diverse to allow that anyone has mastered it, but degrees should not always be required to be practical. Let's not screw up Charlie Eliot's

ideas too much. One should not always be practical—
to hell with pragmatism. A degree doesn't have to
signify that a person has mastered an occupational
goal—we've got the MBAs—let's have a degree that
simply says this person studied and has proven he or she
can think occasionally. That's enough.

Both North Texas and SMU should add the idea of
ideas to its curriculum, though heaven knows what a
student steeped in history, philosophy, and literature will
do for a living. Colleges were not formed to help diminish the unemployment lines. If business can make use of
people who have proven they can think, then more good
on them. The state schools are more reluctant to energize
what it sometimes thinks of as impractical courses and
degrees. Social mobility is the reason most students enter
college. Perhaps we should allow for "other" reasons.

"The multitude of men and women choose the less
adventurous way of the comparatively unconscious civic
and tribal routines. But these seekers too are saved by virtue of the inherited aids of society, the rites of passage,
the grace yielding sacraments given to mankind of old
by the redeemers and handed down through the millenniums (sic). * It is only those who know neither an inner
call nor an outer doctrine whose plight is truly desperate."
Joseph Campbell *The Hero With a Thousand Faces*.

Teach Campbell's dicta. It will do. Educated people
have the best chance of not becoming desperate. Non-
desperate folks are the most pleasant of us. All we have
to do is to discover the nature of an inner call and the
natures of outer doctrines. Both SMU and UNT can do this
if we let them. They would like to do this sort of teaching now, and many of their faculties do. The funding is
probably enough, but funding is based on some wrong

assumptions. Funding of public universities based on the number of students attending is not a good idea. Public colleges tend to recruit more than they can handle— North Texas always has. Public colleges expand into the power vacuum to increase appropriations and salaries. Their reasons for doing so sound reasonable. The economy needs more educated persons. Educated persons, yes. Degreed persons, no. Degrees do not mean education.

A well-known incident occurred, so says the mythology of North Texas, in a barbershop in Denton. A young man entered and proclaimed too loudly that he had just graduated the night before. As he continued talking, he bragged to everyone in the shop that he had graduated without reading a book. The barber turned to a large, powerful man, a Dr. Latham—everyone on campus knew him by sight–sitting in his chair and pointed out to the young man that the man was a professor at UNT. Dr. Latham never looked at the recent graduate and said, "I know you have graduated, but did you receive the education that should come with the degree?"

The story doesn't sound like the stuff of legends, but that this incident, true or false, occurs to the minds of generations of NT students indicates that the students of North Texas are aware of the purpose of schools. Most students who hear this slight story decide that perhaps degrees from any kind of school do not always "take." A story this calm would not "take" on the SMU campus.

No one should fail says the educationsts. Nonsense. Another well-known aphorism of the Ed crowd is "Schools fail, not students." More obvious nonsense designed to appeal to the proletariat. "Teach students, not subjects" is another bit of absurdity the Ed bunch uses to advance its program of finding and "fixing" the problems of education.

If schools are to prepare one for the so-called real life, then students should fail regularly. Everyone should enter the race may be a good idea, but that everyone should earn a ribbon means that the ribbons are of no value. Private schools know this better than public ones—they can afford to; in fact, they can't afford not to know this glaring truth. Both private colleges and public are excellent if we let the professors alone to teach.

The Marine Corps takes a sergeant's word over that of the private's every time. Some abuses occur this way, but the discipline engendered is effective for the Corps. Let's take the word of the educated professors and fund the universities according to some method that requires the faculty to think, not necessarily to become "accountable" by how many pass their courses. Mystery is not accountable. To have faith is not to know. Have faith in the educated to educate. It is the only way. Persons who take the time and considerable trouble to earn advanced degrees in real subject matter, not education, are interested in their subjects, and they will almost always teach better than anyone has a right to expect, considering how little money they make, considering anything.

The accrediting associations were a good idea in their time, but they have fallen into the hands of the educationists. An educationist is a graduate of education programs. Make no mistake, I have a bias, and that bias is that educationists are the least able among us to evaluate the public schools and the universities. For instance, how did it happen that the educationists came to decide how much math, music and English (and everything else) a college student must take to be licensed to teach these disciplines in the public schools? They grabbed the power because the academics were too busy to defend their turf. As William Butler Yeats says in *The Second Coming,* "The best lack all conviction, while the worst / are full of passionate intensity." The worst in education are the ones who know where the problem is and how to repair it. Be careful of these folks, they grab the loose power left lying around while most idealists seek conviction.

When schools become better, there will be fewer educationists, and the educationists know this on some primordial level, like children afraid of snakes. Some problems must be found for educationists to be able to proliferate and to grow in importance, in prestige, and in money earned. Hence, dire warnings (all warnings are dire) boom forth from the educationists that cannot usually be solved by accountability, just in the method defined and constructed by one of their weak-minded gang. Educationists are in large, swarming numbers at North Texas. North Texas has to have them for the majority of its students, or NT would have much less money coming in from the state.

Problems are easy to find. Anyone can find problems in a society that tries to educate all of its citizens. A society may try to educate all of its citizens because such an attempt forestalls revolution and tries without success to eradicate a class system, but we should all realize that the task is impossible. We should rid ourselves of the multiplying number of educationists by severely limiting the number of education schools that award degrees.

The responsibilities of the six regional accreditation associations are to assure the public that everything possible is being done continually to diagnose and cure the education problems as they are discovered by the associations. They do this (discover and cure) by sending educationists like them, the ones who run the associations, to teach the teachers. Never do they send math professors to teach the math teachers more mathematics, nor do they send English professors to teach English teachers; they send an educationist to teach all the disciplines how to teach students, not teach math or English. The educationists teach everyone how to teach. Not possible. The educationists *are* the problem, not the ones to solve the problems.

Take a look at a Rice catalogue and notice that this obviously superior school employs only two full-time education professors for those students who, after earning academic degrees, decide that they wanted to become missionaries to the public schools. This system seems right. In a better world UNT could do the same, but the funding method of the moment would cause UNT to dry up if it did not churn out educationists who are the largest group (of students?) at North Texas. These educationists always want to increase their kind. In this increase lies power. And bitter folks who have not done well in academia are inclined to support the educationists in their proliferation. Many think that these are the ones who have the answers to the problems of the society and its education process. Many poor students become administrators because they see education as a series of pointless hurdles that did little for them by way of changing them. They want to make up for a world that did not recognize them as good students.

Counselors, for instance, are prepared (?) only in graduate education courses. There are no undergraduate counselor courses. What one usually finds in counselor education courses are students who failed to excel in any academic area. If Ronald Reagan had been working as an actor, he would not have been apt to run for office.

There is something to the idea that persons move one level above their competency.

Principals and superintendents are more often than not former coaches. Coaches almost always see the world from the viewpoint of the group ("No I in team" their locker room signs continually proclaim) almost never from the individual position, and it is the non-conformist, non-group oriented persons who have the most to offer the group. Ironic, but true. Notice how Jesus and Socrates were non-conformists, helping the group. Jesus worked on the sabbath, touched the dead, and his worst offense for the Jews was throwing the money-changers out of the temple who were a part of the inherited class of persons, priests. Priesthood was an inherited function, and the priests liked their place in the hierarchy of the group. Examples of the contributions of the non-conformists, individualistic persons are so numerous as to be obvious. SMU turns out more conforming students than does UNT, and this is SMU's biggest problem.

Matthew Arnold pointed out that in democracies schools face the perhaps insurmountable problem of the people having power. When the masses learn they have power and learn how to use it, their children receive diplomas and degrees. Schools become less effective all the time. Arnold painted a bleak picture for democracies who require an educated electorate. His predictions become more and more true.

The United States has been awarding academic degrees for almost four hundred years, (Harvard was founded in 1635), but education degrees have been in existence for less than a hundred years. The number of education degrees awarded add up to more than all of the academic degrees ever awarded in the United States, though the academic degree has about a three-hundred year head start. We need fewer of these parasites, but we are creating, minting more than ever. We multiply our problems by doing so. Southern Methodist and North Texas know what to do. Let's let them. Have faith.

Which school is better? Tough call, but SMU is better in the areas it emphasizes such as statistics, economics, anthropology and some studies it offers that NT does not such as engineering, theology, and law, but North Texas is better in music, in wider areas of degree choices, and in general attitude of its students. And North Texas offers medicine, which SMU does not. The atmosphere of an academic community is better at North Texas, except in its large education department, and atmosphere is important to learning. Take your choice, if you have the money, but bright students learn anywhere.

MOVIES

———————————■———————————

*T*he following movie list in not complete, accurate, or even sensible in many ways, but these are movies that made some sort of impact on me. For instance, I continue to see my ideal of manhood as portrayed by Gregory Peck's character in *The Big Country.* I continue to grade men by Edna Ferber's criteria—right, wrong, or foolish. For me, Peck's behavior is the way a man should act, and I think in those terms today as I did almost 50 years ago when I first saw that film.

Many of these movies motivated me to learn more about the subject of many films, and many of the movies helped to transmit my culture to me better than other methods. Movies are the literature of the 20th and no doubt the 21st. centuries, and no aspect of our culture has been ignored. Nothing has ever been effectively censored for long in American and British movies—a large plus. In addition, we have delved into the cultures of many other places.

I have thought of approximately two hundred movies that I have chosen not to list, either as good or bad. These movies, of no doubt some value, had little or no influence on me of which I am aware, so I omit them. I realize that many good movies might have made some impact on me if some other movie had not gotten there first. For instance, the Mel Gibson movie *Galloppli* would have made a big impression on me and colored my behavior and attitudes had I not seen *Paths of Glory* first.

I feel constrained for some odd reason to point out that my favorite categories of movies are war, western, manners, and comedies. I have no idea why, nor do I care to know about myself enough to know.

I have used no research documents except my memory and the help of Jim Lee, who gave me the names of six actors and one movie to consider, which I believe to have merit enough for me to be entered in my list. The spelling of the actors names are my own and only approximations, but I expect to be able to enter Heaven on the basis of the accuracy because we are forgiven so I am told for our sins and no doubt faux pas. And because compassion is the basis of Christianity. I feel constrained to say that I have seen many of these films several times.

Best Movies—Film Noire The films I classify as Film Noire are not the same as the rest of the world sees in this nebulous category, but my category is as good as anyone's in this situation because Film Noire movies are usually not very good such as *Double Indemnity* and *The Postman Always Rings Twice*, or detective movies with Alan Ladd or Dick Powell are known as not particularly good in films with depressing endings (and depressing middles and beginnings). These films are often the opposite of tragedy in that one finds no universal grievings, only pathos and sorrow for the species–Thomas Hardy attitudes on film. In the last few years Hollywood and TV have striven to make the genre more respectable. The attempt to make these films interesting largely fails. Some films that were not intended to be B movies are now labeled Film Noire, such as The Maltese *Falcon*, as part of the attempt to generate interest in audiences that watch old films on TV like AMC and Ted Turner's place. *Falcon* was a good movie when it was made, and it was not "Low Budget" as most Film Noire's were. The category is misleading and nebulous, hard to define and usually not very good all the way through. If film noire movies have trouble with a plot, they usually hide it and make believe the film is a reasonable story when it often has large holes in the reasoning that many critics, living on earnings discussing films do not want the audiences to detect an entire genre that is often weak. One film I don't care for with Dana Andrews and Gene Tierney, made after *Laura*, pretends an important conversation held by the detective and a criminal cannot be heard by the taxi driver. With a larger budget that scene could easily be taken care of. The ones I list may not fit the category of some critics, but the films I list have merit.

Laura circa 1944 Dana Andrews, Gene Tierney, Clifton Webb Good combination detective / love story. Gene Tierney was at her lovely best for this one. Worth watching just to look at her. Clifton Webb, an obvious homosexual, was not a good choice for the would-be lover, but the movie survives this flaw. Time was a clever factor in this film and in this respect, forgive the pun, the film was ahead of its time. The audience sees only a portrait of Laura for several minutes while we learn that detective Dana is looking for her murderer. She comes in after we are sure she is dead, and we will have to see her only in flashback. We feel sorry for Dana and ourselves until she walks in. Fooled me. Now we see a detective story that has us think of something like *Vertigo* about thirteen years later. We are afraid he will lose her twice.

Citizen Kane circa 1948 Orson Wells, Everett Sloan, Joseph Cotton. Overrated, but it is an excellent film, and one that will stay with the viewer. Many, at that time, different camera angles provide different ways of seeing and understanding. Nice (wonderful actually) experiment. The black and white is an advantage for this film, though most of the time Ted Turner is right—films should be in color. But CK is artful in the chiriousco sense and a beautiful endeavor to note. The influence of this film cannot be overrated. The America Film Institute has recently, 2003, rated this film as the best American film–heady praise.

Fargo circa 1999 Bill Macy, Steve Buscemi, Harve Presnell, Frances McDormand Funny and bloody at the same time. Makes a nice feminist statement too, without offending even the most chauvinistic of us. Macy hires a man to kidnap his wife for ransom because he needs the money to pay back and hide the money that he has been stealing from his father-in-law. You just cannot trust such people as you hire to kidnap someone, and Macy is a boob. Nothing goes well for him. A woman cop is good on the case and after a dangerous day, she comes home to comfort her husband who has had a bad day at the office working on trivial matters, or some such. Funny, bloody, shocking.

Godfather I and II circa 78 & 80 Al Pacino, Robert Duval, Diane Keaton Captivating in that although we cannot approve of any of the characters, there is something about them we root for. Perhaps we need to believe that some justice can exist when the law will not work to protect us. In fact, the law is often our enemy, and the movie is well done and makes us almost like those who are not reasonably likable. Rather like Shakespeare—think of Iago, who is witty and likeable, though he is the Devil. When Claudius the villain is at prayer, feeling his guilt, we understand him well enough to feel sorrow for him too. Claudius is sympathetic when he is on his knees suffering the torment of the guilty, praying for forgiveness though he knows that he continues to want that for which he committed the murder. Somehow we see the characters in *The Godfather* movies, though not the third one, well enough to feel strong emotion when they fall, though fall they should. These two movies are among the best ever produced.

Pulp Fiction 1994 John Trevolta, Samuel L. Jackson, Tim Roth, Harvey Keitel *

Uma Thurman, Bruce Willis, Christopher Walken, Rosanna Arquette Again, I like almost all characters in the film, but for the two brutal perverts in the homosexual rape scenes. That bit of gore is satisfying though when we see them suffer. That suffering we like. Unique way of unfolding the action too. The plot is convoluted, though the story, as we remember it, is sequential. Nifty bit of story telling. The unfolding is the movie.

Inductive reasoning required—always a plus.

Reservoir Dogs circa 1992 Tim Roth, Steve Buscemi, Harvey Keitel, Chris Penn. Harvey Kitel and Tim Roth are magnificent and the story is compelling. Kitel, an unmitigated villain, is likeable. No small achievement. Quentin Tarantino proves himself as an excellent director / storyteller, far beyond director Spielberg in this case. *

Lolita circa 1960 James Mason, Peter Sellers, Shelly Winters, Sue Lyon Compelling, though one never likes any of the characters. The movie defies everything I know about story telling, but it is compelling nevertheless. (I must come to the conclusion that I don't know enough about story telling.) I think I could see myself making some similar mistake as James Mason, though never, I hope, on his scale. The murder Mason commits is not dramatically justified and detracts from the emotional impact of the story. An older man in love with an extremely beautiful young woman who is the daughter of his wife. Lots of intriguing sickness here. Funny Peter Sellers gives us the only respite from the sick stuff, though the stepdaughter is a knockout and as such something of a respite herself. Many of us can see ourselves tempted to be fools too, apparently. At least we understand even if we disapprove. The point is that we cannot approve of any of the characters, and even though we would never be able to insert ourselves in any of the roles (a requirement for Aristotle) we watch. No one will get up and leave this movie.

Goodfellows circa 1998 Ray Liotta, Robert De Nero, Joe Pesci Bloody and entertaining. I think we see the "goodfellows" as such dumb asses that we have sympathy for them, but not much. Just an interesting side of the world that most of us, thank goodness, know little about. Like looking at dinosaurs, I suppose. We know they were here, and we are glad we are not too close, but we are interested. Something is appealing about the idea of family as all important in protecting us when so often the law does nothing for us.

(I'm not sure what movies fit into **Film Noire** exclusively— none, I suspect. I think the subject of the film will put the film in one of the other categories too.)

Best Movies—western

High Noon 1953 Gary Cooper, Grace Kelly, Lon Chaney, Jr., Lloyd Bridges, Katy Juardo, Thomas Mitchell Reminds me of Sinclair Lewis and William Faulkner in that the movie shows the evils of a small town. In Cuba we find an apt expression: "A small town means big troubles." Many folks (John Wayne and Senator McCarthy) hated this film because it failed to portray Americans as people who always will do the right thing when they know what the right thing is. Cooper was the American hero, obligated to help his community to help himself, himself bereft of help from the community he has been helping for years. The American hero is tall, taciturn with the big stick at the ready. Plus, the hero is obligated to help us, but not to be one of us. *High Noon* shows the best qualities of the American hero in Gary Cooper. Even if you don't like the movie, and I find that impossible to consider, there is Princess Grace to look at. Coop moves on to grayer pastures contemptuous of his former community. Great scene as he throws his badge in the dirt and heads west after luckily surviving a gunfight against all odds. Compelling movie *

Shane 1953 Alan Ladd, Jean Arthur, Van Heflin, Jack Palance, Ben Johnson. Medieval heroic tale. The hero moves on like The Lone Ranger after he helps. He does not have to deal with the everyday problems that we don't want our heroes to be contaminated with "The proud man's contumely" and that sort of thing. He doesn't have to seduce or fight off the seduction of Jean Arthur by simply moving on. The *ubermench* has to change his environment to live up to our hopes; otherwise, he might become

Hitler. Nice gunfight by the poor hero who doesn't want to do the wrong thing, but he has to consider the difficulties of omission and commission. No answer, but he makes the right choice we think, and evil is defeated after a hell (pun intended) of a fight. Superb

The Shootist 1976 John Wayne, Ron Howard, Lauren Bacall, Richard Boone, Jimmy Stewart, Hugh O' Brian Wayne's best role by far is *The Shootist*. He is pretty good in *Red River, The Searchers,* and *The Quiet Man,* not too bad as Rooster Cogburn, *True Grit* only—the sequel to *True Grit* is dog dooky (a technical term, I know.) The eye patch helped him considerably in the Cogburn role. I have enjoyed many of Wayne's movies, but I like his personality, and I am willing to overlook many of his poor performances because of his personality, his ensemble cast, and the direction. Wayne, in *The Shootist,* is truly a man looking death in the eye and though he doesn't flinch, he knows what he is going to miss when he enters the dark. In spite of his childish philosophy when he tells a young and hairy Ron Howard that he doesn't treat people badly, so he won't allow himself to be treated that way, we put up with him because he is sympathetic in his bravery with no one to hold his hand. We want to say to Wayne, however, if a bad guy is as big as a 6ft.13 inch NFL lineman and just as quick came after you, wouldn't you run, Marion? Nevertheless, a fine, fine movie about a situation that most will face. Only a quick death of the young can save us from his fate. The last head nod by a dying Wayne is too much, but otherwise a fine piece of thoughtful entertainment. The need to show Jim Stewart again at the end of the movie is a "break" that tells us we are watching a movie and takes us out of the film. However, I forgive the filmmaker for the otherwise fine work.

She Wore a Yellow Ribbon (war also) circa 1949 John Wayne, Vic. McGlaughin, John Agar, Harry Carrey, Jr., Ben Johnson, Jo Anne Dru. In this movie we see the hero, John, try to go west as traditional heroes do, but he is called back before he can journey too far (in any sense of the term "too far"). Hence the modern western is forstalled. The end of the journey occurs later in say, *Lonely Are the Brave* with Kirk Douglas. This movie, *Yellow Ribbon*, has great characters and is an appealing film. Ben Johnson makes the movie. Johnson is, even at this early stage of his career, almost a perfect actor.

Red River circa 1947 John Wayne, Montgomery Clift, John Ireland, Joanne Dru, Walter Brennan, Colleen Gray. Epic journey filled with hardships, which are overcome by a hero—a modern hero. Montgomery Clift transcends his father figure, the more reactionary John Wayne. Wayne has to learn from his son of sorts, who always appeals on some level. Lots of memorable characters in this film. It even has a good part for John Ireland. Walter Brennan is his usual self, which is a character we usually like. Wayne is better in this movie than in most of his sadly less than mediocre work. (Watching Monty Clift, the effeminate, fight John Wayne requires suspension of disbelief.)

Rio Grande (war also) circa 1948 John Wayne, Ben Johnson, Harry Carey Jr. Victor McGlauchen, Claude Jarman Jr. J. Carol Nash, and Ken (Festus) Curtis who was one of the *Sons of the Pioneers*. He sang in *Rio Grande*, and he was in *The Searchers* as the slightly demented, goofy suitor. *The Searchers* is often thought of as one of Wayne's best movies, though I think it overrated). I have a bias against films with Natalie Wood. I think *The Searchers* would be better if John had whaked Natalie. The whacking would not have been much of a loss if John had done her in. The act, the whacking, (I expect I have seen too many Godfather type movies) would show the undoubted competent hero with an enormous flaw. Then we would have had a tremendous tragedy. As is, *The Searchers* is relegated to a weak film level, in my opinion. *Rio Grande* is a good film with Maureen O'Hara, as usual, failing to get the credit for her fine acting.

Ft. Apache (war also) 1950 John Wayne, Henry Fonda, Ward Bond, John Agar, Shirley Temple. Pedro Armendarez. Explanation of the martinet anti-hero suggested by the movie to be Brevet Gen. (Lt. Col.) Custer. Nothing commends this movie more than the fine acting of Henry Fonda and Ward Bond. Wayne is worse than usual in a film that seems to have been created for him. He is certainly not convincing at the end of the film when he has become the commanding officer. We see no new maturity in him though he has become the C.O. Perhaps the directing is at fault. Victor McGlaughin, usually a journeyman actor, is guilty of immense overacting in this one. Pedro Armendarez, on the other hand, is excellent. Wayne should have picked Armendarez for his ensemble cast used in all of his movies. *FT Apache* is one of the John Ford trilogy paying homage to the Cavalry that helped tame the west. Taming the west means killing all the Indians possible. It is unpopular and seen as almost immoral today to say unkind things about the American Indians, but their culture was not a good one, and it had to go if we were to fulfill our manifest destiny in order to build a world where we could make atomic bombs and pollute the universe in order to make the planet almost uninhabitable now. The Indians would have done the same thing if they had caught up with us technologically, pollute the universe in such a way as to make the species close now to making itself extinct.

The Outlaw Josey Wales 1976 Clint Eastwood, Sam Bottoms, John Vernon, and the ugly woman Eastwood was living with who almost ruined all of his movies, Sondra Locke, and the Indian who was in *Little Big Man*. Chief Dan George? Great movie about the western hero as the knight is trying to move on, but he is programmed to help anyone who needs him, and he is determined not to be defeated. Clint Eastwood is wooden, but in this film wooden is okay. *

The Unforgiven circa 1995 Clint Eastwood, Gene Hackman, Morgan Freeman, Richard Harris. A great movie that almost defies explanation. No character is sympathetic except Morgan Freeman, and he leaves much to be desired in a hero. Every character is a villain, but somehow Clint Eastwood gives (sells) a superb performance, and his logic about the nature of mankind is chillingly accurate. We deserve only pain, but the idea of heaven is that we can all obtain more than we deserve. Nice thought. Nothing new, but the view of mankind is efficiently and ruthlessly played by one of us. Somehow we can sympathize with a character who knows himself and the rest of us as well. Gene Hackman, as always, is one of the best actors ever to portray us. The movie is puzzling because we usually need a hero or a central character with whom we can sympathize. To sympathize we need to see ourselves in the possible situation. Without being able to project ourselves into this situation, we always, I once thought, are incapable of caring what happens. In this movie, I see no one to like, but I am interested in the film from beginning to end. A mesmerizing movie. *

Best Movies–Modern western (cowboys of this day)

Jr. Bonner circa 1970 Steve McQueen. Robert Preston, Ida Lupino, Joe Don Baker A kind of *Gone with the Wind* theme. A good way of life is gone with the wind, but in this case the hero goes down "head bloody but unbowed." In addition, this flick is never sentimental—no bathos. Robert Preston is magnificent as the father who continues to dream though his years for dreaming should have ended long ago. Somehow Preston never seems to be the village dolt, nor is he a complete boob. We think he may be a hero, although a failed one who will continue to strive (and fail). He's better than Willy Loman for some reason, though they have much in common. We see his son, McQueen, "Haulin down the road" (rodeo-ing) much as his father has done. He is not a boob either, but his days are past his best, and he also won't be defeated and can't win. The father son relationship is priceless. McQueen's best acting occurs in this film. Watch his face to see the movie. He doesn't not have to say much *

J.W. Coop circa 1971 Cliff Robertson Surprisingly good, low-budget film about another modern cowboy who will not quit. The circumstances are not the same as Jr. Bonner, but the more single-minded Robertson gives an excellent performance. If a person has to make a choice, and I'm sure he or she will not, *Jr. Bonner* is a better flick because the complications to the plot are more unified, thus intriguing. I recommend both films for the complete view of the cowboy and his means of striving to be the best cowboy he can be, a kind of religion where the cowboy is a tough judge of himself. The last scene with Robertson lying in the rodeo arena clutching his prize buckle, as he perhaps lies dying is one of the best single shots to tell a story I have seen. *

Lonely Are the Brave circa 1962 Kirk Douglas (The reverse of Shane—the hero is out of step with society, so society will destroy him. He can't move on as Shane did. Old civilization has him. *Hud* can't move on either; consequently, he becomes the "Man Without Qualities." *Hud* and *Shane* are good movies, but they are different reactions to a world that won't let them, Kirk in this case, "head west," but requires Alan Ladd, as Shane to move on." In *Lonely are the Brave* we see the best Kirk Douglas movie in a long career, although that may not be saying too much, however, Douglas is killed by an eighteen wheeler partly because he won't give up his horse to complete his escape. Walter Matthou is superb as a sheriff who comes to respect Douglas, no matter that he does his job as sheriff as well as he can.

Best Movies—family

To Kill a Mockingbird circa 1961 Gregory Peck, Robert Duval. This one should become sentimental, but somehow, oddly, it doesn't. It is what it purports to be from the beginning—nice, sweet, and often moving film. This movie may be the most well-known movie ever. Even more have seen this one than *Citizen Kane*, I expect. Peck is good as he most often is, and Robert Duval gives his best performance, something like the silent Raquel Welch in 1,000,000 BC, but without the pulchritude.

Life is Beautiful 1998 Roberto Benegini I don't know why this one is good, but it is. It is another holocaust movie, and one would think we would become tired of these, but the father, son relationship in the concentration camp is indeed beautiful.

(There must be many more family movies that are good, but I cannot think of them.)

Best Movies–fantasy and animation

Harvey 1950 Jimmy Stewart, Josephine Hull, Jesse White, Cecil Kellaway, Wallace Ford, Harvey Pukka. Sweet, though unrealistic fantasy with a nice, if exaggerated, point. Pleasant, pleasant, pleasant. Stewart once said of this film that he regretted it. He said that he played Elmo P. Dowd as if Elmo were a dypso. "How little one knows oneself." Did he think he was Joan of Arc? Stewart's best movie.
Snow White C. 1934 Magnificent animation and good music. *

Chocolate 2002 Johnny Depp, Juliete Binoche Fascination with the alchemy of chocolate mixed with love and understanding of all levels of society. The church is portrayed well too–an oddity for Hollywood, but this one, I think, must have come from outside the environs of the mindset that often enervates Hollywood. *
Don Juan de Marco circa 1996 Johnny Depp, Marlon Brando, Fay Dunaway Much of it straight from Bryon's poem. Clever in that the way to show and believe in the reinvigoration of life and the ability to love works. Marlon Brandon and Fay Dunaway, not often my favorites,

combine to give a strange, but compelling view of an aging marriage that continues to continue in a fine fancy. Depp, a good actor, portrays a modern boy, as well as Don Juan, as more acted upon than actor—thus the seducer and the boy are saved from our ostracism while we are saved from realizing our own voyeuristic inclinations.

The Wizard of Oz 1939 Judy Garland, Jack Haley, Burt Lahr, Ray Bolger, Margaret Hamilton, Billie Burke, Nigel Bruce. What can one say; it is good.

Best Movies—love stories

Waterloo Station 1937 Robert Taylor, Vivian Leigh Sad, not realistic, but sad. The sociology is as wrong as *Pretty Woman*, but the truth that we see in this movie has some ideas worth considering. Just what is bad, and when must we forgive? More importantly, how do we forgive ourselves? A woman thinks her lover is dead and becomes a prostitute. He returns. Tough. When we sell our souls we always think it is not worthwhile to have a soul or, and this is more common, we will buy our souls back. The horror is we cannot buy them back; we do not know how. We have been too corrupt. We change. Only forgiveness can redeem us, and not knowing we can be redeemed, we destroy ourselves, one way or another. The human condition is sad.

Casablanca circa 1943 Humphrey Bogart, Ingrid Bergman, Claude Rains, Paul Henreid, Peter Lorre. Tough Humphrey has a heart of gold when he sees the needs of the world outweigh even his love. Not sensible, but poignant. Lots of wartime propaganda, but a good film, nevertheless. Claude Rains is a great foil for Hump. Peter Lorre is good in this film, believe it or not. I only value a governmental system that helps me protect my loved ones. Hump boy gives up Ingrid for the greater good of the greater number. Nonsense, but admirable at that time in that way. I wouldn't have given her away when I was kid; I continue to feel and think the same way. I think that 99% of the time we must hang on to the ones we love and tell the world to go fuck itself.

Love is a Many Spendoured Thing 1955 William Holden, Jennifer Jones. Star- crossed lovers—sad, sweet sadness that shows love, though genuine, can be defeated by unseen, but felt, world forces unleashed with the absurdity of war in a world desperately needing clarity from love. Not much of a thought-provoking movie, but the two lead characters go beyond the film's obvious limitations until the film is worth seeing, and remembering. The actors save the plot. We love them.

An Affair to Remember circa Late 40s, early fifties. Cary Grant, Debra Kerr The attempt to give to the loved one is noble in a world that sees little that is noble. Sometimes we wonder if we missed seeing the nobility. Nice thought to have. Love increases the love of the loved one. Poignant, stupid, but good enough. In a silly plot, Grant and Kerr are both sympathetic, even lovable. They are better than the script. As Tom Hanks says in *Sleepless in Seattle*: "That's a chick's film." Yeah, but a good one.

Murphy's Romance circa 1988 James Garner, Sally Field Adult love with realistic approach to problems which are major, though they seem so ordinary as not to be significant. Great movie. James Garner is the best at acting when he is not speaking. He is the best listener of anyone I have ever seen. Sally Field is a likeable and good actress, but she is no match for Garner. He makes the movie. *

Best Movies—drawing room—manners, behavior of any type even the behavior of nature just so the behavior as well as character carries the theme.

Executive Suite 1950 William Holden, Frederic March, Louis Calhern, Paul Douglas, Walter Pidgeon, Dean Jaggers, June Allyson, Barbara Stanwyck, Shelley Winters, Nina Foch, Tim Considine Superb movie that tries to describe the present by the future. Short term profit for the stockholders or self respect in doing the right thing now for the future. I have seen a university make a come-back by taking the "far view," as advanced by William Holden in this film. And I have seen a Jr. College assassinate itself by doing the expedient thing. The Jr. College folk would have done well to have seen, understood, and remembered this movie. The university I was doctored by valued the future, but doing the right thing for the future cost the president of that fine institution his future, and oddly the hero knew he would lose. Not many like Charles Austin, formerly president of Texas A&M University–Commerce. The film taught me to look for such opportunities to do the right thing. This little-known movie has great performances by every character. Fredrick March and William Holden went on to do more great films, but no one will ever see Louis Calhern, Paul Douglas, or even Barbara Stanwyck do better, or do as well. Nina Foch is riveting in her brief appearances too. Dean Jaggers is always special and good, and so is Walter Pidgeon when he is in his range, as he is in this one. A quick profit from an inferior product looks good to stockholders, but better quality insures pride and longevity. The debate in this move shows the temptation to savor the moment is a strong temptation. *

Zorba the Greek circa 1960 Alan Bates, Anthony Quinn Zorba's attitude is the lesson for us all. The conflicts are universal, and the film is a good lesson on what is important. Zorba is the ancient Greek with a love for life, all of it, though he knows most lessons are painful. Quinn is great in this one, and so is Alan Bates, who was an underrated actor. *

Moonstruck circa 1990 Cher, Nicolas Cage, Olympia Dukasis, John Mahoney Anita Gillete One can "settle" and become affected by and with true love. Cher, usually nauseating, is good in this one. Everyone is slightly addled or pixilated and profits by the pixilation. Good film which shows love for the old as well as the young. One smiles as he walks out of the theatre.*

The Magnificent Ambersons circa 1949 Joseph Cotton, Tim Holt. Sociology in the changing world—a kind of *Gone with the Wind* without the war. It is set in the early twentieth century as times are changing with the industrial revolution. They ain't gone as fer as they can go. Great scene when Tim Holt answers the question of what he plans to do with his life and he looks slightly irked at such a middle class question and answers "a yachtsman" as he and his date dance sideways away from the camera. Priceless moment in moviedom. This movie is as good if not better than *Citizen Kane*, although the ending is slightly lame, but one may and should overlook the ending. Holt is a fine actor, but he languished in B films for most of his career. B westerns—a waste of talent. No one in the "know" has held the thought for long that talent is the vehicle by which move actors prosper. Pity.

The Grass is Greener circa. 1952 Cary Grant, Robert Mitchum, Debra Kerr, Jean Simmons Fun movie about love and infidelity in the most urbane way. No one looks ridiculous however foolishly each one behaves. Not great acting, not a great plot, but fun with understanding as a nice point to make in a civilized society. Cary Grant is good as is Jean Simmons. The other two hang on and are not so bad as to detract from the fine performances or the glowing feeling in the audience. *

The Pleasure of His Company circa. 1956 Fred Astair, Gary Merril, Lilly Palmer, Tab Hunter, Debbie Reynolds Former husband arrives to attend his daughter's wedding and tries to take over the former wife's and almost new daughter's life. (He has ignored his daughter for many years.) He discovers what he has missed and that hurts, but he is not destroyed. He is a new kind of hero with a peculiar new kind of flaw—a kind of Updike character. Surprisingly fine flick. *

An Officer and a Gentleman 1982 Debra Winger, Richard Gere, Lou Gossett, David Keith, Robert Loggia. Interesting movie that compares the Byronic hero with the American hero. America wins as the Marine sergeant (Lou Gosset) creates a new kind of hero from the Errol Flynn, Richard Gere trademark Byronesque, old world hero, portrayed by Gere. Gere recognizes his debt. We often don't, alas. *

Cannery Row circa 1982 Nick Nolte, Debra Winger (Comedy too) Commedia dell' Arte proletariat losses made to seem less than they are by attitude. Beautiful scenery unlike almost any other movie I have ever seen. The music is magnificent also. One loves all the characters. Reminds me of *Tom Jones* circa 1960 and *Waterloo Station* 1937 in that Debra Winger is a *Pretty Woman* whore untouched (somehow) by her trade. Great fun in a fantasy about a group of bums who remind me of the Dwarfs with

Snow White. * The music and the scenery and the narration by John Huston make this film one of the world's best. It lost money. The critics yawned at the hoke, but some hoke is made in heaven.

Indiscreet circa 1955 Cary Grant, Ingrid Bergman, Brit actor who played the part of the brother-in-law is a fine comedic actor; he also plays the part of the King in *The Court Jester.* A "turn" in Don Juan caused by true love and a clever woman. Grant tells every woman he seduces that he is a married man, but he is single. Nicely done, fun movie. The part of the seducer, witty and urbane, is made for Grant. Ingrid is good too. Both characters charm us.

The Quiet Man 1950 John Wayne, Maureen O'Hara, Victor McGlaughin, Barry Fitzgerald and his brother, and Ward Bond This one is "Don't miss." A beautiful movie in many senses. A man tries to come home to a place that was never his home and discovers that he must prove himself to everyone in this environment too, even to his wife. We agree. He has to. And this aspect of the movie seems to be in contrast to the point of *The Big Country.* Why not? Iago contradicts himself when the time is right, and he is the Devil. The good are allowed contradiction too, especially when they come to see themselves in a true light *

Educating Rita circa 1984 Michael Caine, Julie Walters— the truth of the movie is painful and illuminating because of love and the social scene. It is typical Brit stuff with regard to the impact society has on mankind. The professor, the Don, is well done by Caine. The woman from the working classes, cockney-like, learns the orthodoxy of university life and masters it along with Caine. With her new mastery, she can now choose what kind of a life she will lead. Caine had not wanted her "spoiled" by the phony life he sees himself leading, but Rita knows she has to be able to choose or she will not be content. No one is content in a prison. The haircut scene is worth the price of admission. What do professors want if not adulation? (Not money)

The Last Picture Show circa 1971 Jeff Bridges, Ben Johnson, Cybil Shepherd, Timothy Bottoms, Cloris Leachman, Randy Quaid. An unblinking look at teen and adult life in a little Texas town in the fifties. Poignant, moving, and sympathetic toward everyone. I want them all to do well, though I know that the likelihood is that none of them will. Bottoms, Bridges are great and Ben Johnson is as good as an actor can be. Johnson gives perhaps the best performance I have ever seen as Sam, the Lion. Even Cybil Shepard is good in this one. Randy Quaid is good too. Cloris Leachman (too darn ugly) hurts some, but not enough to destroy the excellent film. With a little make up Cloris could have just been plain, rather than god-awful ugly The expectations of the young when confronted with the social class problems they have never known in high school, but will experience the remainder of their lives.

Radio Days circa 1989 Woody Allen, Mia Farrow The same comments as can be made for *Last Picture Show* are applicable, everybody is adorable. The difference is that *Radio Days* has to do with the initiation of proletariat northeastern city kids. Brooklyn, I think. Of course, the humor is in the cynical looking back for Allen. All Allen movies are the same, but good anyway, somehow. Nostalgia is the glue that keeps us in our seats. One of Allen's very best movies *

The Best Years of Our Lives circa 1947 Frederick March, Myrna Loy, Dana Andrews, Teresa Wright, and the no-hands man, a real wounded veteran who won the academy award for his part as best supporting actor. Good, but overrated picture about the return of the vets after WW11. Three lives of service men examined across the social spectrum and that is an important aspect of a movie that wants us all to reunite without the inevitable class distinctions. The distinctions are thought not to be significant, though the lower classes will always think that they have been cheated, and often, of course, they have. The Republicans think that if they, the lower classes, had been better at the game they could have cheated and prospered in this great system too. The picture is insightful and important, but it has not aged well. The insights of that day are old fedora now, something like Shakespeare's brilliance reduced to today's clichés, but a good evening's entertainment, and something to think about. No answers, but good questions.

From Here to Eternity 1953 Burt Lancaster, Debora Kerr, Montgomery Clift, Donna Reed, Frank Sinatra, Jack Warden, Ernest Borgnine. Especially good film about the Pre-World War II army and an insightful look at the life of the soldiers. They live like all of us, but in a close environment, thus the results are seen faster and sometimes more clearly in the clear hierarchical manner of the army. The film has an unerring eye and ear. Verisimilitude is enough this time. Kudos for Debra Kerr, always a lady, but not often much more. In this one, she shines. Jack Warden is extraordinary in a small part. Sinatra is especially good in what may have been his only good performance. Donna Reed, Burt Lancaster, and Montgomery Clift, as well as Ernest Borgnine, are all far above what anyone would have any right to expect. Other actors shine too. *

The Graduate 1967 Dustin Hoffman, Anne Bancroft, Murray Hamilton, Kathryn Ross, Norman Fell Initiation theme of a young man just out of college who is about to enter a world he has little interest in. His life becomes more complicated when he falls in love with the daughter of a woman, the wife of his father's partner, he has been having an affair with. Lots of humor, but often one feels uneasy seeing that which we might rather not be told about in the upper-middle classes. *Raising Arizona* makes fun of the lower classes. This picture shows the foibles of the more prosperous and well educated. Kathryn Ross is an esthetic delight.

The Sting circa 1972 Paul Newman, Robert Redford, Robert Shaw, and the woman who was the Captain in *Private Benjamin*. View of the con artist world as seen by Hollywood. Likable fantasy-type film because we get to see the bad guy, who always thinks he is smart, get out-smarted. A feel-good film. Newman and Redford are more beautiful than the music, and the music is fine, fine, which makes a big contribution to this one. Beauty is always a seller, and a good thing too.

Chariots of Fire circa 1985 Ben Cross, John Gielgud and several nice-looking young men. Somewhat like *The Sting*, but the view is of those who have money, power, position, talent, but are nevertheless left out of the "best" circles. A comeuppance movie reminiscent of F. Scott Fitzgerald and Jackie Kennedy Onassis. Takes place at Oxford or Cambridge, (Cambridge, I think), which are interchange-able for me, just after WW1. A different class is coming on the university scene. Moneymaking and professionalism are changing the social scene. The movie thinks the change is a good thing, but actually all the votes aren't in yet. The transfer of power moving to the middle classes is beginning in Chaucer's time, and according to Evelyn Waugh isn't completed until after WW11. Now we are seeing the values of the lower classes taking over, and we of the middle classes don't want to relinquish the good stuff. Could it be that democracy is just a nice way to protect our class and our money? If democracy does not protect capitalism, will we like it? I think not. See this one and decide with whom you side. Maybe more amateurs would be best. (Universities would not have to hire non students to play games for us, and we would learn that those who should be our best (the ones who make up universities) do not become corrupt.)

They Might be Giants circa 1974 George C. Scott, Jo Anne Woodward Anything is possible. Bread mold might be a cure for many diseases, and the ones who seem to be nuts are sometimes really nuts, though they are often the innovators who are doing good by all of us. We learn to be open to mystery in a spiritual world even though logic and reason may be the way the spiritual world works too. The mysterious is satisfying, and who is to say God doesn't work with logic? Just who is nuts? The title is from *Don Quixote*. Remember Quixote doesn't say the windmills are giants. He says they might be giants. He's right.

From Three till Noon circa 1973 Charles Bronson, Jill Ireland Strange movie about a man and a woman who cannot become who they imagine they were. The circumstances make us aware of injustice and odd justice, and plain justice—none of which do we always want. We see much irony in the big moments of life. This movie is

Bronson's best. He is on his way to rob a bank with associates when he is deterred by circumstance. He meets a beautiful woman who comes to love him. He is captured and sent to jail for a crime he didn't commit. When he gets out, she remembers him the way she wanted him, not the way he is. Her imaginings have become world famous in the novel / autobiography she writes. He is confused; her fate is more bizarre and less believable. Suicide is always unconvincing, and an easy way out for screenwriters. *

The Caine Mutiny circa 1954 Humphrey Bogart, Van Johnson, Fred McMurry, Jerry Paris, Jose Ferrer Much better movie than it gets credit for. Humphrey Bogart gives the best performance of his life, (to change as the moment goes on is always tough for actors. Only the best can do what Hump Bogart did in this movie, and he gave many good performances. We have to see Bogart change as he sees himself change. This type of awareness is always difficult to comprehend and difficult to recognize in oneself or in others. Others always deserve our sympathy because of the human condition, which is we are flawed, but we don't want to see the flaws in ourselves, and even more, we don't want to see the flaws in our leaders. When we puritans see the flaws of our leaders we are horrified. Point: Adolph Hitler lives up to our American puritan standards of sexual behavior whereas Eisenhower, Lyndon Johnson, FDR, John Kennedy, and Bill Clinton did not. Bogart was not a good leader when his men and circumstances demanded that he be at his best. He needed his men more than they needed him, but they let him down more than he let them down. Ironic, interesting, thought provoking. I would require this film for the naval academy midshipmen. The academy probably hates it and would crucify anyone who offers it to the students. *

Treasure of The Sierra Madre circa 1941 Humphrey Bogart, Walter Houston, Tim Holt, Bruce Bennet. Gold fever ruins Humphrey, but Tim Holt learns from foils Humphrey and Walter Houston about how to live and what to search for. Bogart, Huston, and Holt are really good. *

Quest for Fire 1982 A look at early man who seeks the light and warmth of fire, as soon as he discovers that it can be produced by man. Early man seems to be too much like us. What are we searching for? Is it easy to see if we know how to look (at them). First fire then the wheel, what's next? The internet? *

Inherit the Wind circa 1961 Frederic March, Spencer Tracey, Gene Kelly, (first Darren in *Bewitched*). An intriguing, insightful look at the Scopes trial, which is not over yet, though the trial was in the twenties. We're still opposed to knowledge that we don't approve of, that does not fit into our personal schemas. Sad, but it is worth knowing that we distrust knowing. Read *All the King's Men*. Mankind is condemned to look, to search, even if he knows the knowledge may destroy him, but more likely we will kill anyone who wants us to know. See Socrates and Jesus then suffer fools gladly. To complicate the matter, we are afraid of the Frankenstein monster too. I remember mothers of my high school friends picketing this film as I went to see it at The Oaklawn Theatre in Dallas. They loved the idea of creationism, and were afraid of the idea of evolution. They refused to see the film and tried to stop everyone from seeing it. Frederick March and Spencer Tracy do some good talking in a talky movie about ideas and freedom to pursue freedom for unknowable value. The search is good even, perhaps especially, if we can't see the outcome. The Frankenstein Monster is something we should be aware and wary of. Can we control the Atomic world? Nah

Shawshank Redemption circa 1999 Morgan Freeman, Tim Robbins The hero overcomes the worst of injustice and adversity then helps another worthy who had fallen but who had merit not realized by an unjust society. An optimistic movie, actually. Sad, but like tragedy, exhilarating when we see the indomitable spirit of mankind. We know of injustice even when we are very young, but we like to see one of us change for the better as we grow older, and we want to see our young selves again as we thought we were. Only injustice prevented our view of ourselves from becoming reality, so we want change and justice, but we are afraid of change too because we think we may be on the path we thought we were on. (I've confused myself.) Morgan Freeman is this movie, but Robbins is good.

Bull Durham circa 1996 Kevin Costner, Susan Sarandon, Tim Robins. Susan Sarandon makes this film. I have never seen a better performance except Ben Johnson in *The Last Picture Show*. Her appropriate tears when Costner, who is not self-pitying, asks her if he might find the success as a manager he missed as a player, is worthy of the best in us and among us. The world is tough and neither nature nor others help much when all we often need is understanding. Sarandon provides Costner with the understanding and love we need to give and receive. A baseball film that is not hokey, and the metaphor is good in that it never lets us feel sorry for ourselves. Some other setting for this movie might have become cloying. "Sixty Minute Man" (1952) resonates through one of the best moments of the film. I remember that song as the first Rhythm and Blues song I ever heard. I wonder who chose that song for this pic, and I wonder why. Great choice. Fine movie.

Bonnie And Clyde circa 1967 Warren Beatty, Gene Hackman, Fay Dunaway, Estelle Parsons The story of ruthless killers made to seem victims as well as villains. I tend to believe that most evil comes from you and me because we can't see the result of our actions. Moral: read many books, and see lots of movies. The more stupid we are, the more evil we usually can become. It is easy to be evil when we are stupid. Usually we never know what we have done. Sad. I like this movie; I am not sure why, except society had little compassion for those down and out in the depression. Maybe that's why Dillinger and his crowd are sometimes seen as heroes. They tweak the collective noses of authority for a while. Dummies are evil and perhaps slightly to be pitied. Is this enough to sustain a movie? Must be. The movie is good.

Hud circa 1961 Paul Newman, Brandon de Wilde, Melvin Douglas, Patricia Neal Likable anti-hero Hud / Paul Newman is explained when depicted realistically. Hud is in a world for which he was not prepared. His answer is to protect himself as he knows how to, even though the self-protection will lead to his downfall, and he probably knows this but not what to do about it. Sell the sick cattle, save ourselves is Hud's choice, but his father calls him an unprincipled man and will not destroy others to save himself and Hud. The father is right, but Hud has a point. Who is to throw the first halos at goodness? Little brother de Wilde walks off at the end in disgust with the older brother who has no good qualities. Hud, Newman, is unrepentant, and we continue to like him even though we cannot admire him. (So much for the nobility of the tragic hero.)

Tunes of Glory circa 1960 Dennis Price, Alec Guinness, John Mills Social situation when a up-from-the-ranks Lt. Colonel (Guinness) becomes the temporary regimental commander only to be replaced by an upper-class, less deserving man who is a full Colonel (John Mills). The Guinness character, the up-from-the-ranks man is intolerant of the upper class twit John Mills, who kills himself and leaves the Guinness character to realize his flaw. However, the Brits believe that the Guinness character can do little else in a society so constructed—a convenient belief for the Brits, and often true, though it not need be. This idea of the power of society and the helplessness of the individual is one most of us want when we are not world-beaters. Convenient and often true. The suicide is not justified, but the film survives the flaw. *

Best Movies—Epic (usually a bad category like film noire)

Big Country circa *1958* Gregory Peck, Carol Baker, Burl Ives, Charles Bickford, Jean Simmons, Charlton Heston, Chuck Connors. Lots of conflicts resolved to my satisfaction. Heston Vs Peck, the new green hand vs. the bully and native.) Bickford vs. Ives for the lord of the manor title. Connors vs. Peck. Bad dumb guy who can't help himself vs. good man of conscience who has the painful duty of being true to himself. (Are you listening, Polonius?) Peck vs. Bickford the prospective father-in-law who believes he has all the answers. We know that Peck is the better man, but no one else does.) We always have trouble knowing the good from the bad because we cannot see the results of our actions. This is the strength of good stories. Carol Baker vs. Jean Simmons for Peck's love after he has proven to Baker that he is worthy, he then learns she is not. He should not have to prove himself to a woman who loves him or thinks she does. Ives vs. Jean Simmons in an important business deal that simply helps to move the plot along. *

The Man in the Gray Flannel Suit circa 1957 Gregory Peck, Frederic March, Jennifer Jones, Kennan Wynn, Lee J. Cobb Peck proves himself a man of conscience after a big mistake. Fredrick March seems to be the too-simple, bad, rich guy; but he has a good point to make about hearth and home vs. success. The question of what to choose is not as simple as we most often like to believe such decisions are. The film reminds me of the ancient Greeks in that what Odysseus learns, he teaches, but he is not home with the wife and kiddies. Society needs both kinds, but society cannot decide which hero is better on any occasion. The world needs Frederick March, and it needs Gregory Peck. Which do you want to be? With this decision the viewer must decide what major aspect of life you wish to miss. Tough call. Calls for thought. Hard to surpass this theme, plot, and action.*

Best Movies—musical (music only)

Show Boat 1951, Howard Keel, Kathryn Grayson, Joe E. Brown, Marge and Gower Champion and the almost mean mother of Kathryn Grayson is the fine character actress, Agnes Moorhead, I think who was so important in *The Magnificent Ambersons*. Not a bit of bad music in this film. I can think of no other musical I can say this for. William Warfield sings the best song ever sung in a movie. This is the best musical ever made.

Seven Brides for Seven Brothers 1954 Russ Tamblyn Howard Keel, Jane Powell Pleasant film. No one will mind having spent the price of admission on this one.

Calamity Jane 1954 Doris Day, Howard Keel Two great songs by Doris, and in one scene she is as pretty as any woman has ever been. Her acting is about as bad as her singing is good. However, I recommend it for the beauty of Doris and the song: "Secret Love" by DD

Love Me or Leave Me 1955 Doris Day, James Cagney, Cameron Mitchell. Cagney is terrible. Good music, fair acting by Doris and good songs from the twenties. The music is worth the price of this one.

Music Man 1962 Robert Preston, Shirley Jones, Paul Ford, Hermonie Gingold. Good music most of the time. Good enough. "Marion the Librarian" is a pleasant few minutes, both for the music and the dancing to the music.

High Society 1955 Bing Crosby, Grace Kelly, Frank Sinatra, Celeste Holm, Louie Armstrong, Louis Calhern, Sidney Blackmer. Remake *of The Philadelphia Story*, but the princess Grace is truly lovely and makes the film good.

The Blues Brothers circa 1979 John Belushi, and Dan Akrod Good enough.

The Student Prince 1954 Edmund Purdom (voice of Mario Lanza) Ann Blythe

Lovely Romberg music. Hokey old plot, but nevertheless I liked it. Hoke is fine on occasion.

Best Movies—dance only

Anything with Fred and Ginger in 1930s
One flick with Fred and Eleanor Powell Late 30's also
The dancing of Marge and Gower Champion is magnificent in *Show Boat*.

Best Movies—war

The Bridge on the River Kwai 1957 Alec Guinness, Jack Hawkins, William Holden, Sessue Hyakawii (manners too) The insanity of those caught in a war is depicted in a compelling way. The brightest are the worst. Jack Hawkins and William Holden are at their best, which is very good. The question is not about death, but about life. Alec Guinness is excellent in this one too. Hawkins is the Oxford Don who has it all figured incorrectly. Holden is right, but makes no claim to sense until he has learned from experience. Guinness is bright and good, but temporarily insane for justified reasons. Holden makes the movie, but Sir Alec got the Oscar *

Zulu 1963 Michael Caine, Stanley Baker, Nigel Green, Jack Hawkins, Ulla Jacobsen Highly unified true story that has everything. The Alamo with the good guys as the winners. This one and *Twelve O' Clock High* are my personal favorite war movies. *

Full Metal Jacket circa 1986 (?) Matthew Modine, Lee Armey You want to know what the Marine Corps is? See this one. Armey was a real DI, a retired Marine Gunny Sergeant, and he says exactly what I heard when I was in boot camp. I don't think the Corps changes. Even the song, the Mickey Mouse song the entire large outfit is singing at the end of the movie really happens in the Corps all the time. The song is a favorite of all Marines. The depiction of the boot camp experience is exactly right. The hopeless Marine who goes berserk is also almost always in every boot camp platoon. (Usually, they are sent home and do not murder the D I, but many want to and some do.) All Marines know the folklore of the murdered DI. The combat scenes with Modine are especially good. *

Platoon circa 1988 Charlie Sheen and several good actors—Tom Beringer, William Dafoe and others too realistic to miss. No commentary about politics or difficult decisions, but the most realistic war movie I have ever seen. *

Twelve O' Clock High 1950 Gregory Peck, Dean Jaggers, Gary Merrill, Hugh Marlow, Millard Mitchell. Probably one of the ten best movies ever, certainly one of the best five war movies ever. Peck, Jaggers, and Marlow are incomparable. Nobody in the movie is bad, but Millard Mitchell as the commanding General is not good. Fortunately he is on the screen infrequently. I am unable to explain why this film is so extraordinarily good. I want to; I can't. Mankind against madness, and in this case mankind prevails in the midst of absurd destruction. *

The Bridges at Koto Ri 1954 William Holden, Grace Kelley, Fredric March, Mickey Rooney, Earl Holiman All the characters, even Mickey Rooney, are loveably caught in a silly, desperate situation. Mickey Rooney and Fredrick March, the enlisted man and the Admiral, have the same feelings, but not the same thoughts. The domino theory is questioned, and even though the movie comes down on the side of the Admiral, the actions belie the words. The viewer is left with the thought as well as the feeling that all the loss has been an enormous waste and there is no way to justify it. America has fought only one holy war, and Korea was not it. *

Command Decision circa 1949 Walter Pigeon, Clark Gable, Brian Donlevy, Edward Arnold, John Hodiac. This one is required viewing at the United States Air Force Academy. *Decision* is a good film about leadership in war, and the horror of daylight bombing over Germany in

1943. Had to be done (the bombing), I think, but casualties were inhumanity at its maddest.

The Americanization of Emily (Drawing Room also) 1963 James Garner, James Coburn, Julie Andrews, Keenan Wynn, Murray Slaughter (Mary Tyler Moore show), and Melvyn Douglas Places war where it should be after we get over the horror. War is absurd, madness. This film is funny, but penetrating. Also it is a little-known movie. See it. Clichés become stupidly funny. One of the very best movies ever made. See it and listen to the Paddy Chevsky's (however he spells his name) ideas about war and why such madness continues. *

The Enemy Below, circa 1969 Curt Jurgens, Robert Mitchum, The character Heine is played by Theodore Bikel. Interesting war of nerves and games. I thought about listing this one as one of the worst then I thought I'd just ignore it, but I came to remember it better and better, and I have concluded that for a movie to linger so, it must be one of the best. The two ship captains guess each other's thoughts too often, but the effect is thrilling, enthralling, and somehow soothing. Odd, I know. Like Shakespeare's stuff we like the good guys and the bad guys. Every fall has the power to generate compassion in us. How nice.

The Memphis Belle circa 1990 Matthew Modine All incidents in this especially exciting movie happened, but not in one mission. It took twenty-five missions for this miracle to occur. See it. The compression is so good that we almost have to reason inductively.

Paths of Glory circa 1957 Kirk Douglas, Ralph Meeker, Adolph Menjou, George McReady One of the finest movies made about the futility and senselessness of war. See it. The black and white film is a help for this movie. This movie reminds me of *Billy Budd*. How poignant can we be? Plenty*

The Best of Enemies circa 1960 David Niven Magnificent comedy about war. A little- known movie that should be much better known. This comedy teaches. *

Battleground: circa 1948 Ricardo Montebon, George Murphy, Van Johnson, Marshall Thompson Not really a good movie, but it makes some interesting points about war, bravery, and cowardice. Nothing *Lord Jim* doesn't say, but this is more subtle and more interesting than Conrad, and Conrad was fine.

Worst War Movies:

In Harm's Way circa 1972 John Wayne, Kirk Douglas, Burgess Meredith, Brandon de Wilde, Patrick O'Neil, Patrica Neal, Stanley Holloway Bad movie, but there is something about it I like. I cannot find its merit, but I like it and continue to list it as a bad war movie. Stanley Holloway should have his grave profaned for this movie he is so bad.

The Longest Day circa 1962 John Wayne, Robert Ryan, Red Buttons, Richard Burton, Richard Beymer, Peter Lawford, Robert Mitchum, Eddie Albert, and almost everybody else who was ever in any movie. Phew, a real stinker

The Sand Pebbles circa 1970 I also like this one very much though I think it often, more often than not, bad. I cannot list it as one of my favorites or as one that made a change in me. Steve McQueen, Candice Bergen, Richard Attenborough, Richard Crenna (with a riveting performance) I have seen Crenna since he was Ogie Pringle and Luke, but this role is one of the best performances I have ever seen by anybody. Steve McQueen is certainly good in this one too. And Richard Attenborough is as good as anybody. Candice Bergen is lovely but no more important than a child's doll in this film. She actually detracts. Probably not her fault as much as the director's. This movie is close to being a great one, but it falls short for many reasons. It tries to be good though. One of the bad guys is shown as being only misguided, but likable Nice try, but not there. Some great moments make the movie worth seeing, but don't expect too much. I'm ambivalent, I know. I've changed my mind. This movie is good, but war has little to do with the film's impact. I have no category for this one. Give me a c-. Dadgum, we ought to be able to stick everything into some little boxes, shouldn't we? What would sociologists do without categories? This many themes movie has the most to do with man as machine vs. machine, I think. See it, and tell me.

Saving Private Ryan circa 2003. Only truly memorable scene is the time when Hanks turns a German soldier loose, rather than kill him. The decision turns out to be a bad one for Hanks, which shows the awful predicament man is in at war. After having seen this one for the 3rd time, I am now a fan of the movie.

The Thin Red Line. 2002, perhaps. I can't remember the name of any actor. Stinks. I mention it to get even with it—a sort of catharsis.

To Hell and Back circa 1956 Audie Murphy, Tom Drake's brother and other bums-notably the "other Maverick" in the TV series. I paid a dime to see this one on a marine base, and I wanted my money back.

Patton circa 1981 George C. Scott, Tim Considine, Karl Malden. *Patton* was filmed with four endings. I have seen them all, and none is satisfactory. Too much Patton. We see his flaws all too clearly and his supposed genius seems to be more of a result of a kind of ego centric insanity. No hero, no tragedy, no great story in spite of the history lesson.

Thirty Seconds Over Toyko circa 1944 Van Johnson, Spencer Tracey. Just a bad war propaganda film. It is bad enough to mention.

Best Movies—comedy Comedies are, to me, inexplicable, but priceless. Usually much better than tragedies because we see characters succeed because of their flaws. Rather religious, actually, though the theology is bad. In this category I considered Charlie Chaplin, Buster Keaton, Harold Lloyd, and Laurel and Hardy. The Silents are often very funny, but ultimately language is funnier, and one may have sight gags too. Comedy is written in the vernacular, not Latin, not elevated; hence, it is not supposed to be seriously dramatic as are tragedies. Comedy, oddly, has always regarded humans more realistically than tragedies because it focuses on the weaknesses and foibles of humanity with its serious limitations of bodily functions and animal nature. The most dignified among us occasionally become the fools. Comedies are known by other terms that help us understand them. Farce and burlesque come leaping to mind. Comedy, not farce and burlesque, which are subdivisions of comedy, has weightier, more elevated dialogue, more sustained plot and more life-like characters than farce and burlesque. In addition, a difference lies in less boisterous behavior, usually. Comedy uses wit and humor to deflate the pompous. The Three Stooges, Jerry Lewis, the Marx brothers, and Abbot and Costello are examples of farce. The plays of Oscar Wilde, and the Novels of Evelyn Waugh are often called Drawing Room Comedies, which are more comedic than farcical.

A Thousand Clowns 1966 Jason Robards, Barbara Harris, Martin Balsam Marvelous comedy about a man's attempt to drop out. He seems beautifully insane, but we know he is the only sane one. When he returns to reality, we are slightly sad, but we know the conversion has to happen for verity and love's sake. This movie is a different version of *Harvey.* Stewart had Harvey, though. Robards has a son who needs his father in the
Rat Race. *

Animal Farm, circa 1980 Chevy Chase. A fine fun look at little town America. Chase's best movie for me. The little town is a mirror of big towns with all of the problems, but in fewer numbers. Chase learns to be one of them after he gives up trying to make them into something in his dreams. He learns that the ball that comes across the plate is nothing until the umpire calls it then it is what the umpire (Chase) calls it. Chase learns acceptance brings love sometimes. He relaxes with himself, accepts himself, and lives happily ever after.

Caddyshack, circa1978 Bill Murry, Ted Knight, Chevy Chase Superb nonsense. Ted Knight is excellent. The entire cast is magnificent. Hard to beat for good friendly laughs.

Young Frankenstein circa 1970 Gene Wilder, Terri Garr, Cloris Leachman, Marty Feldman, Madelyn Kahn, Peter Boyle, Gene Hackman Everybody is marvelous in this one, but Gene Hackman is the best in his small part. Cloris Leachman is awful, again. The dancing scene with Wildman and Peter Boyle is perfect sight and sound. *

Hollywood Knights circa 1980 Robert Wuhl, Michelle Peiffer, Tony Dansa *

A rip off of American Graffiti, but better done. See it.

Farris Bueller's Day Off 1986 Matthew Broderick, Allan Ruck, Mia Sara, Charlie Sheen and Jeffrey Jones as the principal. (Jones also great in *Amadeus.*) One of the best comedies.

The Search for the Holy Grail circa. 1982 Monty Python Group: John Cleese, Michael Palin et alii GREAT * Silly as a film can be. Constant laughs.

Animal House 1977 John Belushi, Tim Mathesion, Peter Reigel, and John Vernon, also great in Josey Wales, is superb in this one too. Look for Vernon in a little-known movie entitled *Charlie Varrick*, and you will see his range, which is apparently limitless. *Animal House* is hard to beat for fun. *

Raising Arizona circa 1984 Nicolas Cage, Holly Hunter, John Goodman, Randall "Tex" Cobb Too good to miss. I love to see the Jerry Springer folks made fun of. *

Four Weddings and a Funeral circa 1999 Great British group with Hugh Grant, Andi McDowell Hard to beat this one for fun in character. See it. You'll like it or there is something wrong with you. I really don't know what Zany means. Manners and a few farcical scenes. See it to learn how to pronounce St. John, and learn about the Holy Goat.*

The Gods Must be Crazy I don't know any of the actors, but this is the zaniest movie I have ever seen. Don't miss it. Maybe hard to find, but it is something new. *

Annie Hall (Drawing room also) 1977 Woody Allen, Diane Keaton. This one is funny because of Allen's insights, which are paranoid to the nth degree. "Jew eat?"

SOB 1981 Julie Andrews, Richard Mulligan, Robert Preston, William Holden Richard (?) One of the best comedies. It is based on an incident that three famous men claim really happened to the body of John Barrymore. Errol Flynn, W.C. Fields and a person whose name I am forgetting all claim the incident happened. I'd like to think so. Nevertheless, a truly funny movie. Robert Preston is too too good. And the fun poked at Hollywood is deserved by Hollywood.

Roxanne circa 1986 Steve Martin, Darrel Hannah, Fred Willard, Rick Rossavich (Magnificent, better than Cyrano, by far.) See this one. Beautiful scenery, and we love every character. The handsome dumb and the beautiful smart learn and teach. *

Support Your Local Sheriff circa 1970 James Garner, Jack Elam, Harry Morgan and a fine actress Henry Morgan and James Garner, both excellent comedic actors get big help from Jack Elam. The film is helped by the very funny actress, whose name I cannot remember. She was in *Will Penny* with Charleston Heston. She was good both times, both roles. James Garner made a living with this character beginning with his TV series *Maverick*. Worth anybody's while, whatever a while is.

My Favorite Year 1982 Peter O'Tool, Joseph Bologna, Lanie Kazan Peter O'Tool heretofore famous for a mincing *Florence of Arabia* is actually good. Too bad he was never good before or after. Bologna is good, as is the young man whose name I have never known. (The central character.)

Arthur circa 1986 Dudley Moore, Liza Minnelli, John Geilgud Dudley Moore is believable if you think drunks can be cute. A funny fantasy. Liza darn near ruins it, but maybe one can see only half of the movie and keep one eye shut when she is on the screen. To give her some credit, and it's close to being a gift, she has one scene on the street after she has been caught shoplifting that is good, funny. John Gielgud helps her beyond measure, though.

Cannery Row 1982 Nick Nolte, Deborah Winger Better than the book. The music and the scenery are magnificent, and the movie is faithful to the funny, funny books *Cannery Row* and *Sweet Thursday*. The movie is one of those rare ones when the film is better than the books and the books are superb. *

Mr. Blandings Builds his Dream House circa 1948 Cary Grant, Myrna Loy, Melvyn Douglas (Not a great movie, but influential on me. First "father doesn't know better" movie I saw.)

Home Alone circa 1997 Macaulay Culken, Joe Pesci, Daniel Stern, and a fine actress who played the part of McCulen's mother, Catherine O' Hara. The actor who played the part of the father is good too. He was in *Trip to Bountiful*. Superb farce. Great kid actor.

Best Movies—musical but not just music

Show Boat circa 1951 Howard Keel, Kathryn Grayson, William Warfield, Joe E. Brown Ava Gardner (Voice of Lena Horne, I think) This one is probably the best musical, just for the music, of all time. Not an even only fair song in this one. All the music is superb.*

Oh Brother, Where Art Thou? circa 2001 John Turtorro, George Clooney, Holly HunterTim Blake Nelson, Charles Durning (also seen in *The Best Little Whore House* and *The Sting*) (comedy also) The best rending of American folk music I have ever heard in a movie. The music is good enough to sustain the movie, though George Clooney is excellent. Holly Hunter is not good. Lucky she had a small part. She almost ruined *Raising Arizona* with her over acting, but she was good enough in that one. Tim Blake Nelson has a great singing voice, and he is funny. *

Grease circa 1977 John Travolta, Oliva Newton-John Hard to do better, but the movie would have been much better if the middle-aged woman who played Rizzo had been replaced. She comes close to ruining this one. Everybody is going for laughs but Rizzo. She is in a different movie from the kids, (she is scary) all of whom are close to thirty or slightly more. Rizzo is more (35, I discovered). The angel guy, (one of the Darrens—the guy with Annette Funny Jello in *Beach Blanket Bingo* or some such) a former teenage singing star, is a great choice. *

Oliver 1968 Ron Moody and two kids Nice dances and fun songs. May be the last good musical.

My Fair Lady circa 1960. Audrey Hepburn (voice of Marnie Nixon) Rex Harrison, Wilfred Hyde-White, Stanley Holloway, Theodore Bikel What else can one say? I think Julie Andrews would have been better, but the film is a good one, and Audrey is good enough, though I have never cared for the voice of Marnie Nixon. Why not let Audrey sing if Harrison singsays? Resacitie? (I don't know the word for talky singing.) You look it up. Start with the Rs.

The King and I circa 1956 Debra Kerr, Yul Brynner, Rita Moreno. Good, even though the King of Thailand, Siam, didn't like it. Nice music and acting in a good fantasy. Yul Brynner is especially good, Debra Kerr, a seemingly lovely and sweet woman was not much of an actress. I saw this one on the stage with Patricia Morrison, who was much better in this part. Julie Andrews would have been better in *My Fair Lady*, too. I like the usually lady-like Deborah Kerr, however.

Thoroughly Modern Millie circa 1969 Julie Andrews, Mary Tyler Moore, John Gavin, Bebe Daniels, The Big Mouthed Blond—a Broadway type, who originated *Hello Dolly* on Broadway. Attractive (beautiful) people singing and dancing in a fantasy that is good precisely because no one will ever take any of it seriously. Laugh and look— well worth your time.

Saturday Night Fever circa 1977 John Travolta Everyone is trying to escape his or her fate. No one succeeds, but maybe one will, we hope. The music by the Bee Gees is good too. *Fever* is now often laughed at because disco has fallen into popular disfavor, but it will be back and the movie is good, much better than most people realized. All the characters are trying to get across the bridge (Brooklyn Bridge in this case, but it is a metaphor.) Alienation theme running through all the situations of the characters.*

Amadeus circa 1994 Tom Hulse, F.Murry Abraham as Soleri, and Jeffrey Jones.

Good because of Hulce making Mozart a fascinating genius. Without Hulce the movie would have failed. Of course, Abraham and Jones are truly good themselves, but the star of the flick (after Hulce) is Mozart.

Best Action Movie: *The Wild Bunch* circa 1971 William Holden, Ernest Borgnine, Ben Johnson, Robert Ryan, Strother Martin, L. Q. Jones, Warren Oats. One of the best commentaries on action—makes *Hamlet* seem like a comedy in the final scene when Gertrude, Claudius, Laretes, and Hamlet die. One supreme moment makes Holden, Borgnine, Oats, and Johnson all lovable in their sacrifice. They kill a hell of a lot of bad guys though. Must be God's plan, or at least He must approve we think. Robert Ryan is the best one in this movie, but he has a great many good performances to his credit. He was always underrated.

Best Movies—foreign

All at Sea circa 1948 Alec Guinness British (Comedy) *
Amilie circa 2003 (?) French (Comedy) *
Seven Samuri circa ? Japanese (war—drawing room-manners) Re-made in this country as *The Magnificent Seven*.
Tunes of Glory circa 1960 Alec Guinness, John Mills, Dennis Price (manners) *

Kind Hearts and Coronets circa 1947 Alec Guinness, John Mills, Dennis Price (comedy of manners with much farce too.) Really British *

Best Movie—Christian allegory

Cool Hand Luke circa 1974 Paul Newman, Strother Martin, George Kennedy, Harry Dean Stanton See this one and think of Christ as Luke. The devil motif in the guard who shoots Luke is clever. The actor playing the part of the apostle John, George Kennedy, is especially good in this film. Strother Martin is always Strother Martin, and he is usually good. I like him in this one too. The Devil motifs in this one make it worthwhile, but without them the film remains one of the top ten, I think.*

Best Looking actresses in the history of the world: Grace Kelley in any / every picture; Audrey Hepburn in *Charade*, and *How to Steal a Million, The Children's Hour* (nothing else); Vivian Leigh in *Waterloo Station;* Julie Andrews *in SOB,* Dana Wynter in *Frauline,* Margaret Sullivan in any Tarzan movie, Doris Day in *Calamity Jane,* and *Love Me or Leave Me.* Claire Bloom in *Limelight* 1951 Hedy Lamar in anything in the 1930s. Kathryn Ross in any potboiler.

Best Looking actors: Jon Gavin, *Thoroughly Modern Millie, Psycho;* Sean Connery, in anything apparently (according to my wife); Robert Taylor (when young—try 1936 *Camille);* Jeffrey Hunter *in 1949 Take Care of My Little Girl.* Richard Gere is handsome according to my wife, and I have always admired her taste in men. She assures me I am more handsome than Gere. Faint praise, I think, but how can I disagree with her?

Best actors mentioned above: Mel Gibson, Ben Johnson, Gene Hackman, James Garner, Tim Robbins, Robert

Preston. (See *The Music Man, SOB, Victor Victoria, Beau Geste,* and *Jr. Bonner* for Preston's value.).

Best actors unmentioned above: Jack Nicholson , Sean Penn, Cornell Wilde (*The Naked Prey*)

Best Athlete in Movies: Fred Astair (no contest**)**

Worst actor mentioned above: Alan Ladd, Mickey Rooney, who always gave more of himself than anybody wanted.

Worst Actors unmentioned above: Rock Hudson, Sunny Tufts, Victor Mature, Stewart Granger, Lyle Bettenger, and Tab Hunter

Best actresses mentioned above: Donna Reed (*From Here to Eternity*); Susan Sarandon, *Bull Durham*; Maureen O'Hara, (*The Quiet Man* and *How Green was my Valley, Rio Grande*) Michelle Peiffer (*Scarface, Witches of Eastwick, Grease 11* and more*)*; Mia Farrow, though I have some personal, irrational no doubt, dislike of her (*Radio Days, Broadway Danny Rose, The Great Gatsby* are superb acting jobs).

Best actresses unmentioned above: Loretta Young, Blythe Danner

Worst actresses mentioned above: Cybil Shepard (in anything) but *The Last Picture Show*; Liza Minnelli, she almost ruins *Arthur,* Judy Garland (except *Wizard of Oz*)

Worst actresses unmentioned above: Raquel Welch, (except for *1,000,000BC;* she had no lines but the ones that defined her. She didn't speak. She is also good in *Bedazzled* because she has few lines and is type-cast— thank goodness. Normally she is awful); Debora Pagent, Natalie Wood, Betty Grable, Betty Hutton, Drew Barrymore, Debbie Reynolds, Sandra Dee, Joan Crawford (in any- thing). These women are bad, bad, bad.

Most Underrated Actors: William Holden (always good), Tyrone Power, Paul Newman see *The Verdict*, and *Absence of Malice* and *The Road to Perdition*. In addition, see *Hud* and *The Sting* and *Butch Cassidy and the Sundance Kid* for great performances by Newman. Dennis Hopper, Humphrey Bogart, (occasionally not good) Gregory Peck, Morgan Freeman, Cary Grant, Tony Curtis (see the film noire flick he made with Burt Lancaster, and see *Captain Newman, MD*)

Most Overrated Actors: Jack Lemon, Richard Burton, Marlon Brando, Robert De Nero, Tom Hanks, (though he is good) Robert Duvall, except for *To Kill a Mockingbird* and the two *Godfather* movies he was in, and Rod Steiger except for *No Way to Treat a Lady* in which he was good.

Great Comedic Actors: Eli Wallach, James Garner, Walter Matthau

Great Comedic Actresses: The Old lady who played the part of Miss Marple in all of the Agathie Christie flicks, and Myrna Loy. (Women are usually not funny, though I have no idea why.)

Most Overrated Actresses: Meryl Streep (though she is good). Shirley McClain (who is always horrible).

Most Underrated Actresses: Maureen O' Hara. See *The Quiet Man, How Green Was My Valley*; Debra Winger in *An Officer and a Gentleman, Cannery Row*, and *Terms of Endearment*, though I hated *Endearment*.

Worst comedic actresses: Lucille Ball, Carol Burnet (Both of these were, are truly terrible and never gave me a smile.)

Best Mother /Daughter Actresses: Betty Field, Sally Field; Blythe Danner, Gwyneth Paltrow, Margret Sullivan, (or is it Margret O' Sullivan?) Mia Farrow.

Best Father / Son Actors: Martin Sheen, Charlie Sheen, Keenan Wynn, Ed Wynn

Worst Father / Son Actors: Robert Mitchum and his sons— though Mitchum is often good, his sons are awful. John Wayne, Patrick Wayne. John Wayne is most often a bad actor who simply portrays his idea of how John Wayne would like to believe that he would behave if he were in those situations. Wayne's only great performance is in *The Shootist* and in that he is superb. It took him a lifetime to find and give that performance, but the waiting and practicing was worth it for that film.

Worst Mother / Daughter Actresses: Judy Garland, Liza Minnelli, Debbie Reynolds Carrie Fischer I suspect that Carrie Fischer could have become a fine actress and outlived the *Star Wars'* thing if she had not been a dope-head. Her performance in *When Harry Met Sally* showed promise, now unfulfilled and now probably unfulfillable. She was awful in *The Blues Brothers* too.

Best Dancer: Male: Fred Astaire (no other great ones) I think Gower Champion might have been a great dancer (see *Show Boat*) but he seems to have other ambitions such as choreography. Gene Kelly was the dancing equivalent of Mickey Rooney and he ruined some movies that would have been especially good. *Singing in the Rain* and An *American in Paris* are diminished by the painful and too, too long Ballets (?) in them

Best Dancer: Female: Eleanor Powell. Almost Honorable Mention Cyd Charise.
Ann Miller is the dancing equivalent of Mickey Rooney, too too much.

Best Singer Female: Doris Day: Honorable mention: Jane Powell, Katherine Grayson.
Jeanette McDonald is not bad.

Best Singers Male: Nelson Eddy, Gordon McCrea (neither could act, but both could sing exceptionally well).

Best songs sung in any movie: "Old Man River" William Warfield in *Show Boat 1951*; Harve Presnell singing "They Called The Wind Mariah" *in Paint Your Wagon 1969*; "Seems Like Old Times," Diane Keaton in *Annie Hall 1977* (And I am rarely a fan of Diane Keaton's.) Mia Farrow sang something good in one of Allen's movies too, though I cannot remember which movie.

Most Overrated Movies: *Star Wars, Citizen Kane, Birth of a Nation, Patton*

Best Performance ever given in movies by anybody: Ben Johnson as Sam the lion in *The Last Picture Show*

Worst Performance ever given by an actor (or actress) who was / is often thought to be good: Doris Day in *Calamity Jane*

Worst Acting family: The Barrymores, especially John Barrymore who was always God-awful, Lionel has his moments as did Ethyl; Drew is as unacceptable as a tattoo.

Most Underrated Movie: *Hollywood Knights*. This movie is a rip off of *American Graffiti*, but it is much better done, and *Graffiti* is quite good.

My Favorite Movies (almost in order) *Zulu, 12'0Clock High, The Americanization of Emily, The Quiet Man, Jr. Bonner, Radio Days, Full Metal Jacket, Four Weddings and a Funeral, SOB, Hollywood Knights, J W Coop, Chocolate, The Pleasure of His Company, The Shootist, Raising Arizona, The Unforgiven, Zorba, The Greek, Amalie, and The Twilight Samuri,* though these last two are French and Japanese, respectively (nineteen)

Most Detestable Movies: (that were thought to be good) *The English Patient, The Bridges of Madison County, Lost in Translation, Ben-Hur, Gigi, Titanic, The Lord of the Rings* (Computer generated movies are a bad sign because as actors become less important. Character is less important; the movie is almost always bad. The Bond movies were a precursor of one- dimensional characterization.)

Best Movie Lines:

"It just doesn't matter" Bill Murray *Meatballs;* "Badges? We got no stinkin badges" *(?) The Treasure of the Sierra Madre";* " Louie, I think this is the beginning of a beautiful friendship" *Casablanca;* "What did you have in mind" Jimmy Stewart in *Harvey;*

"Can't you even try to keep from forgetting that?" (the very best line in all of moviedom) John Goodman in *Raising Arizona;* "Oh Billy, Billy, Billy, Billy, Billy, Billy Billy" Ted Knight in *Caddyshack;* "Do you think he wants some cheese?" Dudley Moore in *Arthur;* "I shot an arrow into the air; she fell to earth in Barkley square" Dennis Price in *Kind Hearts and Coronets.* "Whatcha got?" in *The Wild One* Marlon Brando 1954. "I coulda been a contender, I coulda been somebody" Marlon Brando in *On the Waterfront* circa 1955. (I have never been a fan of the "Here's Looking at you, kid" by Hump Bogart in *Casablanca,* though I like that film.

Best Movie Kisses: Jennifer Jones lays one on Charles Boyer in *Cluny Brown,* a black and white minor movie of about 1959. Gwyneth Paltrow, all of her many kisses in *Shakespeare in Love* 1998, are the stuffs that dreams, and other things, are made of. "It is impossible to say just what I mean, but as if" . . . magic lanterns and screens and that sort of thing.

Best movie of S pear's stuff Mel Gibson's *Hamlet* C. 1996 Mel Gibson, Ian Holm, Glenn Close, Alan Bates, and Rip Torn, I think. This is the best *Hamlet* by far, far, far. Laurence Oliver plays Hamlet as if he is effeminate and reluctant because he is effeminate. Burton and Braneaugh, if that is his name, are too too excruciatingly boring. Gibson has it all right in my opinion.

Oddity #1: I like most of Woody Allen's movies, though I more often than not dislike his ideas. He is anti-intellectual, though he is bright and creative. I especially have taken a dislike to a scene in *Annie Hall* when he and Annie are standing in line to go into a movie and Allen gives us this fantasy, a fantasy he no doubt has and relishes, of a moment when Allen overhears a professor at Columbia abusing an author's work and Allen takes the prof to task because the Prof. cannot see the meaning—"the author's meaning," which is to say that Allen believes that the meaning of the author's work can only be ratified by the intentions of the author—nonsense. Allen sneaks in this idea of the ill-educated on too many occasions for me. I find myself wanting to explain to Allen that if the work of art is to rise to the level of art then it cannot be restricted only to that which the author meant to say. What an artist does, paints, or says must go beyond the meaning of the artist in order to rise to the level of art. We all represent much more than we know and if the canvas or manuscript is to be limited to the author's meaning, much of its value will be lost.

Oddity # 2: Cary Grant made many movies that were especially entertaining, funny, and good, but I can find no influence on me in them, worse luck: *Bringing Up Baby*, *The Philadelphia Story*, *To Catch a Thief*, and *I Was a Male War Bride* (hokey, but somehow entertaining) *Arsenic and Old Lace* are good movies. (Josephine Hull was as good in *Arsenic and Old Lace*, as she was in *Harvey*.) I would love to be influenced by Cary Grant, but Groucho got to me first, and try, as I often do, I am more Groucho than Cary. Pity. I can't list Groucho either, however.

Notice # 1: Hitchcock's movie *Psycho,* is a shocker, but it is only a shocker. The listed movie is *To Catch a Thief.* I liked it, but my gosh how could anyone not like looking at Grace Kelly in that one? Other than the ineluctable beauty of Grace Kelly, *To Catch a Thief* is only a fair movie, not especially good. Movies such as *North by Northwest, Vertigo, and The Birds* are not good. Hitchcock most often stinks. He can only shock and that is a piece of cake. He needs to give his audience a perceptual set in order for them to see the idea and, more importantly, have the "ah hah" inductive moment he strives for. In so far as Hitchcock fails to do what he hopes to do with the gimmickry of pin spots and that sort of audience manipulation, he is a failure. We don't understand movies where we are only shocked. When the movie Psycho I saw first in 1961 was over and the audience poured out into the street, I could see heads together, striving to understand what they have seen, Audiences who are shocked are not set for the action, not "perceptually set" for the scene and fail to understand it until later, if at all. It is easy to shock us when nothing prepares us for what we are about to see and hear. A perceptual set is a recognized psychological term most authors and directors understand. Hitchcock did not know some facets of his profession. It is easy to shock, but it is cheating. Hitchock reminds me of Hemingway trying to write a tragedy but failing to understand the concept. Tsk, tsk.

Notice #2: I list no movies by the admittedly great playwright Neil Simon, though I almost listed the initiation

theme of his early army days movie with great performances by Christopher Walken and Matthew Broderick—
Biloxie Blues? Some idiot does a Jerry Lewis imitation,
however, and hurts the movie, makes me uncomfortable.
Biloxi Blues, I think. The movie centers on Simon's days in
the army just as WWII is coming to a close. Good movie,
not great.

Notice # 3. I cannot make myself list four movies with the
fine actor Sidney Poitier. I thought of listing *The Defiant
Ones* with Tony Curtis; however, I think Curtis by far the
better actor of the two, and Poitier is good, not great).
Guess Who is Coming to Dinner, Lillies of the Field, and a
Patch of Blue are good movies, but Poitier seems to me to
portray nothing more than a smart, nice black man. As an
actor, I don't see much to him. He didn't hurt any movie,
but neither did he make them great, and I can think of
several movies that I think he was at best not good in.
Apropos of little, perhaps nothing, the best black actors
I have seen are, in my opinion, Denzell Washington, Lou
Gossett and Morgan Freeman. I think these three as good
as anyone and a great deal better than most everyone.
These three have great range; Poitier seems to me to be
a kind of John Wayne portraying himself, as he would like
to be in various situations. Had Poitier not been black, I'm
not sure how much acclaim would be his. He was Black at
a nice time to be Black. He was a Black actor. Freeman,
Gossett, and Washington are fine actors, period. (I realize
I am sounding like a scene from *Guess Who is Coming to
Dinner*.)* My personal special special favorite

THE HERO

▬

*H*ave you noticed how well *Spiderman* has done at the box office? And yet another version of *Star Wars* has come along, and it too has done extraordinary business. Box office records have fallen. Why? We need; we want heroes. It's that simple.

Today many people have wondered almost all of their lives about where have all the heroes gone. Since September 11, we have found that they are here among us as they have always been. We need heroes, and we are all glad and proud to note that they are in large numbers all around us. Many of us look on the police and fire departments across America with new eyes, noting the qualities of heroes that must have been with us since there has been an America, and we are pleased to note that there is something good about a culture that has always produced heroes.

In all cultures of the western world, i.e., the Greco, Roman, Judaic, and Anglo-Saxon worlds, heroes take on mythic proportions because the hero is extremely important to our psyches. In ancient Greece, the hero, Aristotle tells us, represented the major houses or families—described as being of "noble proportion." The hero story was one for and about the upper classes because the upper classes were the only ones who knew how to read, could afford to buy books or go to school. Of course, literature was written by the upper classes, about the upper classes, and for the upper classes.

Today, however, tragedy (the domicile of the tragic hero) is extended to the common man. Tragedy as a concept has become democratic and thus even more important than it once was. In ancient Greece, the life of the peasant (there was no middle class) was brutish and short. No one expected the plebian classes to experience anything but pain. Only when there were many among the population who could have some hope of a happy and content life did mankind think of loss of life as tragic, and only in the comparatively recent past has the majority of mankind expected pleasure from the hero story.

In modern life, common people can rise to the level of the tragic hero because we have been taught that we have the right to pursue happiness. When we don't achieve what we have anticipated, or when we have suffered an extremely painful blow from life, we now think that the common run of mankind can rise to the level of the tragic hero. Tragic heroes now can be sales clerks, tire salesman, firemen, or even teachers. They can inhabit any level of society.

The level of pain never determines who can be a hero. In normal pain- experiencing brains, the amount of pain suffered is the same. The measure of tragedy is never the amount of pain, but rather the reaction to the pain determines the tragic hero.

Perhaps the worst pain a person can suffer is the death of his or her child. The poet Walt McDonald has told us that if we are lucky we will outlive our parents, but if we are unlucky, we will outlive our children. It is the reaction of the person to the pain that renders him or her heroic. If one's child dies, then none among us will seriously blame the bereaved parent for his or her suicide, psychosis, drunkenness, promiscuity, or any of a myriad of destructive ways of handling the concomitant angst associated with life's worst blow.

Pathos, the opposite of tragedy, occurs when we see one of our own defeated by life. We may not blame the defeated one, but we are saddened because we have seen one of our own rendered ineffectual by a painful blow—the psychotic, the drunk, the promiscuous, the neurotic have all lost the battle. What we enjoy, not in any macabre sense, is to see one of our species suffer life's worst blow, but not be defeated. The hero is the one who says that he or she will continue to be the best that he or she can be. When Mrs. Rose Kennedy was informed that her son Robert had been assassinated like his brother John, Mrs. Kennedy was asked how she would be able to go on with life. Her answer is the essence of tragedy and the hero: "I will not be vanquished," she uttered. The indefatigable, indomitable spirit of mankind is the basis by which we judge the tragic hero. When we see a hero, then we know that *when*, not *if*, life's worst blow comes to us, we too may be able to display the indomitable spirit that we all need so desperately in order to have the courage to persevere. Mankind has always needed heroes and the tragedy of life and literature has provided the examples we need.

We never look at the hero to see his or her pain, but rather we watch tragedies to feel the pleasure we know we will find in seeing a hero overcome pain to continue to strive against an awe-inspiring universe that often seems indifferent to mankind's needs and desires.

The only difference between the ancient and the modern hero is that now the hero is potentially all and any of us. Mankind has always needed heroes in a world that often seems dark, hopeless, and pathetic.

Heroes have always thrived in cultures that have believed in freedom. Freedom given to us by our God, a freedom that we approve of in our government, is the measure of America and of our place in the world.

In the western world, the idea of freedom was pronounced by the ancient Greeks, whom some say were not really free in their pagan religion because they had soothsayers whose prediction always came true. True, except that the predictions of the tribal shamans were always conditional. Oedipus is told that *if* he is not careful he will commit sin. Oedipus then commits sin, and exactly the one he was running from, but he need not have. Oedipus commits the sin of hubris, the inordinate pride that the Greeks were always warned of. We must be careful of the same sin; we must not believe that we are driven by bad luck, abusing parents, or even the devil. We know that with God's help we can control the devil, and we can control ourselves. To believe that we are not to blame for our sins, to believe that bad luck pursues us, or that we have no real responsibility for our lives is the way toward chaos.

We must believe in freedom, or we are then denied the dignity of a life in which we can make mistakes that a Christian can be forgiven for. John Calvin's belief in predestination and Sigmund Freud's theories of determinism have robbed us of the idea of freedom to be heroes. If we cannot have villains, but merely mentally sick people who commit unspeakable crimes, then we cannot have heroes. If sick persons are not responsible for their crimes, then it must be equally true that our heroes were also merely determined to do as they did. When the firemen and policemen went up the stairs in the World Trade Centers, they were merely conditioned to do so, some would have us believe, but they knew better than anyone else the dangers that they chose to face.

God gave us free will, which allows us to choose evil or to choose the heroic path. If He had not given us free will, then we would be extensions of God, not His creations. The truth is that our God has given us freedom of choice and that freedom has been ratified by a democracy that fosters, even produces, heroes in great number.

On some level, even though we often want to avoid the responsibility for our actions, we know we need heroes, and heroes are popular. They can even be rented for a few hours of movie fantasy, but real heroes abound in America and they always have.

RAMBLINGS FROM A DISEASED MIND
OR THE IDLE THOUGHTS OF A IDLER

———————————■———————————

*T*he soul is a lonely possession. As it has desired to enter a body, it has lost communion with a world of souls. Now it seeks refuge, love, but the desired one must be equally lonely–teeming with physical life and a curious desire to make another of its kind a less lonely possessor and become, in the act, less a lonely possession. A body determined (in the Freudian sense) to return to the minerals should wish to return home with one well-known soul. Comfort for souls and bodies, not surprisingly, lies in giving and receiving. The plan is not perfect, but perhaps a harbinger—most likely a harbinger.

But this is not all. Souls must know they are lonely. Too often defenses are successful, and shades must learn to avoid the traps of the journey: suicide, psychosis, alcoholism, promiscuity, funny pills, lung stuffing smoke, and over indulging with food, drink, excitement—sin with the bad breath of the Devil.

Peace. Peace is all. If the bell rings once or twice signaling a deed worthy of an angel, the lonely possession/possessor cannot hope for more.

Nature dangles, like a diamond necklace, conjunction to keep us in line to the guillotine. We tread lacking bliss to keep our place in the queue, believing the line lasts forever, but knowing a cruel queue is better than the chaos of no queue. Troubled, we are in the eye of God, that strange ubiquitous numinous.

Women know all these facts, having learned early, perhaps in the throes of the loneliness of the search, but they do not want details, and blissfully, dreamily do not acknowledge them. Women, when mothers, know souls better than corporal possessions. If a woman loses her way on the journey and does not know souls better than the secular, she fills the void with things. And it is sad to see one so well equipped for the journey lose her way.

I seek design, a deciphering prayer, but offer no assurances because, as you know, I have only glimpses—through a glass darkly, and these are shards.

REX RESPONSE, ACTUALLY
AN ESSAY AUG 1, '06

———————————————■———————————————

*R*ex, this morning, which now seems so long ago, you said that not everyone gets to, or can, "dis" Poe and Cisco. I think I'll explain a little of both to you. First: Poe.

Poe was important to American letters in that he was of a help to making the detective story respectable. It wasn't academically first rate for some time, but the genre now has some credibility, and Poe is partly responsible. That is a plus for him, I think, though I know several professors around the state who continue to be arrogantly opposed to that type of story.

Secondly, Poe helped to make the gothic tales more readily acceptable in this country. Bram Stoker and Mary Shelley might not be nearly so well-known had it not been for Poe. That genre, however, is of questionable value now. It is, as you can see, cyclical. Some decades we produce none of it then there is resurgence in interest. Poe's name during the revitalization periods takes on more luster with even some who are not eighth graders, normally his staunchest supporters.

The gothic tale, however, had its inception when thinkers were beginning to worry that the industry—the so-called industrial revolution was beginning–and scientists might be able to create something that mankind could not control—the Frankenstein monster. That worry is now obviously one of merit. And we now see a race between technology and philosophy that might have dreadful import for the species Homo sapiens.

Oddly, Poe's greatest and perhaps lasting importance may come not from his creative endeavors, but rather with his comments on how to write, though much of what he says is nonsense. He once said that nothing that is written should be so long that it cannot be read in one sitting—patent gibberish that were it taken seriously would rob mankind of much of its best thinking.

Ah, but Poe's poetry has almost no merit, though I am aware of some few scholars who believe that it has great merit. Poe has his champions even outside the eighth grade.

The major problem with Poe's so-called poems is that they are not sensible. Poe started a school of thought among the French—the so-called French Symbolist Movement where the idea is to generate emotion by the sound of the words, not its sense. The French have only admired the Americans Ben Franklin, Edgar Allen Poe and Jerry Lewis. One can hardly have respect for anyone or any culture that sees Jerry Lewis a thinker. I do not believe Poe to be any better than Lewis.

Poe thought to generate strong emotion is more important than to transmit ideas. He based this presumption on the premise that some words are able to generate emotions that are not concomitant with their meaning. In this he is quite right, but these words are few—certainly not enough of them to justify a revolution in thinking about poetry. And Americans have always believed that emotion is generated when the meaning is conveyed. The French have produced many fine philosophers, perhaps more than their share, but their poets are more often than not, not first rate.

Poe was not an educated man, especially in the humanities. He flunked out of the US Military academy then made a penurious living by writing. Not being educated in the arts, Poe did not know of the methods of writing. For instance, the English language is one that makes sense by word order—our syntax is subject-predicate-object or predicate nominative. Of the four thousand or so languages or so spoken on this planet, very few use word order as thoroughly as we do. If we say that the bear ate the man or that the man ate the bear, the difference is profound, but the words have not changed. Only the order of the words has been manipulated. Our syntax is such that we use subject, verb, object (if one has an object) in that order, so that we know the actor, the action, and the recipient of the action by the order of their words. Hence, in our poetry we use rhyme and meter in their best mnemonic sense, so that the sound may emphasize the sense. To accomplish this feat, we must know when to rhyme and when to vary the meter. Poe knew nothing of either activity. Because of our predilection for word order as an important factor in conveying meaning, we expect the rhyme to be made when sense is made because such rhyme accentuates the sense. And the reader remembers the sense more easily and better or longer. Poe had little interest in making sense.

By the way, languages that do not use word order to convey sense as vigorously as we do have methods that are also beyond Poe's opportunity to use. For instance some languages conjugate as many as five parts of speech. The German language, our closest neighbor linguistically, has a complicated method of ders and dains or some such to distinguish masculine plural and feminine singular and all points between with an ability to know the subject from the object without word order being important. I don't speak German, but many of my friends used German as their foreign language on their way to the doctorate, so I use their knowledge, such as it is in my hands, to make my point. I do speak French, and the French have methods of conveying information with only occasional emphasis, and they count the syllables in their poetry; hence, their poetry is known as syllabic while ours is accentual / syllabic.

Rhyme is easily dispensed within poetry. Conservatively one notices that more than sixty percent of the world's finest poetry does not rhyme. Even Shakespeare refuses to rhyme when he has something important to say not in the context of the sonnet, a form much loved in the six-teenth and seventeenth centuries because of the renais-sance, and it is a form I love. The form is loved by many of us today. In Shakespeare's more mature plays, he rarely rhymes, though in his tragedies and history plays, fully two thirds of his work, his many major characters speak in blank verse, unrhymed iambic pentameter, and the poetry is exemplary.

Meter is harder to control in poetry than rhyme–much more difficult to control–so more craft is needed. Poe uses less craft than is called for because he did not know how to control craft. Poe merely thought that he was better at meter, rhythm, than most writers because he did not know that the variations are as important to poetry as harmony is to music. His poems are thuddingly regular because of his ignorance. The thudding quality is only acceptable to those who are young and those who know nothing of prosody. Critics argue now that somewhere between fifteen to thirty percent of sound feet should be variants. Remember, Poe used none.

For instance, Poe used internal rhymes of all three types because he wanted the rhythm and sounds so important to the French Symbolists (his disciples). What he loses is sense. In *The Raven*, for instance, we hear, or more accurately we are told, of the "rapping rapping" on the door. Internal rhyme in English language poetry is untenable because of our emphasis on sense.

The raven is a birdie that has come calling from the "Plutonian shore" that sometimes says "Lenore" and other times says, "never more." It is difficult to say what he means by these elliptical statements, and I prefer my messages not come by way of bird.

The friendly reader says that the bird is a messenger from the Roman equivalent of hell—the dominion of Pluto and a long way from the Christian concept of hell—to tell the central figure that his girlfriend, his love, is dead, and he is never to see her again. If she were to be in hell, he might well rejoice in knowing that he is not to be cast into perfidy with her.

In short, Poe will time and time again sacrifice sense for sound when the sound ought to amplify the sense and make it more amenable-accessible. He sacrifices sense and revels in his self-generated, self-assurance that he is better in his craft than others when in fact the truth is that he knows little of craft or how and when to employ it. He is, most often, a crummy poet who makes little or no sense, and his meter is childlike. Other than that he is great.

As for the other matter you must think deplorable, my attitude toward Cisco, I can only say that I regret living in a community that has no choir in the high school, no rocket club and no Latin club. I was surprised years ago when you became upset with me because I refused to be a cheerleader for a community. I had never thought of liking or disliking a community for what it does and does not have to offer. I like Cisco well enough that I had rather live here than in Dallas; I had rather live in San Francisco than in Dallas, and I would rather live in Colorado Springs than any of those places I am mentioning. I lived in Dallas, San Francisco, and Colorado Springs before I lived here. I stayed here because my mother needed to be near her mother, and I could help her. Finally one becomes too old to have the nomadic opportunities that we have available in youth. I simply bemoan the loss of opportunities much more than I either like or dislike a place. It really does not seem to me that one likes or loves a place. One simply counts advantages to the disadvantages and chooses what seems better at any one moment. The trouble is that one may become stuck in a place that he would rather not be. That does not mean that one likes or dislikes a place. However, I am always surprised to see that some of the indigenous personnel here have feelings for place. I think that odd.

I am aware that thinking and feeling are not the same. I think Dallas too crowded, and I think San Francisco too foggy, though not too crowded; Colorado Springs is often too cold and Texas often, much too often for me, is too hot. My thoughts are not my feelings.

Joseph Heller once said in the voice of Yossarian that the enemy is the one that gets you killed, no matter his uniform color. Perhaps if one is born in a parochial place then that view of life is the one that directs his or her life. I don't know. I don't have much in the way of feelings for any place, only thought.

By the way I was surprised and pleased this morning when you said that you bore me no animosity. You said, "not going to frown at you," which I now realize probably does not mean any animosity, but I choose to see your words in the best possible light because I have heard from more than one source that you were beginning to organize a letter writing campaign against me, somehow with letters to the *Ft. Worth Star Telegram*. You know how gossip is. I choose to ignore it.

You know I miss those morning sessions you guys held at Dan's place. Many people always pretended to know what you guys were saying. Now, alas, no one purports to know your thoughts so completely.

The "hate" letters I receive are few and unsigned. I receive many fan letters and those are signed. The ratio of for and against is far better on the side of good or for. However, I don't mind the bad; they are often funny and almost always illiterate.

JACKIE BIBBY—THE RISING STAR: TEXAS SNAKE MAN

———————————————◼———————————————

*I*n case you've ever wondered, the holders of world records, as documented by *The Guinness Book of World Records*, receive a certificate, nothing more. For world records in bravery, foolishness, and often just plain stupidity, they get a piece of paper that seems to them a kind of immortality. In Jackie Bibby's case, he seems woefully under appreciated. Bibby, an ex-con, who served 26 months of an eight-year sentence in Huntsville for drug dealing, holds four world records for snake handling. In addition to regularly kissing a cobra on its head (not a record), he has crawled into a sleeping bag with109 rattlers, held eight (large) rattlesnakes in his mouth, sat in a bathtub with eighty-one rattlesnakes, and sacked ten rattlesnakes in 17.11 seconds—all world records. Chevy Chase, in his now cancelled talk show, called Jackie: "The bravest man I've ever seen." I saw that show, heard Chevy Chases' comment and thought he was reserved.

Mark Young, a more experienced evaluator, uttered stronger praise. An editor with *Walden Book Reports* in an exclusive interview recently asked Young, editor of *The Guinness Book of World Records For The New Millennium* "What is the wildest or strangest record you've seen broken or attempted to be broken."

"I think the wildest for me was watching a man [Jackie Bibby] sitting in a bathtub with as many rattlesnakes as possible. That was hard to watch."

WBR: "And he lived to tell about it?"

Young: "He did but he was very, very careful about setting that record." Jackie doesn't get into containers with snakes as often as he has them placed in a tub, sleeping bag or coffin with him. Jackie says that more often than not snakes strike at movement, so he is REALLY COOL. He is absolutely still.

On the night of June thirteenth, he set his most recent world record on the *Ripley's Believe it or Not* show. The record, which Jackie held was for seventy-five rattlers, but he broke his record with eighty-one rattlesnakes tub bound with him. The young lady with whom he was in competition began to involuntarily shake after about twenty rattlers had joined her in the tub. She had the snakes removed then she got out. Seemed reasonable to me. Jackie, on the other hand, has some inexplicable knack for knowing when a snake is about to strike, and he has one of his helpers take the dangerous one out. But the ever-cool Jackie has himself lifted out of the tub, coffin, sleeping bag, still filled with large rattlesnakes, very slowly. He quietly, as if snakes could hear, (they can't) says softly, "Lift me out slowly, don't yank me."

Jackie believes, and who is to dispute him, that snakes have a kind of herd instinct. They feel safer when there are many of them about. When the snakes feel safer, he is safer, Jackie asserts. He has his "container" filled carefully with snakes, but he has them placed at his feet as rapidly as is safely possible. But his real secret is to remain extraordinarily calm, and he does not move a muscle, voluntarily or involuntarily.

Jackie has been bitten five times that required hospitalization and stutters with a slightly glazed look on his face when he says that the pain is immense. Jackie is a man who handles snakes almost every day in ways that most all of us would consider insane or inhumanly fearless. For a man who chooses his words carefully, the normally eloquent Jackie can't find words for the pain. That Jackie is truly afraid of snake bite pain is shocking because it has always looked as though that through some quirk of genes or nurture, Jackie didn't, couldn't experience the same pain and fear that the rest of us do. It is difficult to realize the strength of the ego needs a person must have to overcome such fear. Can a man with such strong emotional need be rational?

"It is really beyond the scope of my language skills to explain the pain," he said, looking down at his boots. I asked Jackie how he got started as a snake handler, and he told me that he entered a contest when he was eighteen and won, got his name in the paper and got the all-important (to him) the adrenaline "high" he needs so much.

That answer didn't mean much too me, and Jackie couldn't understand what I couldn't understand. I told him that I could have passed by pavilions of such contests and it would never enter my mind to enter the contest. He just looked blankly and said, "I dunno, seemed normal to me."

I first met Jackie when he was a student in my English class at Cisco Jr. College in 1969. Jackie didn't have much interest in classroom doings and withdrew passing—WP. I saw him a few months later and he was a prosperous-looking bull rider, trying to fill his card, earn three thousand dollars in a year, to gain membership into the PRCA–The Professional Rodeo Cowboys' Association. Not long, a few months later, he was a soldier, looking good with his airborne insignia shiny as his new pick-up. Soon thereafter, another few months, I remember being startled to read a letter to the editor, a long preachy letter, from The Texas Department of Corrections—prison, written by Jackie. For almost two years, Jackie's letters appeared about once a week in the bi-weekly county newspapers and satisfied the local inhabitants that the Texas prison system produced a perfect, model prison, doing what it should be doing— punishing and rehabilitating. Jackie cleverly proclaimed his regret for his life as an evildoer. I remember thinking that he was an effective writer, and just plain smart. His letters were read, discussed, and popular throughout the county.

When Jackie came home I told him what he already knew, that his letters had made him a celebrity around his home country. Not overly impressed he said, "You know, when the oil played out in the thirties, the smart people left Eastland county while the others stayed here and bred. Ain't too hard to impress some folks." Years later Jackie told me loudly, not surreptitiously, that far from being rehabilitative. prison was a dealer's paradise. He could get whatever he wanted in prison except women, he said. The omission struck Jackie as unreasonable.

Out of prison and "clean," although he had a few illegal relapses, he came back to school and took my class again. I had him speak to all of my classes. He was eager to do so and wanted to make up for his former life by helping others. Like most people who meet Jackie, I discovered I admired him a great deal. Although he is a tough, brawny-looking guy, he is eloquent, seems honest, and is interested in keeping others from the world of drugs, which Jackie refers to as "The Shooting Galleries."

Jackie, always a seeker of the adrenaline high, became a rodeo bull rider briefly after giving up on college.

"I rode a few, but I got on a bunch."

In the army after his brief rodeo career, Jackie volunteered for Airborne and loved the experience of jumping out of planes and became a skydiver. Later, as a civilian, he became one of those who jump from buildings, bridges, and mountains—a base jumper. He got the double-dose high of jumping and thumbing his nose at the law, who particularly frowned on the jumping from a building, under construction, at night, in Houston. Looking back without any touch of nostalgia, he uses a well-rehearsed line that must be a big hit with the people who listen to his testimony: "Nothing but bird shit and idiots fall from the sky." He counsels against looking up to, or for, either. Although he has given up sky diving, he zips around the Davis mountains in a hot hang glider looking like a bald headed Tom Cruise, or maybe more like Goose, coming off a carrier.

Jackie says of his dope days during his cowboy and Army life that he found using and selling to be easy.

"Hell, in those Merle Haggard *Okie From Muskogie* days, cowboys were thought to be patriotic for drinking beer and nobody thought cowboys, and even in the army I was a known cowboy, were going to be doing dope. Man, it was all too easy. I made more money in the army than the generals, unless they were dealing too."

Jackie, who admits to having been in more jails than he can remember, and having been married to more women that he can remember, can explain just how he became who and what he was and is. Most of us can't do that—and maybe don't need to as badly as he does. Learning how he became an alcoholic and user of anything injectable was the path Jackie took to find his cure.

"You have to know that how you came to be a doper is a reasonable process, not something of a big bang of bad luck. The process is something you can understand; otherwise, you'd give in to the Devil and believe you couldn't help yourself. You've got to know God can do for you what you can't do for yourself or you'll be whipped," Jackie said.

Jackie also knows why he puts on snake shows all over the world, and suffers the occasional snakebite:

"When I'm in a sleeping bag full of rattlesnakes, or watching fifty of them or so crawling over me I'm no longer a bald-headed, middle-aged man. I'm on a natural high just as good as when I was a doper, but when the show is over, I remember it now. When I was high or drunk, I could only foggily remember, but now I remember and get high again. Man, it's wonderful. A little pain now and then is worth it."

In Jackie's many trips to drug treatment hospitals, sometimes voluntary, sometimes not, he is satisfied that he has found the reasons for his obsession with drugs and danger. It all goes back to his Momma and Daddy, of course. "Hell," he said, "I think God gave us parents and wives just to blame. I don't want to think I'm just a really rotten son-of-a-bitch."

Jackie's parents gave him sips of their drinks until he stole some beer from the refrigerator and ran off to the pasture to drink it. He said that he doesn't know how many he drank, but "plenty" made him feel just like he wanted to. When he started to school, he was afraid of the teachers, the other kids and everything he could see, including the big yellow busses. Jackie began running off from school everyday, and once when the principal chased him, Jackie threw rocks at him until the principal turned around and went to Jackie's mother for help.

The next day when Jackie returned to school, he found he was a hero with the other kids. That did it. He has wanted the feeling the beer gave him and the adulation of the other kids every day since. A few years later in jr. high, Jackie took his motorbike to downtown Rising Star, north of Brownwood, almost every night and did stupid tricks that often tore-up his bike and himself to earn beer and the odd joint now and then from the older boys. The cuts and bruises and the jeering remarks from the older boys suited Jackie just fine. Just as long as somebody was looking at him, he didn't care what the reason was. He would get drunk and tear-up his motorcycle as often as he could to get high and to get the adulation, or even scorn, any kind of notice, from anybody.

"Today, I even look forward to the attention I get from the nurses when I'm in the hospital for snakebite. They're all pretty nice, you know."

Jackie refers to his father, an ex-cop whom he loves dearly, as his chief enabler. His father never told him no.

"He had to arrest me once on a warrant, but he bailed me out again, kinda quick. Man, he loved me, still does, only now he's proud of me, though he doesn't know why I do the snake shows and wishes I wouldn't. He says for me to tell him what I've done after I've done it. He can't watch any show," Jackie said, somewhat wistfully.

"My father and mother drank too much and probably too often, and they weren't exactly alcoholics, but if you see the parents you love and who love you, drinking too much or too often, even if it's just for relaxing, then a kid thinks drinking is okay. Who knows what comes next? Some will grow up to be alcoholics, some won't. Some chemistry problem in some of us. My world seemed normal to me."

"Momma played the mental illness game all her life. Daddy doesn't understand to this day why she left the house for treatment when things were chaotic. She was good at the game," Jackie said.

He became a better game player than his momma ever was. He was in the mental hospital in Wichita Falls often enough to be on their Christmas card list. Likable and jovial as he is, Jackie makes friends everywhere. The warden and other inmates at Huntsville were probably sorry to see him go.

Maybe Jackie's story about how he became an alcoholic, narcotic user is old hat common now, but his attempts at a movie career are unique. Who would crawl into a coffin with a dozen rattlesnakes for a part in *Walker-Texas Ranger*? Jackie has had several bit parts acting on television shows and in movies, and has appeared on *The Tonight Show* with Jay Leno, and done *The Maury Povich Show*, *Ripley's Believe it or Not*, and many others, notably the popular *Don't Try This at Home* in Great Britain. He believes all his chances at show biz as an actor stem from doing odd and dangerous things like crawling into a sleeping bag, head first, with 109 rattlers. He has become well known to several celebrities who have appeared on TV shows when he has put on his literally death-defying shows as a snake man. These new friends have helped him get small parts in movies and TV shows. Jackie claims James Garner, Jamie Lee Curtis and several other celebrities as

"Plain-fun-folks who want to help me. They're almost all good people, these actors," Jackie said. "I never met any ass-actor, but Garner and Jamie Lee seem really interested in me. She damn near fainted at the sleeping bag thing, and then hugged me. I can take a lot of that," he said, smiling big.

"Still," he says, "the bathtub gig-gag is more dangerous because snakes can see and they strike at movement. I always think that they might get into a fight among themselves, and I'll be caught in the middle, but I love it," he said, smiling, laughing. In a coffin for one show, a rattler wrapped around his neck and squeezed until he thought that he might suffocate.

"My helpers had a devil of a time getting that SOB off my neck, and I didn't dare move," he laughs. "You sure don't want to sneeze or scratch an itch."

Jackie is well aware of the hellish puns he makes. He makes some use of the horror so many of us have for snakes when he puts his hands out in the stigmata position, has a coiled rattler placed on his head, two more coiled on his shoulders like epaulets and hangs two snakes from each hand. There is no need to tell the audience to be quiet and still at that point in his show.

Jackie is better known in Europe than he is in Texas.

"People in Europe seem more intrigued about rattlesnake handling than they are in the United States. I think it is more commonplace in this country than it is abroad. My agent in California has several gigs waiting for us in Europe. In addition, we're going to the Orient. I can't wait."

"I've appeared in London, Paris, Amsterdam, and Cologne. Been to Europe seven times," he bragged with his infectious smile.

Jackie received his ninth bite early this year and spent several days in the hospital in Brownwood. Not long after his release from the hospital, he and I were in a local restaurant when his doctor came in with his small son. The doctor came over and introduced his son to Jackie. The boy, about ten, asked Jackie the question that obviously went through his father's mind: "Why do you do it, mess with snakes, I mean?"

"Just so your father would bring you over to meet me," he said. "If I didn't handle snakes, nobody would be interested in me."

Maybe, I thought, but he would always be interesting. He and I had just returned from a hang gliding trip to Ft. Davis where I photographed, marveled, and watched in horror at some of his near misses while floating above and diving around the local mountain scenery of Ft. Davis.

Just recently, Jackie told me that he was lying to me in 1969 when he dropped out of my class. The story he told me, and I didn't remember, was that his father had been working on an oil rig and had his leg cut off in some horrible accident. Jackie had told me he had to go to work to support his family.

"That story worked on you," he laughed. "If I had been dropped with a WF, I would have been drafted to go to Vietnam, but you gave me the WP. The next year though I joined the army. I really didn't want to miss a good war."

I told him it was a good story, and I probably believed him, but in those days, I didn't fail anybody if he was going to have to go to the war.

"Damn," he said. "I wasted a good story, except I've been telling for years at Narcotics Anonymous meetings how you believed me."

I'd probably believe him today too. He is a champion storyteller, actor, and snake man.

Jackie is proud of his day job as a drug counselor in Stephenville, and he believes he helped his mother to become a functioning, good wife and mother, unwilling and unlikely to run and hide under the protective covering of the mentally sick.

Jackie lives not far from Ft. Worth on the Granbury highway. He keeps a very large python as a pet. His door is unlocked, his name is in the phonebook, but I wouldn't go in uninvited if I were you.

For a complete record of Jackie's daredevil itch scratching and acting activities, with pictures, see: texsnakeman. com.

ALL THE KING'S MEN

$\mathcal{R}$obert Penn Warren is busy in *All the King's Men* trying to explain the Garden of Eden myth almost in terms of the Augustinian Theodicy. He is also almost conventionally Christian in doing so. On the last page of the novel Penn Warren says:

> The Creation of man whom God in His foreknowledge knew doomed to sin was the awful index of God's omnipotence. For it would have been a thing of trifling and contemptible case for perfection to create more perfection. To do so would, to speak truth, be not creation but extension. Separateness is truth and the only way for God to create, truly create, man was to make him separate from God himself, and to be separate from God is to be sinful. The creation of evil is the index of God's glory and His power. That had to be so that the creation of good might be the index of man's glory and power. But by God's help, by His help and His wisdom.

In order for man to have free will, he must be able to be evil. That man can choose evil is the exact Augustinian theodicy. To create evil as Penn Warren says is not the way St. Augustine put the case. To choose evil is the Augustinian way. But I am splitting hairs of participles or something. I'm certainly quibbling, but I want to be exact.

Man can choose to be evil whereas if he had been an extension of God and not a creation there would have been no pleasure for God in being worshipped by a part of himself. In other words we go to church and try to love the life Christ told us about because God gets pleasure from us that way. Funny, isn't it? We go to church because God get pleasure from our worship. I can't imagine how this could please Him so much. That we can get some pleasure from thinking we might not go to hell, though we are never quite sure, is incidental. However, man must seek knowledge, that is, no doubt to me, our nature.

Hence, we have a Garden of Eden myth, a true myth, I believe about when man learns that he is no longer a part of God. At this point mankind has to seek something, either good or evil. If we seek God, God apparently giggles.

All of the above is the Augustinian "Free Will Defense." God has been defended by St. Augustine from the charge of creating evil, and we are left with the question of how an omnipotent God could not keep evil out of *our* world and our lives. (I suppose the world is God's.) And if God is all good as we frequently say we believe He is, could he create evil?

Mankind frequently comes up with the idea that God is either limited in His goodness or in His power, no matter St. Augustine. Of course other Theodicies abound that are as logical as St. Augustinians such as the Ireanean one and the one By Edgar Sheffield Brightman, but Christianity has labeled these heresy. If so, by the way, C.S. Lewis has his heretical moments. In his book *The Problem of Pain*, Lewis talks of some people being improved by God post mortem. This is the ireanran theodicy and a heresy. C.S.

Lewis, a heretic? Surely not. He is a heretic if Christianity continues to label The Ireanean theodicy a heresy.

Milton's *Paradise Lost* is the spoonful of sugar to help the Augustinian theodicy go down, should the reader want or need help with St. Augustine. (No charge).

The funny thing is that God, who could part the skies if He is omnipotent, and proclaim that He is here, but this He cannot do. If he put the wings back on a plane that was falling as many inside the plane might well be praying for, we would know that we have a God. But we are not to know. We are to accept Godness on faith. Hence, if falling and praying for deliverance from a crash, one would largely be wasting his or her time. Better to pray for the forgiveness of sins, I expect. Better chance.

God does not want us to KNOW that he is among us. My how our behavior would change if we knew. Perhaps our free will would be lost. Then God is without pleasure. Apparently that will not happen.

However, I can offer one slight bit of affirmation of separateness from God. When I was five years old, I was going to the candy counter alone at the Majestic theatre in downtown Dallas, I suddenly realized that I was not everybody and that I was alone. I think I realized that the movie I left to go for candy was going on even though I was not watching. Everybody was not me. The feeling was not good. I became lonely, and that is the Garden of Eden Myth for me. Gender realization comes upon us at that time. I decided at that day that I was a boy largely out of whimsy. I still think so.

When we go back to God, to be a part of Him, there will be no gender. My quest began at age five. I started early, but I was stupid about how to proceed on this quest. I think the feeling of being alone hits everybody at some time. Some are lucky not to have the awakening until late in life, but I think the feeling of aloneness is universal, and I suspect the feeling is never pleasant. How unpleasant seems to vary widely. When I question people about feelings like mine at age five, I find everyone has had some sort of similar eye-opening moment that was most often unpleasant.

One thought sometimes leaves me in a painful doubt. When I was in the Marine Corps, at least for the first three years, I had no feeling of being singular in this tumbling universe until I was promoted to sergeant, was transferred, and I lost my friends and that strange feeling came back upon me. I remember walking through the barracks one day and I had the painful remembrance of that time at the candy counter. Later, when I was commissioned I lost the alone feeling again for a while—about a year, a stress-filled year. The feeling came slowly back. I noticed its progression. When I became a company commander as a Captain, the loss of myself as a group member became strong. It has not left me since.

I remember being overjoyed at seeing a close friend of mine come into my company as a Gunny Sergeant. I wanted to hug him, but such behavior never occurs in the Corps. He was glad to see me too, and on a few occasions when we were out of sight and sound of everyone, he no longer called me sir, and I did not mind. He was a professional Marine and he knew the ways of the Marine World. We talked about those we knew in those first three years in the Corps, and many of them were pro Marines. I was surprised how many had stayed in the Corps, but later I began to understand the reason. It is a brotherhood, even though that sounds trite or Shakespearean— Henry 5th. The feeling of loss of something not identifiable is common if it begins at age five or many years later in one's life. Some people find destructive ways to hide the feeling of loss—booze, funny pills, eating too much, talking too much or not eating at all. The Marine Corps is a better way until one retires. A good marriage is a help, but it doesn't work for everyone.

Prufrock and Burden as Observers

Jack Burden of *All the King's Men* and J. Alfred Prufrock from "The Love Song of J. Alfred Prufrock" are observers of life. To call them observers is to say they are not participants. Both characters are passive, not active. Each one is more acted upon than actor. Normally, such people are to be pitied, and indeed the reader of Prufrock may justifiably feel pity for J. Alfred, but Burden is different from J. Alfred. Burden is trying to come to a decision about the extent which he should participate in life, while J. Alfred is paralyzed with fear of being an active participate. J. Alfred is right in that participation is almost always painful. No matter that without being active no great happiness can occur.

Prufrock, unlike Hamlet, cannot ever be galvanized into action. He is a lost and lonely soul, and so afraid of rejection that he will never ask a woman to be his mate. He is doomed to watch, fantasize, and mourn his lost life, but he will not take a chance on being rejected.

Prufrock is led to his question, but he will not ask it. In the first stanza Eliot says that Prufrock is led ". . . to an overwhelming question. . . / Oh, do not ask, "What is it?" The most pathetic aspect of Prufrock's character is that he knows he is afraid. He cannot hide his fear of rejection from himself. He knows he is more Polonius than Hamlet.

Prufrock says, "Do I dare" / Time to turn back and descend the stair, / With a bald spot in the middle of my hair— "Do I dare? / Disturb the universe? / in a minute there is time / For decisions and revisions which a minute will reverse." Prufrock no doubt knows he is only an observer of life and having this knowledge makes him sympathetic to some readers and pathetic to others. Prufrock is by choice apart from the joys and pains of life. Jack Burden is, however, another kind of observer.

Jack is trying, because he has no choice, to make decisions about his own lonely nature as well as about the nature of the universe. The distinction between Burden and Prufrock is that Burden has no choice in his quest for knowledge and that makes him an observer while Prufrock is an observer with choice, motivated by fear. *All The King's Men* would be a far different story without the character of Jack Burden. The novel seems to be a story of Huey P. Long of Louisiana. The parallels are obvious and undeniable, but Penn Warren for the remainder of his life continued to deny the story was of Long. That puzzled most readers, but the story is the story of mankind.

Burden is on a quest that represents Robert Penn Warren's understanding of mankind. A questor is necessary for telling the truth. Moreover, there is another difference between Burden and Prufrock. Burden, when he gains knowledge, becomes a part of the world, an actor. He has to be a part of the world because he has been born, he has been made to leave Eden, but he is not alone, and he knows his purpose is to discover.

In one way, *All the King's Men* is a mystery. Several questions come to any reader's mind. Why is Burden an observer? Why does he have to know what kind of man Willy Stark is? Why does he avoid the physical encounter with Anne Stanton, and why does he run from the Cass Mastern story? The answers to these question and a few more comprise the novel.

Burden is an observer because he has to be. Seeking knowledge is the nature of mankind. The story of the quest is as old as storytelling. Not only does Penn Warren make Jack seek the nature of things, but also the author uses psychological terms and ideas to answer the questions. For instance, Jack psychologically identifies with Cass Mastern and in many ways Jack sees himself as Mastern and does not want to complete the Mastern story for his dissertation because he finds out what he does not want to know—that Cass Mastern falls from Grace. Jack also learns that Willy has fallen from Grace as does Adam, Anne, the judge and all the others. This knowledge is the knowledge that Jack does not want. Jack avoids Anne Stanton for the same reason. He does not want to have knowledge, carnal knowledge. Jack must look, seek, but he does not want to know. Jack looks carefully at Anne, but he does not come to know her. He sees her as an innocent little girl; he describes her as having pigtails and as small and innocent as Eve; but he does not want to leave the Garden of Eden (Penn Warren 294-295). Later when Jack discovers Cass Mastern's fall, he is disappointed and afraid because he sees himself, and perhaps all of mankind, as Cass Mastern. Jack runs from this knowledge because he is afraid of this knowledge. Afraid as he is, he cannot stop his knowledge-quest because the nature of mankind is to know. "For life is Motion toward Knowledge)" (Penn Warren 150).

Jack's quest for his father is his major quest of interest. The judge is his surrogate father who, ironically, he later finds to be his real father. Jack questions Adam Stanton when he asks Adam if the judge had ever been broke (Penn Warren 210). Adam is the Adam as Eve is the Eve, and when Adam innocently confirms Jack's question about his father, the Judge, by telling Jack that the Judge had been in financial trouble at one time, Adam destroys himself (Penn Warren 210).

Hence, Adam who is the most motiveless character in the novel, is a mythical Adam more than a psychological character. There is no valid psychological reason for Adam to kill Will. Mythically though, Adam who is good, kills Willy, who is evil, and the war between good and evil continues. However, Adam ironically destroys himself by telling Jack what Jack does not want to know. Jack, the observer, discovers that his real father has fallen too, just as the judge's friend, Governor Stanton has fallen. This knowledge emancipates Jack, and the emancipation of Jack is the greatest irony in the novel.

Jack had to observe, even though he was afraid of what he might learn, but the knowledge that Jack gains allows, even pushes him to become a part of the world. Jack is afraid to gain the knowledge of mankind's fallen nature, but as the novel ends, Jack lingers awhile in the Garden—the city of Burden's Landing and then decides that he and Anne will go out into the world where they will continue to learn and to know pain. They will go ". . . into the convulsion of the world, out of history into history and the awful responsibility of time (Penn Warren 438). Jack becomes a participant in the world, not merely an observer, and this is the difference between Jack Burden and J. Alfred Prufrock—the difference between two characters who once had much in common.

Works Cited

Warren, Robert Penn. *All The King's Men.* 1946 New York: Harcourt Brace & Co. 1996.

Eliot, T.S. "The Love Song of J. Alfred Prufrock." *The Norton Anthology of English Literature.*

Ed. M.H. Abrams. 5th ed. New York: W.W. Norton & Company, 1986. 2174-2177.

POETRY, POETRY HISTORY, AND POETICS

———————————◼———————————

*A*bout 3000 years ago on the island of Lesbos, near the island of Samos, near Turkey in the Mediterranean, a Greek woman named Sappho wrote lyric poems, many of which are extant in fragment form— many long fragments. She is the first lyric poet of whom we have knowledge. At close to the same time the epic poem appeared. The ones most people are familiar with are *The Iliad* and *The Odyssey*. Homer, whoever he was, probably a blind troubadour who had found the traditional way for the blind to earn money, wrote these stories which had no doubt been passed along in the oral tradition for about 300 years before he wrote them. The Greek, Trojan (Turkey) war probably took place somewhere near 1200 BCE, but equally as probable, the written versions are unlikely to have appeared until somewhere between 900 to 700 years before Christ. So, poetry is old and because the Greek plays are verse plays, poetry is the only written literature we have of that time period. It took the printing press in the 1400s before literature could be produced cheaply enough so the slowly emerging middle classes had something to read. After prose, Aristotle's *Poetics* would have to include prose and Aristotle's work would have to have been named Literaturetics, not poetics, which was all of literature,—somehow unwieldy.

Greek poetry was written in dactylic hexameter because that was the way of their language. Dactyls are sound feet in three syllables in the order of a heavy stress, followed by two unstressed syllables. This is represented graphically as /uu. Hexameter, as one can see, is six sound feet per line. Thus they wrote eighteen syllables per line. In English, the most common meter is Iambic Pentameter, which is an unstressed syllable followed by a stressed one—represented as u/. This stress pattern is known as the iamb. This then is, of course, ten syllables per line. Imagine the difficulty of a novel in metric form. However, in Shakespeare's plays, the major characters of the history plays and the tragedies speak in Blank Verse, which is another way of saying unrhymed Iambic pentameter. Imagine how hard it is to write such dialogue for these five act plays. The difficulty of writing a fourteen line sonnet (iambic pentameter in a prescribed meter rhyme) is daunting, but writing a verse play requires enormous, almost unbelievable talent.

The difficulty of such a task accounts for the scarcity of the epics. The major ones generally considered to be masterpieces are *The Iliad, The Odyssey, The Aeneid* (Virgil C.19 CE), *Beowulf* (C. 750 CE), *The Divine Comedy* (C. 1400), and *Paradise Lost* (1667). Other epics exist, but most of them lack greatness, fall short of art. Longfellow's *Evangeline*, which many students through the years had to read in the eighth grade is in Anapestic Hexameter, which is unstressed, unstressed, stressed or uu/. This meter in now frequently called "galloping meter." It sounds like the *The Wililam Tell Overture* or the theme song from The Lone Ranger. It is not long before such a meter begins to cloy, to irritate.—da da DA, da da DA, da da DA. Nobody reads Longfellow now, thank goodness.

Zooming ahead, I come to modern poetry. Modern poetry, in one sense of the phrase, can be said to have begun slightly after the last sound shift. Modern English began about fifty years before the birth of Shakespeare, who was born in 1564. Modern English, an amalgam of Anglo-Saxon English and Norman French, made word order an important part of the method of conveying thought, which is to say the syntax became subject-verb-object in that order. In many languages when the word order is changed so is the meaning. In English, for instance when we say the bear ate the man or the man ate the bear, we have changed the meaning, but we have not changed the words, only their order. Old English and Latin for example were languages that worked in different methods. In English, we conjugate only verbs. Other languages conjugate nouns, pronouns, adverbs, and adjectives as well as verbs. In these languages word order does not carry the same meaning in the way we do in English.

In addition, while on the subject of language, the time is right for mentioning the role stress plays in conveying meaning. Stress in our language conveys implied meanings in the way that other languages most often cannot. As example, if a person says: the young GIRLs are pretty, aren't they. The stress on the word GIRLS, may, probably does, imply that the young boys are not so pretty. However, in the same sentence one might stress the YOUNG girls are pretty, aren't they? The strong implication here is that the older girls may not be so pretty. In addition, that same sentence that stresses AREN'T THEY? is an insistence that the speaker is to be agreed with. Thus, in English our stress that not only carries meaning, but it is used for beauty. We use controlled stress patterns to carry a sort of music can be. Stress patterns should be controlled in many forms of poetry. Take the sonnet again as the best possible example. Read and listen to yourelf this sonnet by Shakespeare:

30

When to the sessions of sweet silent thought
I summon up remembrance of things past,
I sigh the lack of many a thing I sought,
And with old woes new wail my dear time's waste.
Then can I drown an eye, unused to flow,
For precious friends hid in death's dateless night,
And weep afresh love's long since cancelled woe,
And moan the expense* of many a vanished sight.
Then can I grieve at grievances foregone,
And heavily from woe to woe tell o're
The sad account of forebemoaned moan,
Which I new pay, as if not paid before.
But if the while I think on you, dear friend,
All losses are restored and sorrows end.

Hard, if not impossible, to beat this music of the iambic pentameter in Shakespeare's hand. This sonnet is number thirty of approximately 154 by William Shakespeare. The number is hard to determine because he included at least three sonnets, perhaps one or two more, in his plays. When one considers the difficulty of this rigorous discipline—fourteen lines of five sound feet with two syllables each or a total of at least 140 syllables in the poem with a prescribed rhyme scheme that makes beautiful sense, one realizes that Bach and Shakespeare and perhaps a few thousand others from the beginning of time have been touched by God.

But back to accent: approximately 400 words in English are spelled the same, but have different meanings. The word REcord is a noun; reCORD is a verb and the words have entirely different meanings, which we know by syntax and sound. More examples: think of the record. Is it a verb as in the sense You, record this. In this instance the position of the word <u>record</u> in the position of the verb. <u>You </u>is the subject; <u>record</u> is the verb. This we know from the position in the sentence. The English language syntax is subject-verb-object, in that order. Thus, if one says to another "The record in on the shelf." We know that record in this sense is the subject. One way to ascertain is by sound; the other way in the written language is position in the sentence.

Notice the word CONtest and contest: contTEST is the verb. CONtest is a noun, thus fit to be subject or object. Again, one should notice that meaning in English is expressed, and it may be implied. And the difference between a subject and a verb may be due to accent or stress. We have a nice language to convey meaning and beauty. Other languages have limitations that English does not. It is safe to say that the great Eskimo novel will never be written. Of the approximately 4000 languages spoken on this globe, only a few have the potential of English. The Spanish language has the potential for great beauty—many fine poems and novels in Spanish, but so far it has not been the vehicle for science.

Most essays do not take the textbook time to delve into detail about the music of poetry, but without much detail, notice the rhyme in English. It is largely a mnemonic device, but rhyme at the end of the line is a recent (since the last sound shift in English) occurrence. In English, we native speakers have come to expect a kind of sense to be made when rhyme is made—a mnemonic device. English is known as an accentual-syllabic language. French, on the other hand is a syllabic language, which is to say one cannot expect French poetry to accent a word in order to elevate it or give it a special meaning other than that for which it has occurred in its history. "The young girls are pretty, aren't they?" in French has no particular meaning by implication. English is better in some fine ways. French is a language of euphony, which is to say the speakers look for the beauty of the sound and the rhythm, sometimes at the expense of meaning, especially for non-native speakers. In other words, one must almost be born in a French speaking country in order to understand its idioms.

Many, perhaps most people, think of poetry as the least of the art forms. Often people probably believe poetry is a lesser art form because it is so easy to dabble in poetry. One needs only pen and paper or word processor to play poet. Most people have tried on some occasion to write a "Roses are Red," or a limerick, or the words to songs or poetry and have discovered that it is rather easy to find rhyme. Thus, they conclude that poetry is an easy endeavor and not particularly pertinent to their lives. Actually, fine poetry is almost impossible to produce. And poets should be, in my opinion, venerated here in the U.S. the way they are in South American countries, for instance. In the U.S. poetry is certainly the most maligned of the art forms. Several reasons for this downfall exist.

In any other art form a would-be artist must make an extended effort and everyone knows this. In order to play a musical instrument a wanna be must purchase the instrument, and be devoted to the instrument for a minimum of two years, several hours a day, at least in order to be in a high school band. How one considers sculpting is beyond comprehension. Money, time, and considerable effort, plus talent somehow discovered are required in order to think of being an artist. Poetry, on the other hand, is for dabbling at no cost of time or money. Not understanding the difficulty of the art form, most people came away from dabbling unimpressed. Then too, note that poetry is taught poorly in the public schools because we require too many English courses to be taught. So many English courses are taught that the non-English majors are often used to teach English. The difficulty of teaching students to write, which means to think is daunting. These stymied English teachers do not know enough about poetry nor writing to teach it.

Hallmark greeting cards are a problem too. What one finds in such cards is verse, not poetry. In this case, "verse" is pejorative. Then too, we have lately the phenomenon of "cowboy poetry." The so called "cowboy poetry" is frequently amusing, but it too is not poetry. Much more often than not it is rhymed short stories. I like much of it, but it is not poetry. Almost all adjectives placed in front of the word "poetry" are pejorative.

Another reason for the demise of poetry in the last fifty years is the rise of technology. The poetry of the Romantics in the late 1700s and the early 1800s, this is the poetry of Wordsworth, Coleridge, Blake, Byron, Shelley, Keats, was directed to the newly emerging middle classes. A higher education was not necessary for the understanding of poetry that was often meant to infuse the middle classes with vigor to fight for the political power that normally comes with the rise of middle classes. Poetry since we have records of it has always been directed to the well-educated upper classes. They were, of course, the only ones who could read, go to school, buy books and so the poetry was about them, to them, by them. Only in the British Romantic period does this direction of poetry begin to change. The Romantic poetry was easy to understand and the emerging middle classes were being taught to read. It is often said that in the Romantic period about fifty percent of the population could read on some level. I doubt that the percentage of close readers extant today is different from the Victorian Age.

However, in the Victorian age which followed the Romantic age, poetry began to be re-directed to the upper classes. Victorian poetry was harder to read, but it kept its audience. Alfred, Lord Tennyson, himself middle class in spite of his title, received a now famous letter from the British Railway System asking that he not announce his arrival or departure times because the attendant crowds disrupted the train schedules. Poets since about 1965 have been able to travel unnoticed, more is the pity.

The major Victorian poets are Alfred, Lord Tennyson, Robert Browning, and Matthew Arnold. Those close to them in power of the word are A.E. Housman and Thomas Hardy. Other good poets exist from that time period also, but the ones named are considered the best.

The Victorians differed from the Romantics in interesting and perhaps somewhat predictable ways. First, the Victorians disliked the subjectivity of the Romantics and made their poetry more objective. In doing so, they began to direct their poetry to the upper classes again. Hence, the Victorians wrote poetry harder to read than the Romantics. The Romantics wrote poetry to celebrate God through nature, as well to agitate for social reform. In their objectivity quest, the Victorians used settings for their poetry from other time periods and places other than England. Quite different from the Romantics who had to write about the here and now in order to make their points about what had gone wrong in their society.

Robert Browning used the Renaissance in Italy as the setting for many of his poems. Tennyson and Arnold went back to ancient Greece more often than not. The point here is that everyone has difficulty in being objective about what is happening at the moment, but when the time and the place differ from the present, the difficulties in finding objectivity decrease. The Victorians did not tell the masses what was wrong in their present day so much as to present the eternal verities: honor, love, duty, courage. These verities are harder to successfully write about because they are often inferred. However, the Victorians wrote poetry that was harder to read and consequently lost some of their audience, though certainly not all as the famous letter to Tennyson indicates.

During the Victorian period the better educated audience for poetry got together on Sunday afternoons to hear the poems of the Victorians read by those they deemed to be good readers. However, as time passed the moderns, largely led by T.S. Eliot and William Butler Yeats wrote poetry that was increasingly difficult to understand. And this increasing difficulty happened at the time of the rise of technology. Poets should have tried somewhat, at least, to compete with recorded music, radios, and the rise of prose the flickers: movies, but no they became inflamed with Greek Mythology, and in the case of Yeats, passionate with Irish folklore about which most English language readers were unaware and disinterested in. Yeats goes on with his personal arcane beliefs about history, which became for him occult, and became for most would-be readers boring: too difficult to understand. Both Eliot and Yeats needed readers with especially good educations. College professors loved them, but most readers yawned and said too tough to understand for me, and poetry began its march towards death. Pity.

Both Eliot and Yeats are great poets and those who have read and understand them are passionate about their heroes, but they killed poetry and made train and plane travel in anonymity possible for poets. For the last forty or so years, poets have been trying valiantly to write accessible poetry so as to gain an audience. So far, their efforts are unnoticed. There is no help on the horizon. Publishers can't take the chance on losing money, so the trouble in finding books of poetry, real poetry, not drivel by Jimmy Stewart, and the blond Thighmaster seller (Suzanne Summers), is almost impossible. Only the subsidized university presses will publish poetry today, and it is a good thing to do to keep the venerable art form alive. More dark days lie in wait for fledgling poets. Emily Dickenson, a superb poet, once said: "Publication is not the business of poets." She is right. Please re-read the poem by Dylan Thomas at the beginning of this little book. See who he writes for.

Poetry once transmitted sophistication to the young. Now, Tom Cruise and others of his ilk became the purveyors of cool. Professional athletes and actors transmit the would-be and often-is culture today. We have no difficulty understanding them.

In a country that allows boxing as a sport, the purpose of the sport is to drive the blood from the brain of the other fighter. Barbaric. And in a country that pays actors and professional athletes far better than it pays its medical researchers, we find our values skewed, and classical music and poetry languishing, panting for an audience. William Carlos Williams, an internationally known pediatrician and superb poet once said: "You cannot get the news from poems, but men die miserably every day for lack of what is found there."

Another reason for the demise of poetry as an art form is the "Verse Libre" movement (free verse). Free Verse for most people seems to be a deterioration of the discipline of poetry. Free verse requires neither rhyme, nor metrical patterns. Thus, bright students often ask the question of if the poem doesn't have rhyme and meter, why isn't it prose? The question is a good one. The answer is that rhyme and meter are not the only ways to elevate language. Free Verse poets are careful to eliminate the prose elements from their poetry. They are careful to omit the inessential elements of prose. Poetry requires most of the time, inductive reasoning rather than deductive reasoning of prose. Inductive reasoning requires reasoning from the specific to the general whereas deductive reasoning proceeds from the general to the specific.

Prose proceeds from line to line making sense, one hopes. Sentence two makes sense in light of that which was said in line one. So that when we finish an essay or a book, if it has been carefully written and carefully read, we know at the end of the last word of the last line in the book what the author is saying. Poetry, on the other hand, may be written in a way that the second line seems to have no relationship to the first line. However, when the reader finishes the poem, sometimes more than one or two readings may be required, he or she will have the Ah Hah experience-the revelation or epiphany hits us at that time and for us that is the time for the pleasure. Why we find such an experience a pleasure is unknown, except mankind has to search so that when we discover, we are pleased. Without inductive reasoning we would not enjoy the television program that has run for more than twenty years known as "The Wheel of Fortune." We watch the program and compete with the contestant to see if we can "see" what the words are. When we are successful, we are pleased and entertained. The quality of poetry that requires us to reason inductively is known as 'compression." A good example in poetry is "The Death of the Ball Turret Gunner," by Randall Jarrell.

> From my mother's sleep I fell into the State
> And I hunched in its belly till my wet fur froze.
> Six miles from earth, loosed from its dream of life,
> I woke to black flak and the nightmare fighters.
> When I died they washed me out of the turret with a hose.

The first line is difficult to understand—"fell into the State"? What state? Nevada? A state of torpor? What does the poet mean? We have to proceed with our reading to discover. The question that leaps to mind when we are reading this poem for the first time is what is the antecedent for "its"? Continuing, we began to gather enough information to have an inkling of the meaning. "Six miles from earth," is 30,000 feet. We are in an airplane. We remember from World War II movie about the turret gunners. The turrets were on bombers, and they were plastic bubbles jutting out from the bottom of the aircraft. Now we know that the fur is the fur of the flying suit. At 30,000 feet the temperature in non-pressurized planes is close to zero. Hunched in its belly is a slang term for the fuselage of the plane, so the reference here is that the poet is talking about his being born from the belly of his mother and immediately finding himself in the belly of the aircraft that along with the poet belongs to the state—the state of America. Now to proceed to the "loosed from the dream of life," which also is puzzling until we continue to read.

The fourth line here is the key to his meaning. "I woke to black flak and the nightmare fighters" refers to the anti-aircraft fire from the ground and the "nightmare fighters" to the enemy attacking planes. In other words, the poet is having an intensely revealing moment that is so intense that everything his first eighteen, to twenty–five years of life all seem inconsequential at this moment. Note that the first experiences we have are especially important at the time, but the poet tells us that those formerly exceedingly important moments have now been like a dream from which at this moment he awakens to a horrible reality.

The last line shows us what we know but do not want to believe. The warrior is inconsequential to the war. A fifty caliber bullet or piece of shrapnel (torn-jagged pieces of meter from the exploding anti-aircraft shells may rip through the man, but not do serious damage to the plane. The plane, unlike the gunner, may be repaired and back into the war in hours.

If one has seen the funeral of the assassinated president Jack Kennedy, he or she has seen the funeral of a very important man. His funeral was a pageant that took three days and consisted of the rider-less black stallion with empty boots turned backward in the stirrups. The caisson carrying the coffin was draped with the American flag and the mourners walking along behind the casket at the death march—sixty steps per minute instead of the regular 120 steps per minute. His funeral was a way to say that this was the death of a very important man. Compare that to being washed out of the Turret with a hose and you see the message of the poet.

Each line of the poems carries important information that the poet wants his readers to have, but if he told his story the way that I have just tried to, we would not have the emotional impact, that burning in the breast, that the best poetry leaves us with.

Briefly, probably too briefly, a discussion of the details of the writing of poetry—methods of elevating the language other than compression is difficult to pen or pin down. Literally hundreds of forms, about two hundred known in English, exist. From sonnet to Octava-Rima to villanelle to many more forms in which the rhyme and meter differ. Form, technique and meaning are the ways to discuss and think of poetry. Ottava-Rima for instance is a form of poetry that requires the poet to write eight line stanzas in iambic pentameter with the prescribed rhyme scheme of abababcc. The sonnet, as almost everyone knows is a fourteen line poem in iambic pentameter with one of two usual rhyme schemes. The older of the two, sometimes known as the Italian or Petrarchan form, uses a rhyme scheme of abbacddcefgefg. This kind of rhyme scheme is designed for what is known as the enveloping method. The main idea is expressed in the As, while the supporting ideas are expressed in the Bs. Tough to make sense in? Yes. The English or Elizabethan form is rhymed ababcdcdefefgg. This form is easier in some ways and more difficult in others. The last two lines of the English sonnet is a couplet that somehow summarizes or makes a comment on the preceding twelve lines. Even Shakespeare had difficulties in some of his sonnets in accomplishing the couplet well. The problem with the Italian form is obvious, except that the Italian language requires vowels more often than the English language. Hence, the rhyme is not as difficult, although the enveloping idea is still especially difficult. Other slight variation may occur in these forms, but think of the difficulty of the meter, the rhyme, and saying something of note. And then think of the hundreds of other forms used by poets, each having a somewhat better method to justify the choice of form.

A poet needs to know the history or the development of his or her craft and such minimal details as the iamb, trochee, dactyl, anapest, and spondee and other arcane matters usually known only to the devoted aspirant, or knowing reader. The purpose of the poets in controlling the rhythm (meter) of their poems is to establish the rhythm in the reader's minds only to vary it at the propitious moment. One of the finest examples I know of is by a now deceased little-known poet whose name is not important, unfortunately. This poet's one really fine poem is entitled "Mining." The title refers to the mining for gold as a metaphor for finding love. The best line in the fine poem reads: "The love that rose came slow as pans of gold." The poem is in iambic pentameter, but the variation that is so important to the poem occurs in this line. The first sound foot is "The love.' This is an iamb because the first syllable—"The" is unstressed and it is followed by a stressed syllable "love." The second sound foot is "that rose" "that" is unstressed and "rose" gets the heavy stress. Thus far we have two iambic sound feet. The third foot is the variation of the rhythm. The "came slow" is a spondaic sound foot that is a variation from the common iambs found all through the poem. Both *Came* and *Slow* are stressed. If the entire poem is unvaried the poem becomes soporific. Variation is similar to the harmony in music. It is necessary.

The third sound foot has both syllables stresses. When the reader notices, and he or she will notice, the change in rhythm to a spondee causes the reader to have to slow down and emphasize the foot. The reader slows his reading pace at the time the writer wants to emphasize the idea of came slow. Love, he says, comes slow as the panning for gold. After the third foot, the line reverts to the iambs of the poem. In other words, the "as pans of gold" are two iambic sound feet, properly used, emphatically used. Some critics say that variation may be used effectively for close to thirty percent of the poems. Fifteen percent variation is a must.

Poets come in groups that can be identified. These groups were and are: Academic poets, Student poets, "Beat" poets, and Poetry Society Poets. The academic poets are just what they sound and seem to be. These men and women who years ago would have been eking out a perilous living by their writing are now employed by universities to teach creative writing. Oddly, as the audience for literature has diminished, we in this country find more students than ever interested in trying their hands at making some literature.

The academic poets know their craft, the history and tradition of their art, and know when to apply the form needed for the kinds of poems they write. They are, for the most part, traditional. Good poets, most of them, but sometimes predictable, though usually interesting. Some critics of present day poetry point to the similarities of these poets who have often been the products of creative writing schools and "workshops." Poetry labeled workshop poetry is usually predictable, and the comment is meant to be something of an insult.

A second group of burgeoning poets are the student poets. These students too are often, almost always, products of the same schools as their professor poets. However, they are frequently more experimental than their professors, and they turn out a great deal of published modern poetry.

A third group known as the "Beat" poets, not a creative name, but reasonable, have as their mentors the Whitmanesque, Alan Ginsburg, Lawrence Ferlingetti school of poetry. This group has some antipathy for the academics whom they consider to be "locked in" to the history and tradition of poetry, thus failing to agitate the establishment and do they what the "Beats" think of as their duty to generate new thought through new forms and themes, failing to achieve variety in technique and form. These poets are often malcontents or subterraneans who complain much about society and its inequities. These poets add much to the field of poetry and have much to say of value. However, readers often have to wade through too much fulminating poor poetry to find that which the "Beats" have to say. Sometimes, too often perhaps, their poetry sounds more like fiction. But these poets have an audience, and they do a great deal to revitalize poetry.

The fourth group is The Poetry Societies, which have been ever increasing in number for about thirty years now. These societies are puzzling in many ways. They are often antiquated in that they admire William Wordsworth enough to emulate him and offer themselves praise because they rarely write free verse. However, in ever increasing numbers and contests, the poetry societies keep the name of poetry in the face of the public. For this accomplishment it is hard to berate them, but too often their poetry is old fashioned and convinces readers that what they had been taught in school was poetry has not changed. In fact, poetry has gone through several revolutions since the publication of *Lyrical Ballads* in 1798.

Contests in art may not be a good idea. The difficulty of proclaiming who is the best artist usually has to wait for time to pass so that the readers may check on the accuracy of the poetry and the method, which may or may not be favorable to many different people. Communication requires a sender and a receiver, but some receivers may legitimately be inclined to yawn at that which many others bow to. The reception of art is subjective. Even the passionate few can frequently disagree about what the best is. Proclamations about art are usually found to be foolish by later generations. Emily Dickenson was told that her poetry was "mere vague jottings." No one reads James Whitcomb Riley today. No one reads Longfellow or Robert Lowell, the elder today. Better not to proclaim who is best today in art of any type. However, we can say what is awful, but we don't have many "Awful" contests, although I wait for the Bulwer-Lytton contest Every year.

- Waste

A STUDY OF THE IDEAS OF ST. AUGUSTINE, BISHOP IRENAEAS, AND EDGAR BRIGHTMAN IN C.S. LEWIS' THE PROBLEM OF PAIN

In the preface of his Book, *The Problem of Pain*, C.S. Lewis says, ". . . I have believed myself to be re-stating ancient and orthodox doctrines."
-Ah yes, Mr. Lewis, we might say, but which ones?

*I*t is clear that when Lewis is discussing ideas which express theology, he believes himself to be referring to Augustinian ideas. Perhaps he is correct, but some of his thoughts cause him to offer an eclecticism which includes the ideas of Bishop Irenaeus. In addition, Lewis embraces some of the ideas of Edgar Sheffield Brightman , though he may not know whose ideas he is happening upon. Lewis only speaks of St Augustine when he deems it necessary to give credit. Lewis must have thought he was writing for a popular audience, not a scholarly one and did not deem it necessary to offer documentation for borrowed ideas.

With regard to Brightman, Lewis was writing his book, *The Problem of Pain* in 1940, and Brightman's two books on the subject of Theistic Finitism were originally published in 1930 and 1931, respectively. Lewis, thus, could have known of Brightman's work, though there is no mention of Brightman in Lewis' book, including the index. Neither Brightman nor Irenaeus is mentioned, though Lewis mentions Augustine four times throughout his book. John Hick's emendations and elaborations of the writing of Irenaeus occur after the writing of Lewis' book, of course.

At any rate, Lewis had read Augustine, and occasionally thinks with Brightman and Hick. That Lewis had no knowledge of either man does not alter his alignment with their thoughts and indeed make speculation more interesting.

Of theodicies in general, Lewis makes an initial comment that theodicies have never been formulated at the beginning of a religion. His point here is that no one has ever inferred from the course of events to the goodness and wisdom of the creator. Only after a belief in a God has been accepted does man purport to explain how evil does not disallow a belief in God. Lewis' point here is that religion, universal in mankind has no origin in the rational, but religion arises from fear, dread, and awe. Such an explanation of the origin of religion, stemming as it does from the irrational, is odd considering Lewis' main purpose of his book is to give rational explanation (however unorganized) for the experience of gratuitous pain and how it does not or should not prevent mankind from holding to a belief in God. In the *Problem of Pain*, Lewis is attempting to do what theodicies do—to justify God's way of dealing with humans. The worship of gods, whether out of fear, awe, dread, or not, and the ethical discussions of philosophers have little to do with one another, yet the subject matter is the same. Fear, awe, and dread might be some revelation that requires the analysis of philosophers. Lewis makes this point when he says that mankind's philosophers should be about their task of philosophical analysis. ". . . when the numinous power for which they feel awe is made guardian of the morality to which they feel obligation"(22)

Divine Omnipotence

After having established that mankind worships because of some inexplicable universal need or compulsion, Lewis proceeds to the heart of his examination of pain and evil. Lewis says that the problem of pain or dystelogical surd is made difficult in that the terms "good" and "almighty" are equivocal. Lewis seems to be moving towards Brightman's position of Theistic Finitism, which is to say God is limited in power at this point. However, Lewis's first point is about the "almighty" is actually "the free will defense."

One can attribute miracles to God, but one may not logically attribute nonsense to Him. "There is no limit to his power," Lewis says. "If you choose to say God can give a creature free will and at the same time withhold free will from it, you have not succeeded in saying anything about God" (28). Obviously, Lewis asserts, a creature with free will may choose to disregard any revelation about God. Free will is a limitation on the power of God, but is a limitation God imposes on Himself. Lewis simply means that omnipotence does not mean all-powerful, but rather means all the power that exists.

After reading Lewis' thoughts on the subject, one is likely to come to the conclusion that Lewis is a reasonable thinker who may or may not be familiar with the Augustinian theodicy. Lewis may be just one of thousands and thousands who have read St. Augustine's thoughts without having given a close reading to them. Lewis asserts:

The inexorable laws of nature which operate in defiance of human suffering or desert, which are not turned aside by prayer seemed at first to offer a strong argument against the goodness or power of God. I am going to submit that not even omnipotence could create a society of free souls without at the same time creating a relative independent and inexorable nature. (29)

Lewis's statement here seems to place him in the Augustinian camp, but does not because Lewis does not see nature as a product of a fallen mankind producing a natural evil as a punishment for sin and retribution; however, it is equally obvious that Lewis does not see nature as a "vale of soul making" a la Hick. What one sees in this statement of Lewis' is a limited god who lacks power, if not goodness, to alter the laws of nature for the benefit of mankind.

In one extraordinary passage, Lewis employs ideas from three major theodicies. The reader may well walk away mumbling incoherently after trying to inject order into the following passage:

. . . and this is far from being an evil: on the contrary, it furnishes occasion for all those acts of courtesy, respect, and unselfishness by which love and good humor and modesty express themselves . But it certainly leaves the way open to a great evil, that of competition and hostility. And if souls are free, they cannot be prevented from dealing with the problem by competition instead of courtesy. And once they have advanced to actual hostility, they can exploit the fixed nature of matter to hurt one another. The permanent nature of wood which enables us to use it as a rafter also enables us to use it for hitting our neighbor on the head. . .

We can perhaps conceive of a world in which God corrected the results of this abuse of free will by his creatures at every moment: so that a wooden rafter became soft as grass when it was used as a weapon, and the air refused to obey me if I attempted to set up in it sound waves that carry lies or insults. But such a world would be one in which wrong actions were impossible, and in which, therefore freedom of will would be void. . . . That God can and does, on occasions, modify the nature of matter and produce what we call miracles, is a part of the Christian faith. . . (33).

Starting with the end of the above quotation, Lewis has invoked mystery as part of his answer. This is the same sort of mystery Puccetti accuses Hick of being evasive with. Puccetti's claim was perhaps exaggerated, but in Lewis these appeals are blatant appeals to non-reason. One occasionally accepts mystery or the efficacy of feeling over reason (usually as an adjunct to reason), but not in an argument that depends on reason.

The first part of Lewis' statement is a familiar one. The nature of matter cannot be such that wood in a rafter has strength to support, but when wood used as a weapon cannot be used to batter. One does not expect God to be unreasonable with matter. Mankind would perish quickly in such an unpredictable world. This is a Brightmanesque limitation that Lewis fails to cite as a limitation on God's power. Lewis merely says that free will would be void, not that God can give and withdraw free will as the inclination suits him to protect mankind from evil.

In the first part of Lewis' quotation, Lewis uses "the free will defense" when he says, ". . . if our souls are free they cannot be prevented from dealing with the problem by competition instead of by courtesy" (39). In this bit of reasoning, Lewis is using an old familiar argument well known to religious philosophers. Lewis asserts that there is no way to exclude the possibility of suffering; pain, he says, that pain is the order of nature and the existence of free will.

Lewis contradicts himself toward the end of this aspect of his argument when he argues for God's omnibenevolence and omnipotence. "His own goodness is the root from which they (His acts) all grow and His own omnipotence the air in which they flower" (45) Obviously, when Lewis is discussing the nature of matter—the wood—he concedes a universe in which God is not all-powerful. At least a better definition of omnipotence should precede his assertions.

Omnibenevolence

Lewis moves more in the direction of Hick when he comes to his chapter on God's goodness. In the beginning of the chapter, "Divine Goodness," Lewis makes the interesting assertion that there is kindness in love; but Lewis adds that mankind should not make the erroneous assumption that love and kindness are the same. Lewis notes, "As scripture points out, it is bastards who are spoiled; legitimate sons, who are to carry out the family traditions, are punished" (41). Kindness separated from love, he says, ". . . involves a certain indifference to its object, and even something like contempt of it" (41). Lewis continues by pointing out it is only for those we love we require happiness on any terms. His point is that we would rather see our children and lovers suffer than ". . . be happy in contemptible modes. If God is love, He is by definition something more than kindness" (41). If Lewis is correct, the record of mankind shows that God has never shown us contempt. For mankind, we find reproving rebuke.

In his rebuke, God corrects his loved children. This statement, of course, reflects Hick's "vale of soul making." In His reproval, God corrects and moves mankind toward becoming worthy objects of His love. We are says Lewis, something that God is making. God, according to Lewis, goes to great length and great trouble to try to perfect mankind. The irony here is upon occasion mankind must wish for less love from God, not more, but in order for mankind to become lovable, he must be altered by His God. This is a "fallen mankind" (Augustinian). For Lewis that God is improving mankind at the moment, not a Hickian, slowly altering mankind moving toward perfection at an "epistemic distance" from the Creator.

At this point though, Lewis seems slightly more aligned with the Irenaean theodicy than the Augustinian one that one suspects Lewis would acknowledge. Without knowing the full Irenaean and Hickian important of his words, Lewis has said that mankind is born in the image of His God, but must be helped, even in the next world, to become more in His likeness. This is, of course, not punishment, but teaching mankind. For Hick and to only a slightly lesser extent for Irenaeas, God is all good, so He will not sentence anyone to hell forever. This is heresy for much of organized Christianity.

Lewis uses many more analogies in this chapter to try to prove his point. He compares God's love of mankind to a man's love for a woman. In this love, Lewis says that a man in love does not cease to care how the woman behaves or looks when he comes to love her. No woman would regard a man's love of value if he fails to care how she looks or behaves. God's love for mankind is of this same caring nature. Just how the love continues is a different question.

Other analogies abound in this chapter, but his point is clear. One increases his care for the object of his love, so that the love may be made complete and certain. That this complete and certain love may continue always is God's plan, Lewis believes. When Lewis says, "What we would call here and now our happiness is not the end that God has chiefly in view: but we are such that He can love without impediment, we shall in fact be happy" (48). The reader can be certain at least, of Lewis' position for the moment.

It cannot be that mankind shall ever find true happiness in this world. Lewis believes that the improving of mankind continues in the next world. The only comment that Lewis fails to make that would coincide with Hick is that Lewis never says that all objects of God's love will receive it. In fact, in later chapters, Lewis devotes some effort to ratify the idea of eternal hell—a non-Hickian concept. Then too Lewis states for mankind to become lovable by His God we must become altered. This is a mankind for Lewis who because of "the fall," has sinned and is not at present lovable by His God. There are similarities between the Augustinian and Irenaean theodicies, but they are not pointed to by Lewis, even when he has good opportunities. Whether Lewis did not know of the Ireanean theodicy is not important because Lewis could have seen when he was deviating from the Augustinian ideas. Perhaps Lewis knew what he was doing or failing to do, but he did not want to be the rebel. Perhaps, he thought a good Christian does not cause doubt, and perhaps Lewis thought that any admitted deviation from the Augustinian theodicy might seem to be a heresy.

Nevertheless, Lewis deviated. Lewis' position is that God is as good to mankind as He can be, but that some pain improves and instructs mankind and is thus a good. This argument is common, but Lewis is pragmatic in that he sees God as improving a fallen mankind who requires punishment for improvement. For Lewis the improvement continues in the next world, although some will be in hell with no hope of improvement. How good is good then?

Human Wickedness

In discussing human wickedness, Lewis is largely a preacher who tries hard to convince his reader that mankind is wicked. His concern with doing so would seem to be unnecessary except that wickedness throughout history has thrived precisely because the wicked have not seen themselves as wicked. Even Adolph Hitler probably thought himself to be on a path that was ultimately leading to virtue. And if the wicked have thought themselves correct, is it not true that Lewis' readers also need to know that just because one thinks himself correct, one has no reliable evidence upon which to proceed. So . . . the reader continues assessing the origins of evil as Lewis presents his ideas cloaked in a sermon.

Lewis says that mankind needs to recover the old sense of shame. Just how old is old for Lewis he does not say, but "originally" and "old," may be coterminous here for Lewis.

. . . the effect of psychoanalysis, on the public mind, and, in particular, the doctrines of repressions and inhibitions. Whatever these doctrines really mean, the impression they have actually left on most people is that the sense of shame is a dangerous and mischievous thing. We have labored to overcome that sense of shrinking, that desire to conceal, which either nature herself or the tradition of almost all of mankind has attached to cowardice, unchastity, falsehood, and envy. We are told to get things "out into the open," not for the sake of self-humiliation, but on the ground that these things are very natural and we need not be ashamed of them. But unless Christianity is wholly false, the perception of ourselves which we have in moments of shame must be the only true one, and even pagan society has usually recognized "shamelessness" as the nadir of the soul. In trying to extirpate shame, we have broken down one of the ramparts of the human spirit.

Most readers would grant that a sense of sin is essential to an even semi-successful Christianity, but the idea of mankind as "fallen" in Lewis' passage is obvious. This concept of psychoanalysis is a concept proceeding from a fallen, non-Irenaean theodicy. In addition, Lewis says,

> Many schools of thought encourage us to shift the responsibility for our behavior from our own shoulders to some inherent necessity in the nature of human life, and thus, indirectly to the Creator. Popular forms of this view are the evolutionary doctrine that what we call badness is an unavoidable legacy from our animal ancestors, or the idealistic doctrine that it is merely our being finite. (56)

This view of mankind is openly in opposition to Hick's view of "soul making." More importantly Lewis is now not speaking of a loving and reproving God so much as he is speaking of the machinations of a malignant evil manifested in the culpable science of the nineteenth and twentieth centuries. A psychoanalytic monster of Frankensteinian proportions has been loosed by a fallen mankind. The reader sees the danger, or so Lewis hopes.

Lewis' opinion of the fall of mankind is that it exists, according to Augustine, to guard against: ". . . two sub Christian theories of the origin of evil produced impartially the effect to which we give those two names and Dualism." Dualism is the idea that God produces good while some independent and equal power generates evil—Manichaeism and Zoroastrianism.

In the monism of which Lewis speaks only the idea of evil exists, and it is an illusion, if this idea, found in Hinduism, is true, the illusion is strangely pervasive.

The ideas of Monism and Dualism are apparently so offensive to Lewis that he is prepared to accept the idea of "the Fall" as preferable to any other idea of the origin of evil. One interesting point about "the Fall" for Lewis is expressed when he says, "I have no intention of arguing that the descent of modern man to inabilities controlled by his remote ancestors is a specimen of retributive justice" (71). In other words, "the Fall" is not a completely satisfying explanation for Lewis, though he does not rush to other organized thoughts—at least does not rush consciously or overtly to the camps of Brightman or Hick. Perhaps he fears to confuse the average readers for whom he seems to be writing.

Lewis' interesting ideas concerning the "the Fall" deal with his efforts to refute the prospect of modern science having disallowed the idea of "the Fall." It is Lewis against the ideas generated by modern science –the interpretations or meanings of science. Lewis has no objection to science, just the misinterpretation of it.

Many people think that this proposition has been proved false by modern science. "We must know," it is said, "that so far from having fallen out of a primeval state of virtue and happiness, men have slowly risen from brutality and savagery." There seems to me to be a complete confusion here. . . . If by saying that man rose from brutality you mean simply that man is physically descended from animals, I have no objection. But it does not follow that the further back you go the more brutal—in the sense of wicked or wretched—you will find man to be (72).

Lewis continues his evaluation of "descent" by pointing out that mankind comes to know about his ancestors by examining his artifacts. "Clearly the prehistoric men who made the worst pottery might have made the best poetry" (73-74). Lewis is on weak ground in this speculative argument. The poetry of Shakespeare is clearly better than that of the author of *Beowulf*, and many critics would agree that the general poetry of today is better than the general poetry of Shakespeare's day. And no one disputes the idea that the artifacts of today are, or will, signify a better corporate culture than that of Shakespeare's day. The common moral evil of today seems, because of technology, to be no better than that of long ago, but the passage of time and lack of technology dims the memory of special brutality whereas instant communications vividly broadcast the triumphant evil of today, making the present day seems as bad, or worse than former times. Though even today, the passage of time reduces our vivid awareness of contemporary horrors.

Lewis again treads on very weak ground when he uses analyses of animal behavior. So much knowledge has been gathered about animal behavior since 1940 that Lewis is obviously wrong when he says that animals are better in some behaviors than man. Lewis was simply wrong in his choice of animals when he said lions are better to other lions than man is to mankind. He could be right, but recently we have learned that lions are only nice to other lions in their own pride, not all lions.

Lewis' attempt to justify the Augustinian theodicy by pointing to a noble-savage beast is the weakest part of his discussion of the wickedness of mankind. In fact, in Lewis' attempt to justify "the Fall," he formulates an argument that Hick would like. "For long centuries God perfected the animal form which was to become the vehicle of humanity and the image of Himself." Later in this argument, Lewis says, "Then in the fullness of time, God caused to descend upon this organism, both on its psychology a new kind of consciousness which would say 'I' and "me". . .(77). This is the Image and Likeness themes of Hick. Lewis differs from Hick in that he doesn't use the term "likeness," and Lewis conceived that the time that "likeness" descended upon mankind was a time before "the Fall."

Lewis concludes his thoughts on "the Fall" by saying, "That if paradisal man could now appear among us, we should regard him as an utter savage. . . ." As for early man as an archetypal representation of modern man, Lewis says, ". . . man as a species, spoiled himself, . . (73). Thus after interesting speculative forays into other thoughts, Lewis returns to the safe net of Augustinian captivity.

Human Pain

Finally, after having educated his reader to his satisfaction, Lewis addresses the idea which prompted his book—human pain. After what Lewis perceives to be his reader's adequate preparation, Lewis treats the subject of pain primeval as having remedial or corrective good. But there are moments when Lewis says that pain may be a "vale of soul-making." Lewis is purposefully ambiguous, perhaps.

Initially, Lewis states "The Free Will Defense" when he says, "When men's souls become wicked they will certainly use this possibility to hurt one another; and this, perhaps, accounts for four-fifths of the suffering of men" (89). But beyond human greed, brutality, and general churlishness, there is much suffering which cannot be attributed to mankind. Lewis, of course, refers to natural evil. All of man's pain cannot be traced to remediation or moral evil; consequently, ". . . not all medicine tastes nasty. . . ." Lewis has his humor (note The Screwtape Letters); however, there is little humor in most of Lewis' thoughts, but a certain slant of ambiguity remains. Placing one foot tentatively in each camp—Augustinian and Irenaean—Lewis says, "We are not merely imperfect creatures who must be imprisoned: we are as Newman said, 'we are rebels who must lay down our arms.' " The "improvement" is soul making; the laying down our arms is Augustinian.

Lewis spends the majority of his effort in this chapter trying to convince his reader that mankind deserves their pain—preaching to the choir. In addition, Lewis regards thousands of years of free will as having been more deeply ingrained in man's nature than only a few years might have done. Lewis refuses to be pinned down with regard to time, but when he says "years" the reader knows that Lewis views time as having corrupted the desire to battle God deeply into man's psyche. Lewis succeeds in not alienating some readers by discussing the garden as though it were literal, and Lewis carefully avoids the wrath and scorn of scientists who would, perhaps quibble about thousands or millions of years. However, time notwithstanding, Lewis is tacitly agreeing that God might at least partly work his will on mankind by allowing or forcing on man free will. But in addition to free will, mankind is persuaded, for good or ill, by an evolutionary process of time passing. These "allowances" by Lewis also place him in both the Augustinian and Irenaean camps. One of these ideas, free will, is essential to every point that Lewis makes, and one idea, soul making, allows Lewis to equivocate when free will runs into plausibility troubles.

Lewis' principal argument is the familiar one: pain is good for a person. Lewis says, "Paradoxically, mortification though itself a pain is made easier by the presence of pain in its context" (92). This facile argument holds little interest for religious philosophers, but it is evidence of a "soul-making" orientation for Lewis. Remediation or corrective pain holds value for both the Augustinian and Irenaean groups, but Lewis leans heavily on the Irenaean group upon occasion. Lewis says, "God whispers to us in our pleasures, speaks in our conscience, but shouts in our pain: it is His megaphone to rouse a deaf world (93).

Other Irenaean remarks include those concerning pain: ". . . he either rebels (with the possibility of a clearer issue and deeper repentance at some later stage) or else make some attempt at adjustment, which if pursued will lead him to religion" (95).

The interesting points here concern what Lewis doesn't say. For instance, if pain occurs to improve the "bad" man, what about the idea that all are fallen? Why are there such gradations of bad and good except that some are further along the road to remediation? To use this obvious argument might cause some of Lewis' readers to become alienated from his argument. The point might seem to be too much the Irenaean one. Lewis is frequently quiet in such interesting moments. Lewis might see himself as the great reconciler, but he is not intrepid. Occasionally he is paralyzed with such fear—fear of confirming the anti-God thoughts of some readers, perhaps. Having explained the pain of "the fallen" or the "bad," Lewis pushes on to pain caused by natural evil—a more difficult and more interesting subject.

In fact, the subject is more abstract than Lewis might wish. Lewis does not directly address the issue from "natural" causes except to explain as best he can that tribulation for mankind is necessary. He must mean that pain beyond that pain which is inflicted by our fellow man is necessary. "If tribulation is a necessary element in redemption, we must anticipate that it will never cease. . . ." Later Lewis says, "We are never safe. . . " (107). It is not hard to see why. The security we crave would teach us to rest our hearts in this world and pose an obstruction to our return to God. One cannot help but wish that Lewis had not been so circumspect and had explicitly said if he believed that pain would continue in the next world as the soul-making continues. This deduction would appear logical from Lewis' other statements; but he is often vague and inconclusive beyond that which one must occasionally come upon in this type of abstract thinking.

Hence, Lewis lightly treats the subject of "natural" evil and as much as dismisses it as though it is not a thinking person's problem to the extent that he finds moral evil to be. However, the inference to Lewis' predilection for which theodicy, though not complete or final, would no doubt leave many readers guessing that Lewis accepts many tenets of the Irenaean theodicy. Lewis primarily wants to be God's good servant. Like Milton in the first book of *Paradise Lost* who strongly echoes the Augustinian theodicy, Lewis wants to "justify the ways of God to man." But unlike Milton, Lewis selects from three theodicies to do so. Only a very little of Lewis' thinking comes from any idea that God is limited (which omits much of Brightman), but much comes from Augustine, and some of his ideas come from the theodicy of "soul-making," which comes from the emendations of John Hick's Irenaeus thoughts.

One last thought. One reason Lewis does not pay much attention to natural evil, the pain that comes from floods, earthquakes, and tsunamis is that he might have to conclude that God is limited, though that limitation is one God imposes on Himself. Hence, if the wings come off your airplane and you spend the time of your fall praying for God to re-attach the wings, you have wasted your time. Better to pray for the forgiveness of your sins. If God committed miracles all the time, mankind would know that God exists. Apparently God would take no pleasure in worship if that worship is imposed by knowing He exists. We are to take God on faith, not knowing. That gives Him more pleasure. Lewis refuses Brightmanesque edge of thought. C.S. Lewis. *The Problem of Pain*. (New York: Macmillan Publishing Co., Inc. 1976)

For Ireanaeus, humans were not the perfect, pre-fallen creations of the Augustinian tradition, but rather creatures starting a long slow process of growth. Humans are free creatures being processed into becoming children of God. The vale-of-soul making of creatures born at an epistemic (a distance on the diminsion of knowledge) distance from God, not as spatial distance. Through struggle, free-willed creatures who can be made acceptable in the eyes of God. Thus, for Irenaeus no one will be put into hell forever. Such a situation is static, but mankind does not come from a state of perfection from which they fell, but are moving toward perfection. No one will go to hell forever because there could be no purpose in such a situation. God creates and continues to create, even post mortem. For Augustinians, this thought is heresy.

Augustine says that because of the moral evil or the fall of mankind comes all evil, even natural evil—earthquakes, floods, disease. But earthquakes, floods and disease occurred long before man appeared on this earth. Some fossils show that some animals suffered from arthritis. And life preyed on life. Eternal punishment for humans would serve no purpose.

ABOUT THE AUTHOR

—————————————■—————————————

Cleatus Rattan, holder of the Mayborn Chair of Arts and Science at the University of Mary Hardin-Baylor as Professor of English, is a former Poet Laureate of Texas and a Distinguished Alumnus of Texas A&M University at Commerce who is the author of five collections of poetry. His book *The Border* (Texas Review Press 2002) received the *Texas Review Poetry Prize* and was later selected for study by University Interscholastic League for High School students across the state of Texas for UIL competition in literary criticism. Rattan is the first living poet to be so honored. National Public Radio interviewed Dr. Cleatus Rattan and asked him to read four of his poems for the second inauguration of the President Bush, the younger. Rattan attended seven universities and earned five degrees from four of them: Southern Methodist University, the University of North Texas (two degrees), Hardin Simmons University, and Texas A&M University—Commerce. Rattan claims not to be well educated, but he is, he says, frequently educated. *Take Your Time Coming Home* (Texas Review Press 2005) was entered for the Pulitzer Prize. *Funeral for Sparrows*, published by Trilobite Press 2007, was sponsored by the University of North Texas English Department and Friends of the Library at UNT. *Funeral for Sparrows* contains the poem, "Clarity," which received the *Descant* award for Best Poem of 2007.

Cleatus Rattan was elected "Most Handsome Boy" in his sophomore and junior years of high School. He was not nominated for this distinction his senior year. He continues to question the taste of his classmates. Bushism in Florida, he suspects. In that same year, 1952, his junior year, Rattan played the part of Nanki Po in the Immortal Irving High School production of *The Mikado*. Some say the strains of "A Wandering Minstrel I" continue to waft through the hallways of the old, non-venerated building. The reviews were inconclusive, however. In that same year, his junior year, the actor, singer was voted by his senior football team teammates as "The First Man to Hit the Ball Carrier After He Was Down." The thought of such an honor makes his eyes grow moist even now.

Cleatus Rattan was formally proclaimed an "Outstanding Graduate" of The Irving Independent School District in 1992. However, he had to agree to attend the award ceremony and say nice things about his old high school to receive the award. An obvious attempt to make up for the "Most Handsome" fiasco in 1953.

Rattan is married to the former Connie Hood of Borger, Texas. She was a school beauty for each of the three years it took her to earn a music degree from the University of North Texas. Her highest degree is MA in English, considering that their three sons are all doctors of one sort or another (One is a PhD, another is a veterinarian, and the third is a podiatrist), her sons and husband continue to adore her in spite of her lack formal education.

Si post fata venit gloria non proper   Martial

(I have no idea what this means)

(I lied. I know what it means.)

ADDENDUM

INTELLIGENTSIA AND IMPEDIMENTIA

■

Cleatus Rattan

Charlie Eliot and James Conant, former presidents of Harvard worked together at separate times to help education, but in some ways they have failed in their mission. Charlie, known as such by the students at Harvard, decided that the "dead" languages were an impediment to modern education and had outlived their usefulness. *Usefulness* is a difficult concept. For one thing, the study of languages, most languages, and perhaps the study of the ancient languages, Greek and Latin, helps us to master our own language. Language is the method not only by which we have shared ideas, but also it is the method by which we think. To lean a new word is to learn a new concept--a new way of thinking. To increase one's vocabulary is the single most important endeavor a student may undertake, but all students at all universities should at least study modern foreign languages and learn "other" ways of thinking. All else depends on the language. I will brook no argument on this premise. Accept it or go read something else.

Charlie's move was the beginning of the so-called comprehensive education, which was to embrace usefulness. The study of business became an important study for college students. I am not sure that was a good idea. I suggest a liberal arts education followed by a few courses, carefully chosen, business courses or even many courses, if one believes as I do, that *many* would mean no more than about 30 college hours should be devoted to business. Business is a vocational matter and better left to schools other than universities. (The study of economics is another endeavor.)

However, the progress of the business curriculum has reached a feverish state so that the MBA has become the watchword on most universities. More and more courses in business are found on the undergraduate level and liberal arts classes have become fewer.

Of course this is not true on the best universities campuses. A student pursuing graduate business studies at Yale, for instance, can discuss the ideas of Plato with anybody, but this is far from true in the second and third-rate universities, which must accept students not as well-endowed or as well prepared as the best universities insist upon.

Not long ago, the United States Navy had a low moment known as *The Tailhook Affair*. Officers and supposedly gentlemen groped women vigorously and in large numbers in a hotel hosting the navy pilots. Admittedly these men and now some women live on the edge of death at high speeds, and they grab at life as vigorously as they groped these women. Admirals were fired and the navy suffered a large, noticeable black eye. One result of this notorious affair was a study that concluded that the Naval Academy would begin to offer more courses in the liberal arts, courses that help us to understand ourselves. Before *Tail Hook*, the Naval Academy offered degrees only in engineering. These gentlemen knew little of the manner of gentlemen. Now midshipmen may take degrees in literature, philosophy, psychology, and sociology. The Naval Academy is better now it has changed and increased its offerings.

James Conant, a brilliant man as was Charles Eliot, increased the concept of usefulness until it became studies such as woodworking, and auto mechanics and many other non-arcane endeavors that require learning and are indeed useful, but these studies are not intellectual and do not belong in the college curriculum. But, you say, these studies are important in the public schools. Yes, they are important for high school students and for our economy and for our culture, but universities are not designed, nor need they be designed, to handle such vocational tasks. The time to study ideas and look far into our future when we may merge human intelligence with technological intelligence must occur in our universities. We need a curriculum that is designed to help students acquire knowledge that one will be apt to use to continue to acquire knowledge from thinking because technology is growing not at a linear rate, but rather growing exponentially. This exponential growth means we must look far down our path as a species and as a culture, not to study business as a useful endeavor of the moment. That is too narrow for the thinkers we must have. Entrepreneurship, however, will be needed to expand the value of ideas—a matter of only a limited few courses.

This brings me to the study of theology. The trouble with theology as a study is that it is designed to increase belief, and as such it is not as analytical as it should be. Mere comparisons (an area of theological study that does promote some analysis) do not promote thinking, only confirmation or perhaps for some a disbelief. This ambition for a study is not enough.

Thus, I suggest that business majors and theologians should never be in charge of inquiry, which is the best idea and pursuit of universities. Theology, like business, can be an interesting study for those already acquainted with the best ideas mankind has to offer. However, theology is far too limited and far too conservative (excluding a few thinkers such as Marcus Borg, Elaine Pagels, John Shelby Spong and several others) to be of extraordinary value to mankind's pursuit of knowledge. Theology looks back and forward thinking is the necessity for Homo sapiens to continue on this planet.

Of course the theologians won't like this essay any more than the church liked the heliocentric idea or the telescope; however, many of them adore John Calvin—more evidence to curse them with.

Chant with me here: "No Business men, No Theologians In Charge of Institutions Devoted to Thought." Repeat and repeat and repeat. We have little time. The world, lippin full of non-thinkers, is intent in its ignorance and arrogance on destroying the species. We must hurry. The enemy is already inside the gates. We must close the gates on the theologians and the doctors of education administrators who have never read a book filled with the best thoughts of mankind. Think of the disaster of an MBA, EdD administrator.

MORE OF THE SAME

■

Thinking

It is my frequently, non-hurried, clearly considered, and reluctantly-formed opinion that the great majority of Homo-sapiens stumble to death after long and short lives without ever having given birth to even one thought. We are taught firmly and with passion that we are to accept the soporific doctrines and tired and unproven "concepts" of our seniors whom we are fiercely taught to have respect for by bible and convention.

Emerson said, "Whosoever would be a man must be a nonconformist." Most of his listeners and readers agreed with him and began as best they could to conform to his ideas. Jean Paul Sartre recognized Emerson's problems immediately. Sartre refused to accept the Nobel Prize for his works proclaiming existential philosophy. He had to do this in order to convey the idea that no one should accept the body of thoughts of another until he or she had analyzed these thoughts. He could not agree that he held a body of thought that others could line up behind him and say this is what I believe: I am an existentialist. Oddly, if we follow the existentialist Sartre and say we are existentialists, then we are not; but if we say we are not existentialists, then we might be.

The world's great ideas, about which almost no one knows, come from non-conformists such as Jesus and Socrates, and a few thousand others. Jesus was crucified for no greater reason than he thought that the Hebrew way was wrong, even though the ideas had merit. Jesus ate meals with the unclean, prostitutes, tax collectors, and others in an unclean state, at least unclean according to the Hebrew bible. He touched the dead (extremely unclean), touched women in their unclean time or the month (Lev. 20:18). And worst of all, he threw the money changers out of the temple, telling them that they were the unclean. The priestly class (the money changers) were an inherited class.

In other words, Jesus, a good Jew, upset the status quo. In this we see danger, and we rely on the old way as the safe way. The ministry of Jesus, whether one year or three, depending on which gospels one accepts, would not be so long today as it was in his time. With the technology of TV news and the immediacy of the world, Jesus would be deft of thought and feet to escape for more than a few months.

Socrates was guilty of no more than "corrupting the youth of Athens" by teaching them that this world is not the best of all possible worlds. The world is never the best of all that is possible, but those in power do not want, will not allow, anyone to think differently today as was the case then in Athens.

And, Jesus and Socrates sacrificed themselves so that we might learn to think. If they had not been crucified and poisoned, we would not know their names and that alone is the petty reason that they sacrificed their lives. Mankind would have forgotten them had they not died for ideas.

Jesus and old Soc were thinkers, and they wanted others to be thinkers. To try to make others think is to be unpopular and a dangerous undertaking. No one in universities wants to try to teach freshmen because they have never thought, and they resist thinking. Year after year of trying to fiddle with freshmen is painful. Thinkers do not like them, except in some fields. Some fields of what we erroneously call thought are not fields of thought in the analytical, inquiring mode. Business and theology studies, while they require brain power, do not promote analysis in the pure sense.

First, business. The world needs entrepreneurs, desperately and for a variety of valid reasons, which should be obvious. However, the thinking required is more recognition of situations for which methods of solution have already been discovered. To recognize and sometimes to discover which method should be employed may require nothing more rigorous than trial and error. Obviously not many people can recognize the needed methods, nor can many learn of the almost innumerable possibilities. Intelligence is needed to do well in the study of business, but inquiry for the sake of inquiry is a foreign idea for those who inquire for that which is known. The study of business, even though it requires intelligence, is not an intellectual endeavor.

The trouble with theology is that the purpose of theology schools, not philosophers of religions, is to confirm beliefs already held. The theology folk are afraid to inquire. The closest they come to thinking occurs on the rare occasions when they undertake comparative theologies. However, theologians are almost always frantic in their support of already known and widely held concepts. New concepts bring their wrath in the defense of the status quo.

In September of 2011, I delivered a lecture to the theology faculty of my university on the subject of the major theodicies, and I pointed out where they were similar and where they differed. In addition, I noted a popular lay Christian theologian who failed to notice when he crossed into ideas held to be heresy by Christian theologians. I quoted passages from books by C.S. Lewis when he was spouting St. Augustine's (C. 350 C.E.) thoughts (the thoughts held to be the only acceptable ones to Christians) and then I quoted passages where Lewis was echoing ideas held from Bishop Ireanaeus (C. 150 C.E.). Ireanaeus is held to be a heretic, but his ideas are so very similar to those of St Augustine that Lewis failed to notice some of the differences. One theologian widely admired in my university and in many other universities, a man known as an expert on Lewis, refused to speak to me for a year. He seems to have found a way to forgive me now, but his anger was a defense of ideas he held to be special and valid. He refused to accept my inquiry, though most of the theology faculty reluctantly agreed with me, shaking their heads.

Many studies today try hard to make their subjects empirically verifiable. Even historians and philosophers are so caught by the rise of science that they try to use what they believe to be scientific methods. Statistical studies of history and philosophy are trying hard to be born and to mature. We now call such studies the "Social Sciences." What nonsense. We all know what science is, and we should all know that many modes of thinking cannot be known objectively. Someday too late, I suspect, we shall agree that education cannot be successfully measured by objective methods, though we all know who the good teachers are.

Business studies and theology studies are not strictly speaking scientific; hence, they are not designed for analytical inquiry. Scientists inquire with no specific results in mind. An hypothesis is an inquiry to understand, not an attempt to prove an opinion. Analysis rejects bias. Business and theology are all bias. All real thinking rejects bias. Alas, we have far too few thinkers walking around on or even lying around under this earth. Most people have never met a real thinker and even when they do, they fail to recognize them as thinkers.

To seek thinkers one should go to the universities, but we will find too few there too. Universities are merely the best bet we have for thinking, but the prospects are not as good as one would hope.

Appropo of very little, I employ a handyman on an almost daily basis, who has rarely read a book, but he has become a good mathematician, and I marvel at his thinking almost every day. He has somehow taught himself to be a thinker. This phenomenon is not altogether unknown, but it is uncommon. Quite probably many people are of a high enough I Q to think, but the evidence for the transition from non-thinker to thinker is not commonly known. The phenomenon is often observed, but not often understood. It is something of a miracle, and it is most often observed in the university. One of the real pleasures of teaching is to see the transition and professors can only hope they have had something to do with the miraculous transition. To see a student begin to grasp at ideas is the fulfillment that the best professors long for. To see no difference in our students at the end of a course or at graduation is to know depression.

The reverse of the miracle "feeling" for the transition to thought is the constant realization of the waste of human potential. The waste is the bleakest of human tragedy. To realize that half of the brains wasted throughout time from merely being in the female body tells that mankind has long been biased against such a possibility. Only now in a few countries have we become awakened from centuries of stony sleep to the possibilities of making use of all the brains we need so desperately.

However, we have for thousands of years wasted our potential brain power. To think that the persons lie dead at places such as Thermopylae, Gettysburg, Omaha Beach, Iwo jima, Okinawa, The Chosin Resevoir, Khe Sahn, Fallujua and almost countless other places that show the madness of wasted brain power that could have started us on the way to cure cancer or to develop governmental sense is to know of tragedy.

My handyman is truly one of the best thinkers I have ever met, and he is not sure what universities are. He certainly has no experience with them. I'm afraid to tell anyone how long it took me to recognize his thinking. I didn't expect him to be a thinker. I wonder now how many I have missed, but remember the average I Q in this country is 100, and that is not smart. Persons of 110 I Q are required for relatively simple tasks, and note that only about 16% of the population have I Qs of 120 and above. The nausea comes from knowing that we do not always, and perhaps not frequently, recognize some of our best brains because they do not represent that for which we profess admiration. We are collectively too dumb to know who is smart. How sad.

Solution: do not accept the status quo; inquire, analyze. You may upset many of those you love or have respect for, but analysis, the asking of why and how, is necessary if mankind is to have a future, which is not likely. Natural evil: enormous earthquakes, gigantic volcanoes, missiles from space are all likely sometime. Moral evil in the form of bombs and other clever ways of killing one another and perhaps killing all of us in the form of a nuclear winter are also likely soon, but the worst scenarios are the ones coming from overpopulation. We are almost out of water and the man-made heat continues to rise. Many scientists are speaking in terms of west Texas heat rising to the 120s in the long summers. That is desert heat, and we are quickly headed (about the 2040s) there. Think of what that will mean. THINK. Many, many in our overfed and starving world do not want you to think of what they are gaining by what most are losing. Check on all of this. A careful check is not easy. Lies abound, but you CAN check on them, though the process is not only not easy, but also often dangerous.

Cleatus Rattan

Made in the USA
Charleston, SC
10 July 2015